Russian Gold and Silverwork

Alexander von Solodkoff

Russian Gold and Silverwork

17th-19th Century

RIZZOLI
NEW YORK

In the text and captions the figures in brackets next to the names of important masters refer to the Index of marks and signatures on p. 223

This book was printed in August 1981 by Imprimerie Paul Attinger SA, Neuchâtel
Filmsetting: Atelier de photocomposition EP SA, Lausanne
Photolithographers: color: cooperativa lavoratori grafici, Verona;
black and white: Photogravure Bienna SA, Biel
Binding: H. + J. Schumacher AG, Schmitten
Production: Marcel Berger

German language edition, *Russische Goldschmiedekunst, 17.-19. Jahrhundert*

© 1981 by Office du Livre, Fribourg
English translation by Christopher Holme
© 1981 by Office du Livre
First published in the United States of America in 1981 by:

*R*IZZOLI INTERNATIONAL PUBLICATIONS, INC.
712 Fifth Avenue/New York 10019

LC: 81-51103
ISBN: 0-8478-0398-8

Printed in Switzerland

Table of Contents

Preface

The art of the Russian goldsmith is characterized by representative forms and techniques to be found nowhere else in the applied arts of Europe. They present collectors and amateurs of gold and silver objects with frequent problems of formal development and classification in terms of art history.

This work sets out to explain the specifically Russian forms, techniques and nomenclature. Special attention has been paid to the elucidation of historical contexts, with particular reference to laws about the stamping of precious metals and the organization of guilds.

The choice of period for this study, from the 17th to 19th centuries, was determined by the fact that the 17th century was the peak of the Russian goldsmith's art, with its centre in Moscow. That was when it produced, with its enamel and *niello* decoration, a specifically Russian style. This century with its peculiar stylistic elements formed the basis of the Russian nationalist historicism and revivalism of the 19th century. By contrast, the work of Russian goldsmiths in the 18th century was characterized by the production of snuff-boxes under stylistic influences from France and Switzerland.

The Russian goldsmith's art in the closing years of the 19th century as seen with hindsight from Western Europe and America is overshadowed by the gigantic figure of Fabergé, whose unusual wealth of ideas was none the less also based strongly on Russian art forms. The workshops competing with Fabergé, which in terms of artistic originality fall into a different category, such as might be called Russian traditional, have hitherto remained largely unexplored. This is astonishing in view of the fact that it was these very firms which attracted special mention in the Western European publications and exhibition catalogues of the day.

It is well enough known that Russian arts and crafts, especially in the 18th century, were strongly influenced by Western Europe. Even at earlier periods we can observe a mixture of different artistic styles, especially among the products of the Kremlin workshops in 17th-century Moscow.

It is indeed a distinguishing characteristic of Russian art that it absorbs foreign stylistic elements, and this can easily lead to the dismissal of its works as mere copies. In considering more closely, however, particularly the work of the goldsmiths, we observe that, apart from the movements of international fashion, styles and forms are not simply copied but taken over and transformed into a special, that is Russian, style of their own.

The study of the Russian goldsmith's art was begun in Russia around 1900 by Baron Foelkersam, who published extensive monographs and a systematic list of St. Petersburg goldsmiths. A further fundamental work was the book (published in 1951) by L. Bäcksbacka, who enlarged Foelkersam's discoveries and processed fresh documentary material. In more recent Soviet literature special mention must be made of the monographs by T. Goldberg and M. M. Postnikova-Loseva, which give special emphasis to technical and regional details and particulars of Moscow goldsmiths.

Without these publications, which are not easily accessible for reasons of language and the smallness of the editions in which they were published, the present work would be unthinkable.

Unpublished sources used for the history of the goldsmith's art in the 18th and 19th centuries were parts of the memoirs of Pauzié and documents concerning the lives of Ador and Pierre Theremin.

Over and above these, many years' practical experience and handling of Russian gold and silver led to new discoveries concerning marks, signatures and techniques. Valuable hints came in particular from Léon Grinberg, Paris, whose advice was always rewarding. My thanks for friendly help must go also to Dr Géza von Hapsburg-Lothringen. A visit to the Hermitage in Leningrad for research was made possible by the firm of Christie's.

My thanks are further due to the following persons and institutions for photographic material, information, or access to collections:

H. M. Queen Elizabeth the Queen Mother, H. R. H. Princess Eugénie of Greece, Galina N. Komelova (The Hermitage, Leningrad), Dr Marina M. Postnikova-Loseva (Historical Museum, Moscow), Serge Grandjean (Louvre, Paris). Dr M. Leithe-Jasper and Dr H. Trnek (Kunsthistorisches Museum, Vienna), Anna Somers-Cocks (Victoria and Albert Museum, London), Jörgen Hein (Rosenborg Museum, Copenhagen), Robert Ador, Georges van Damme, Countess Mordvinoff, Mme Alain Mouchet, Hans Nadelhoffer, Victor Provatoroff, the Earl of Shelburne, E.R. Wheatley-Hubbard, Dr Giovanni Zagrebelski, Hans Bolin, Jacques Kugel, Messrs. S. J. Phillips, Popoff & Cie, Paul and Peter Schaffer (A la Vieille Russie, New York), A. Kenneth Snowman (Wartski, London), together with Gisela-B. Obenaus, Christoph Freiherr von Seckendorff-Aberdar, Jurij von Solodkoff and all collectors who preferred not to be mentioned by name.

1 Tapering octagonal beaker, parcel-gilt, engraved on each side with a sibyl in a cartouche, above each her name surmounting a line of a prophetic saying, late 17th century, 20.5 cm high. The names are Russian versions of the geographical origins attributed to various sibyls in classical times, Persika (Persian), Lubika (Libyan), Delphina (Delphic), Ximia (Cimmerian), Simia (Samian), Dimophila (Demophile of Cumae), Elistzonta (Hellespontic), Phrugia (Phrygian).

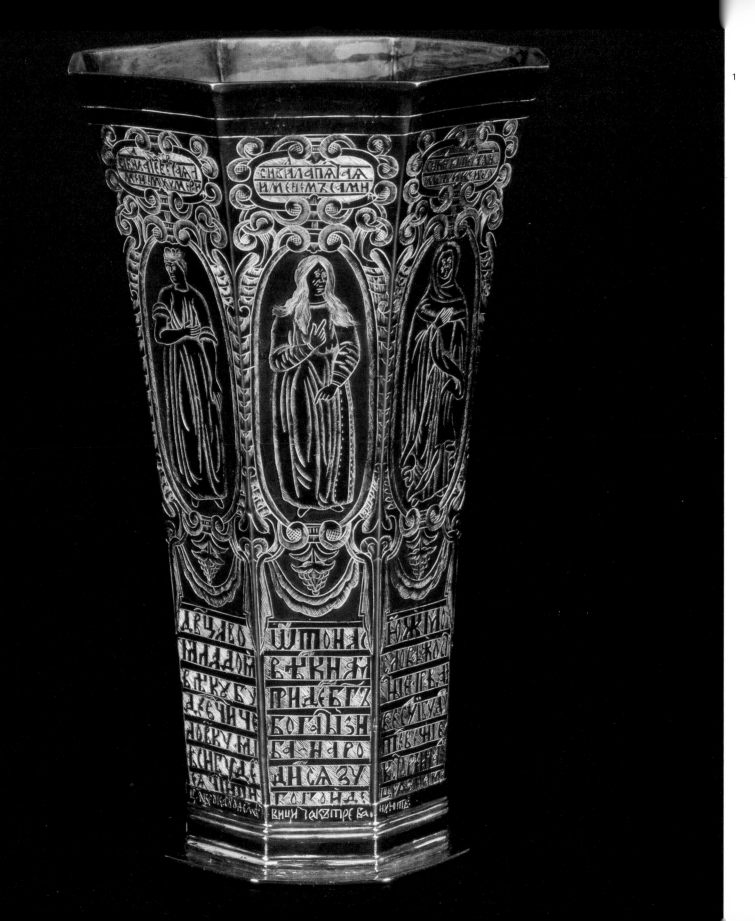

2

3

4

5

6

14

15

16

17

21

22

23

2 Four silver-gilt *charki*, double-walled, 17th century (from left to right) *charka* engraved inside and out with drinking mottoes, in the middle with the figure of a swan, 6.5 cm long; *charka* chased with sea creatures, 7.7 cm long; *charka* with a scene of Jonah and the Whale, in the middle a bird with outstretched wings, 4 cm high; *charka* with a similar scene and a swan in the middle, a drinking motto on the lip, 4.6 cm high (cf. Pl. 7).

3 (left) Silver-gilt, octagonal, slightly tapering beaker, engraved with scrolling foliage and on the lip: 'Beaker of Princess Anna Mikhaylovna Odoyevskaya', 8.5 cm high, about 1700.
(middle) Small silver-gilt *bratina* on toothed foot, the *bombé* sides engraved with two cartouches containing inscription bands with the owner's name: 'Alexey Petrovich, Lord, Grand Duke, and Tsarevich of Greater, Lesser, and White Russia', unmarked, about 1700, 4.8 cm high, diameter 4.2 cm. Alexey Petrovich (1690-1719) was the son of Peter the Great who was executed at his father's orders after speaking out against the reform and secularization of Russia. (National Historical Museum, Moscow)
(right) Parcel-gilt *bratina*, engraved on the lip: 'Bratina of an honourable man, drink to your health from it', arabesque ornaments below, early 17th century, 10.5 cm high.

4 Liturgical *diskos* (used in the Orthodox Church to serve the bread for Holy Communion), of silver gilt and *niello*, depicting the Holy Virgin, the border with a liturgical inscription in *vyaz'*, probably from Moscow, latter half of the 17th century, 20.5 cm diameter.

5 Silver-gilt *charka*, the handle with floral reliefs, on the rim an inscription recording the gift of the *charka* by Tsar Alexey Mikhaylovich to the citizen of Novgorod, Stepan Yelisarovich Karsakov, for tax collections in Pskov, middle of the 17th century, 12.5 cm diameter.

6 Parcel-gilt chalice, engraved with the Deesis in medallions. The inscription on the rim is from the New Testament, that on the foot records that the chalice was made to the order of the Tsar Alexey Mikhaylovich and the Tsarina Mariya Ilyinichna in the Monastery of St. Nicholas at Opochka on the 8 August 7161 (1653), 19 cm high. (From the de Savitch Collection)

7 Interior view of the *charka* in Plate 2 (right).

8 Silver-gilt *charka*, double-walled, the interior chased with the scene of Jonah and the whale with other sea creatures, the exterior with masks and the inscription 'Charka of Grigoriy Ivanovich Panteleyev, Drink to your health and happiness', 17th century, 7 cm diameter.

9 A parcel-gilt shallow *charka* on three ball feet, the handle carved with a bird and fruits in relief, 17th century, 7.4 cm in diameter.

10 Silver-gilt *charka* with pierced handle, the bowl chased with a bird and flowers, double-walled, the exterior with pomegranates and berries, city mark of Moscow (double eagle) about 1700, 3 cm high.

11 Parcel-gilt beaker on three pomegranate feet, engraved with figures in baroque cartouches, Moscow 1695, 9.5 cm high.

12 Silver-gilt cylindrical beaker engraved with the crowned double eagle surrounded by palm-branches, the reverse with a medallion of a harbour scene, master's initials Ya.F., Moscow about 1720, 13.5 cm high.

13 (left) Plain silver beaker, engraved with a medallion containing a view of parkland and a flying Cupid in a cartouche frame with a banded inscription in Russian 'Harmony preserves love', on the reverse a crowned mirror, monogram K R, master's initials (Cyrillic) D Kh, Moscow 1733, 8.2 cm high;
(right) Plain cylindrical silver beaker with three engraved medallions of putti and birds surrounded by scrolling foliage, master's initials of Ivan Mikhaylov (94), Alderman F. Petrov (40), Moscow 1774, 7.6 cm high.

14-17 Silver tankard with engraved decoration, on three ball feet, master's initials of Petr Semenov (178), assay-master Anisim Kuzmin (15), Moscow 1751, 16 cm high. 15-17: Details of the engraved medallions on the tankard.

18 (right and left) A pair of beakers chased with *putti* figures in cartouches, by T. Siluyanov (192, 193), Moscow 1771, 8.3 cm high;
(middle) A beaker with *rocaille* ornaments and scrolling foliage on a matted ground, by E. Ilin (82, 83), Moscow 1753, 8.8 cm high.

19 Silver beakers with eagle decoration:
(left) Master (Cyrillic) P W, Moscow about 1770, 7.7 cm high;
(middle) Master B A (46), Moscow 1771, 7.6 cm high;
(right) Probably by A. Afanasev (2), Moscow about 1770, 7.7 cm high.

20 Silver beakers chased with eagles:
(left) Master (Cyrillic) S F, assay-master A. Titov (33), alderman A. Kosyrev (3), Moscow 1786, 8 cm high;
(middle) Beaker on ball-feet, unmarked, about 1775;
(right) Master (Cyrillic) A D, assay-master A. Titov, alderman A. Kosyrev, Moscow 1787, 8 cm high.

21 (left) A covered beaker chased with scroll medallions, master (Cyrillic) I K, assay-master I. Shagin (118), Moscow 1750, 19 cm high;
(middle) A covered beaker chased with medallions under baldachins, surrounded by scrolling foliage, by Mikhail Klushin (140), assay-master I. Shagin, Moscow 1750, 26 cm high;
(right) A beaker chased with scenes in scroll cartouches, by A. Kostrinsky (16), Moscow about 1770, 15 cm high.

22 A parcel-gilt beaker and cover with eagle finial, one of a pair, chased with a dog-sleigh and rocaille ornaments, master's mark I C and trident (115), assay-master Ernst Ruch (270), Moscow about 1725, the chasing about 1765, 30 cm high.

23 Covered beaker, sides chased with decoration of medallions in baldachin cartouches, Moscow about 1750, 29.5 cm high.

Organization of the Goldsmith's Trade in Russia

In all countries the working of precious metals was subject to special regulations. This was because legal security in the use of precious metals and the traffic in them had to be specially protected because they were at the same time the foundation of the currency. In addition the handling of such metals was often subject to taxes. The stamping of precious metal objects did not become a matter of regulation until later. At first it was their craft which was put under control.

In Russia the organization of the goldsmith's trade in the 17th century followed the traditional pattern.[1]

The goldsmiths were organized in two corporations. These were the so-called 'Silver row' and the *Oruzheynaya palata* (Armoury) of the Moscow Grand Dukes. The name 'Silver row' derives from the original location of the goldsmiths' shops, both in Moscow and in the provinces, which were arranged together in a row on the market-place. This was the only place where precious metals could be dealt in and generally they would also be worked there, on the spot.

In its organization the Silver row was the association of craftsmen and dealers together in a single corporation. Each member was required on entry to bind himself by a deed of guarantee (*poruchnaya zapis'*) to act according to the Tsar's *ukaz* or edicts. The craftsmen in addition had to produce some sort of sample of their work before they were admitted.

At the head of the Silver row were two aldermen (*starosty*), who had to assay the silver content and the weights (by comparison with the 'State Pound'). Later they were entrusted with stamping and with checking that no piece was sold unstamped. The *starosty* also travelled to the trade shows and fairs in the provinces.

Parallel with this was the association of the goldsmiths and silversmiths in the workshops of the Moscow Kremlin, situated in the Armoury to which they were subordinate. This was immediately subject to the Tsar's Court and was directed by a boyar. A particularly distinguished boyar was Bogdan Matveyevich Khitrovo, who directed the workshops from 1655 to 1680. He managed to attract the best craftsmen to Moscow and thus raise the quality of their work to such a level that the products of the Moscow Kremlin can easily be distinguished from all others.

The term *Oruzheynaya palata* had in practice a dual meaning. On the one hand it was the administrative unit for regulating the goldsmiths' trade, on the other it was an independent court workshop carrying out private commissions from the Tsar and in this connection other workshops of a private nature must be mentioned. These were the ones which worked for the Patriarchal Court in Moscow or for the monasteries, such as the Troitse-Sergeyevo monastery. Additionally the Stroganovs in the 16th and 17th centuries installed workshops in Solvychegodsk in which a great number of masters of all kinds were working and which represented a smaller replica of the *Oruzheynaya palata.*

By an *ukaz* of the 19 January 1700 Peter I subordinated the whole goldsmiths' craft to the *Oruzheynaya palata.* The Silver row was now supervised by it in a centralized fashion and sent out iron stamps for marking silver objects to the *starosty* of the Silver rows in Moscow and the provinces. Subsequently, in connection with the reforms of Peter I and the recruitment of innumerable foreign masters there were further changes in the organization of the goldsmith's craft. By *ukazy* of 16 January 1721 (Regulation of the Chief Magistracy) and of 27 April 1722 (Concerning the Guilds) a universal guild system on the German model was introduced for all craftsmen.[2] The craftsmen who had entered St. Petersburg as immigrants in the first years after the foundation of that city in 1703 were principally of German origin. Following German tradition and perhaps also just in order to have a national club, these masters combined as early as 1714 into a guild of their own, without there being any legal basis for it. The Russian goldsmiths followed their example, so that there were now two guilds, one for foreigners and one for Russian masters, in St. Petersburg. The general institution of guilds had one principal difference from the existing Silver row organization, that dealers were excluded from the guilds.

The guild order of 1722 was at first almost disregarded, especially in the provincial cities, and already in 1724 an *ukaz* had to be issued 'On Botchery' forbidding all unregistered masters to practise the trade.[3] In the capital of St. Petersburg, however, the guild organization seems to have established itself very rapidly, one good reason being that it was unnecessary there to clash with the traditional Silver row. In 1725 the guild was officially defined as follows in the language of German officialdom: *'Das Amt der löblichen Gold- und Silberarbeiter in Sanct Petersburg'* (1787: *'Ausländisches Amt der Gold-, Silber- und Galanterie-Arbeiter').*[4] In 1785 Catherine II laid down the individual guild regulations in a law of 21 April, that is, in a chapter headed 'About the Condition of the Crafts' in the 'Charter concerning the rights and privileges of the cities of the Russian Empire'. These were confirmed once more by Paul I in 1799. They provided that at the head of the guild there was to be a *starosta* or alderman elected from the body of the masters. Only masters had the right to vote, and master status could be acquired only by serving an apprenticeship, three years as journeyman, and the submission of a 'master piece'. Only a master could operate a workshop or keep apprentices and journeymen (Russian 'under-masters'). The rights in the workshop passed on death to a 'master widow'.[5]

While in Moscow from the middle of the 18th century the alderman of the year could guarantee the quality of a piece with his own stamp, thus enjoying equality of control with the Court, in 1785 this control of metal quality was transferred entirely to the administration of the 'Assay Palace'.

The period during which the two laws of Catherine II and Paul I were promulgated represents the summit of guild organization in Russia. In 1793 there were in the Russian Guild 44 masters with 16 journeymen and 14 apprentices, in the Foreigners' Guild 59 master goldsmiths, 51 master silversmiths, 27 masters of *galanterie*, and 2 engravers. Jewellers did not belong to the guild, they mostly settled as shopkeepers, who had their own guild organization graded according to capital.[6]

Between 1714 and 1800 the distribution of nationalities among masters in St. Petersburg was as follows: Germans 234, Scandinavians 261, French 44, and from time to time a few Swiss, English, Austrians, and Italians. The number of masters organized in the Russian Guild cannot be given, since between 1864 and 1871 the greater part of the documents were sold as 'waste paper'. Foreign masters, however, were greatly in the majority, until in the course of the 19th century the proportions were slowly equalized. Foreign masters who acquired Russian citizenship left the Foreigners' Guild and became members of the Russian one. This was the case, for instance, with the masters Blerzy and Barbé.

The rigidity of guild organization was already beginning to be loosened in the first half of the 19th century. Other trades, the locksmiths' and the bookbinders', for instance, were amalgamated with the Silversmiths' Guild. One reason for this was the rise of machine and factory production, which will be considered later.

Though the guild system had been more or less strictly established by the middle of the 18th century, there was one interesting special development of the goldsmiths' trade, the Court commissioning service. It is noteworthy that such better known goldsmiths as Pauzié and Ador were not guild members, and yet they worked in St. Petersburg and supplied the Court. This privileged position of Court purveyor holding the Imperial Warrant, was not only allowed but kept going continuously by commissions, a phenomenon which was possible also in such strictly guild-bound countries as Germany and France.

The Emperors' patronage was responsible for a range of pieces of particularly high quality. Unlike Pauzié and Ador, who had direct access to the Empress, masters generally received their commissions through the Court Office *(Pridvornaya kontora)*. This issued not only the drawing but the metal required for the commissioned piece and then negotiated the master's fee. Frequently the commissioned pieces might be replicas or copies of foreign originals. While neither design drawings nor craftsmen's names have survived from the 18th century, there is in the Hermitage an album from the year 1801 with the title *A sa Majesté impériale l'Empereur, Alexandre I. Pot au lait, varié sous trente formes, faisant parties d'autant de déjeuner. Année 1801. F.X. Hattenberger.* Of the artist, F.X. Hattenberger, it is known that he worked in the Imperial porcelain factory and also did sketches for bronzes.[7]

In 1741, for example, the master Ivan Libmann received from the Court Office 2 *pud* 36 *funty* of silver for the making of a *nakhtysh* dessert service.[8] As large amounts of precious metal often had to be handed over to the masters for working, the risk of theft or embezzlement in the workshop was particularly high. The silversmith Johann Friedrich Köpping in 1763 was commissioned to make the 'First Silver Service' for the Court (Index of marks no. 291), and for this the metal was delivered to him together with a military guard. 'Lieutenant Moller of the Preobrazhensky guard regiment was ordered to attend the work with a guard in the house of Master Köpping, to ensure that no silver or money could be abstracted.' Lieutenant Moller was stationed in the workshop the whole time until the work was finished, with a detachment of six soldiers and a sergeant. For the repoussé work in silver Köpping received 5 roubles per *pud*, for the plain work 3 roubles 70 kopeks per *pud* (16.38 kg), and for gilding 70 kopeks per *zolotnik*.[9]

In 1775 in Moscow similar conditions of payment were accorded the German master Georg Rittmeier. He was required to make a silver service (Index of marks nos 67, 68) for the Court to a prescribed drawing. In 1753 he was working for the Court Office in St. Petersburg. The Office handed over the finished silver articles into the keeping of the so-called Silver Stewards, of whom since 1726 there had been two in office at a time. The senior of the two was called the Keeper of Silver. It was their task to look after the silver, repairing and supplementing the pieces where necessary. Of the 19 holders of this title four were master silversmiths: Zolotarev, Palm, the well-known master J.F. Köpping, and Lidmann. They were also partly responsible for sorting the pieces and picking out to be melted down those which were obsolete or beyond repair. They kept the lists of the entire silver collection of the Court, and these also tell us what services were given away by the Emperors as presents. In 1784 the Silver Stewards, who had been independent until then, were subordinated to the Imperial Household, but in 1802 they were transferred to the Court Office. In 1843 the post of Silver Steward was abolished.[10]

Of all those engaged in dealing in the arts and crafts at Court in the 18th century the merchants Libmann and Bernardi and the Court Jeweller Pauzié may be taken as specially characteristic. All three had definite positions of trust at Court permitting them not only to do business but also to take on special services which gave them a certain power.

Isaak Libmann, a banker with the title of Chief Imperial Commissioner, who is frequently referred to in the literature as *Juif de la Cour*, is known to have supplied the Court during the reigns of Peter II, Ivan VI, the Empresses Anna and Elizabeth, with every possible kind of art object, gold, and jewels.[11] The French ambassador, the Marquis de la Chétardie, describes him as an extraordinarily wily person, capable of mixing in intrigues of every kind or starting some of his own.[12] Pauzié mentions that Libmann was thought a great deal of at the Court of the Regent Bühren (during the minority of Ivan VI, 1740-1), who favoured him to such an extent that, as the saying went, it was Libmann who ruled Russia.[13]

Bernardi was Court Jeweller and Purveyor to the Empress Elizabeth during the 1750s. Of him the Grand Duchess Yekaterina Alexeyevna (the later Empress

24 (left) A covered beaker on ball feet, engraved with rocaille motifs, master I K, Fedor Petrov, Moscow 1753;
(right) A silver-gilt miniature tankard on three ball feet; the sides chased with scrolling foliage, engraved inscription inside the cover (Cyrillic) 'Tankard of Mikhail Ivanovich Strezhnev', unmarked, about 1745, 9.2 cm high.

25 Parcel-gilt tankard, applied with a pierced relief with the biblical scene of Tobias and the Angel, the cover with rocaille chasing, master's initials (Cyrillic) N S S (164), assay-master I. Shagin (118), Moscow 1750, 19.5 cm high.

26 A large parcel-gilt bowl in the 17th century Augsburg style engraved with a mythological scene in a central medallion surrounded by flowers and fruits, master's mark V S S, Moscow 1740, diameter 39 cm.

27

28

29

33

34

35

36

37

38

44 ▲

45

46

27 A pineapple cup in the 17th century German style with eagle finial, master's marks A I and A K, about 1750, 16 cm high.

28 A coconut-shell cup mounted in silver. The nut, engraved with a bust of the Empress Elizabeth and her monogram, is supported by a warrior, with eagle finial, master A B, Moscow about 1760, 26 cm high.

29 A cup and cover with eagle finial, the pierced double wall with two portrait medallions, by Andrey Kostrinsky (16), Moscow 1751, 30 cm high.

30 Silver shield like a grenadier's cap, chased with a monogram of the Empress Yelizaveta Petrovna beneath a crowned double eagle and with military and artistic emblems and the inscription 'Marte et arte'. Master's initials of Martin Charles Dubolon (309), assay-master Ivan Frolov (101), St. Petersburg 1759, c. 20 cm high, zolotnik mark 74. (Hermitage, Leningrad)

31 Silver-gilt beaker, engraved with bay-wreathed medallions with the double eagle, a crowned cypher, and a landscape scene, the domed cover with a double-eagle finial, master's initials I.Ya., Moscow about 1800, 20.4 cm high.

32 (left) Oval silver sugar-box on four feet chased with rocaille ornaments and birds, master's mark of Alexey Ivanov (14), Alderman Fedor Petrov (37), Moscow 1770, 17.5 cm long;
(right) Silver-gilt oval sugar-box on four feet chased with cartouches and rococo scrolls, Moscow 1756, 16.5 cm long, c. 1770.

33 (left) Silver-gilt charka, of unusual weight, about 1770, zolotnik mark 74. This type of charka was not chased but cast and then engraved;
(middle) Parcel-gilt charka with chased rocaille design, assay-master's mark BA, alderman with the letters AAA in a heart-shaped stamp, Moscow 1766;
(right) Nielloed parcel-gilt charka with rocaille decoration, Moscow 1770 (G.R. Hann Collection).

34 Trefoil charki from Moscow:
(left) by Stepan Savelev, 1788, 7.5 cm long;
(middle) master's initials (Cyrillic) Th. G., 1776, 6.7 cm long;
(right) master's initials E.A.K., about 1770, 7.3 cm long.

35 Four chased charki with chased gadrooning and engraved scrolling (from left) master's initials A E (8), Moscow, about 1745;
by Alexander Hildebrand (6), 1762;
master's initials M.K., about 1750, 6.5 cm long;
by Vasiliy Popov (52), double eagle mark, Moscow 1733, 5 cm diameter.

36 (left) Parcel-gilt cylindrical charka with engraved eagle designs, by Fedor Kryzhev (223), Moscow 1771, 5.8 cm long;
(middle) Silver-gilt octagonal charka with engraved geometrical designs, by Joseph Nordberg (298), St. Petersburg 1835, 6.8 cm long;
(right) Parcel-gilt charka with four chased rococo cartouches, master C I T, assay-master N. Moshchalkin (163), St. Petersburg 1795.

37 (left) Plain cylindrical parcel-gilt charka, the handle in the form of a mermaid, rare stamp of a provincial city: Vladimir, 1763, master M C (148), 6.8 cm long.
(middle) Bell-shaped beaker set with coronation jetons of different emperors, unstamped but about 1825, 5.6 cm high;
(right) Parcel-gilt charka signed with the initials of Johan Heinrich Sart (284), St. Petersburg 1759, 7.2 cm long.

38 Four cylindrical charki, Moscow (from left):
Master Yakov Maslennikov (216, 217), 1757, 5.6 cm long (with handle);
Master with the initials (Cyrillic) Th. M.S., 1778, 6 cm long;
Master Petr Semenov (176, 177), 1766, 5.8 cm long;
Master Gabriel Zontag (62, 281), 1776, 6 cm long.

39 Sugar box in cartouche form, chased and engraved with rocaille decoration, the cover chased with a shell and with bullrushes, master's initials B.A., Moscow 1766, 17.5 cm wide.

40 (left) Parcel-gilt Jewish ceremonial box in the form of a citron on a leaf-shaped tray, master's initials (Cyrillic) GR, probably Grigoriy Ratkov (66), assay-master CA (180), Kostroma 1769, 24.5 cm long;
(right) Parcel-gilt tankard with repoussé portraits of emperors within foliage cartouches, Moscow 1743, 14.5 cm high.

41 Silver-gilt tea-pot engraved with monkeys and birds in scrolling foliage, with ivory handle, master's mark I C with a trident (115), Moscow 1743, assay-master K. Grigorev (256), 14.5 cm long.

42 Silver-gilt cup and cover, the prize for a horse race, engraved with a rider on horseback in a bay-wreath cartouche surmounted by the horse's name 'Convoy', on the reverse a presentation inscription dated 1790, the cover with a medal to the sea victory of Count Alexey Orlov, by J. Gass, master's initials AP, Moscow 1790, 21 cm high.

43 Silver-gilt tankard engraved with putti in medallions and with foliage ornaments, mark with the initials of Petr Semenov (178), assay-master Ivan Shagin (118), Moscow 1752, 15.9 cm high.

44 Plain gilt covered écuelle, the cover with flower-spray finial, signed Schlepper for Berthold Christian Schlepper (241, 322), St. Petersburg 1776 (?), zolotnik mark 74, 24 cm long.

45 Butter-dish and cover, the silver-gilt sides with silver lattice work, rocaille handles, and a rose finial, master's initials (Cyrillic) P. Ts., Moscow 1777, 20.3 cm wide.

46 Silver filigree basket and cover with interwoven and soldered silver strands forming foliate friezes and columnar bands separated by fillets, master's initials H V (?), assay-master M. Karpinsky (139), Moscow 1806, 20.3 cm wide.

Catherine II) writes in her memoirs, in connection with the arrest of Count Bestuz-hev and Bernardi in January 1759, 'Bernardi was an Italian jeweller. He was no fool, and his profession procured him the entry into the most exalted houses. There was not a house, I think, which was not in some way under an obligation to him or for which he had not performed some small service. Since he was constantly going in and out, he was entrusted as occasion offered with messages from one to another. A line in a note reached its destination through Bernardi quicker and more surely than through the servants. That is why Bernardi's arrest put the whole city in a panic, for he had run errands for everybody, for me as well as others.'[14]

It can be said of Pauzié too that he was not only Court Jeweller but that he occupied a position of trust which made it natural to involve him in diplomatic errands. As he describes it in his memoirs, he had no difficulty in gaining access to the Empress Elizabeth. Not only was the organization of the Imperial household at that time relatively small but Elizabeth was an Empress with a particular fondness for jewellery and objects of art. Even at night the master was liable to be summoned to the palace to receive from the Empress 'a commission for some creation which had just occurred to her'. Even the Austrian Ambassador, Count Nicholas Esterházy, was only able to gain an audience with the ailing Empress through the intervention of the Court Jeweller. Both Peter III and Catherine II too treated him with similar confidence and dispensed with the usual Court ceremonial in receiving him.[15]

Other purveyors with the Imperial Warrant were, during the reign of the Empress Anna (1730-40), the Berlin merchant Peter Kakow who sold silver, china, and crystal, and in the time of the Empress Elizabeth, the English dealers Simon Chaser and James and Charles Woolf. At the court of Catherine II there were Sila Glazunov and Adadurov, then about 1800 Dementev and Rozhin, and later too the merchants Yakovlev and Kudryashev.

After 1840 we have the beginning of what was a typical 19th-century develop-ment, the increasing bureaucratism of the Imperial Household and its progressive enlargement, together with the introduction of the Imperial Warrant as a title stamped on articles of gold or silver. The masters who held it were entitled to adorn their signature with the Imperial double eagle, with presumably favourable effects on their general custom. The quality of pieces distinguished by this warrant is in fact particularly high.

The most important holders of the warrant in the period after 1840 were the *Magasin anglais Nicholls & Plincke* in St. Petersburg, a firm managed by Englishmen which overwhelmed all their smaller competitors. Only big firms such as Morozov, Grachev, Khlebnikov, Sazikov, Ovchinnikov, and ultimately Fabergé were able to compete with the *Magasin anglais* and in the end get the better of it.[16]

From the middle of the 18th century onwards a development took place in the organization of the workshops which continued into the 20th century. This was the creation of 'factories' for goldsmiths' and silversmiths' work which were expressly so designated and called by the same name in Russian (*fabrika*). One of the first factories was established in Moscow in 1757 by the merchant Vasiliy Matveyevich Kunkin, who owned the monopoly for the manufacture of church utensils from precious metal. In 1752 some 70 'masters and workmen' were employed there, with the owner acting only in a supervisory capacity.[17] Another 'factory' was that of the Popov brothers in Velikiy Ustyug (see the section on *Enamel*), which was founded in 1761 and bore in its stamp the letters U.V.F.A.S.P. in Cyrillic as an abbreviation for *Ustyug Velikiy, Fabrika* [of] *Afanasiy* [and] *Stepan Popov*. It is quite clear here how the concept *fabrika* as a 'factory' had completely established itself in Russia. In the laws too, as for instance in the 1785 Charter for the Rights and Privileges of the Cities of Catherine II, mentioned above, there are references to factories and manufactures.[18]

From early in the 19th century onwards larger factories began to assume the business leadership in Russia. Among them were the firms Gubkin, Sazikov, and Ovchinnikov in Moscow, with Morozov and Fabergé in St. Petersburg. The methods of work were becoming increasingly mechanized, along with increases in the work force.

The smaller workshop proprietors could hardly compete with these more powerful businesses. For this reason from 1898 onward they began combining in *artels* (cooperatives), more than twenty of which are known. The articles produced by independent *Artel* masters were sold in retail partly by big businesses and partly by dealers.[19]

Notes

1 For the following comments see Postnikova-Loseva, *Russkoye yuvelirnoye iskusstvo*, p. 194 ff.
2 Polnoye Sobranie Zakonov (PSZ) VI, 3708 (1721), VI, 3980 (1722).
3 Foelkersam, 'Inostrannye mastera...', p. 97.
4 Bäcksbacka, *St. Petersburgs Juvelerare*, p. 10.
5 PSZ XII, 16188 (1785), XXV, 19187 (1799).
6 Bäcksbacka, *St. Petersburgs Juvelerare, passim*, Foelkersam, 'Nekotoryya svedeniya...', p. 11; Foelkersam, 'Inostrannye mastera...', p. 98; Foelkersam, *Opisi serebra*, p. 62.
7 Foelkersam, 'Inostrannye mastera...', p. 109.
8 Foelkersam, *Opisi serebra*, p. 7.
9 Ibid., pp. 64 ff.
10 Ibid., pp. 7 f.
11 *S.I.R.I.O.* (Collection of the Imperial Russian Historical Society), vol. 84, p. 47; vol. 96, p. 161; vol. 106, p. 579.
12 Chétardie to Fleury on 19 February 1740, in *S.I.R.I.O.* vol. 86, p. 238.
13 Pauzié, 'Zapiski', p. 81, cf. Foelkersam, *Opisi serebra*, p. 223.
14 Catherine II, *Memoiren*, Frankfurt, 1972, p. 339.
15 Pauzié, 'Zapiski', pp. 99 f.
16 Foelkersam, *Opisi serebra*, p. 21.
17 Postnikova-Loseva, *Russkoye yuvelirnoye iskusstvo*, p. 197.
18 PSZ XII, 16188 (1785).
19 *Ves' Peterburg*, 1914 and 1916, *s.v.* Gold and silver objects, Jewellers.

Styles and Influences in the Goldsmith's Art in Russia

17th Century

In the 17th century the goldsmith's art in Russia, centred on Moscow, was at its peak. Especially at the beginning of the century, the forms were simple and original. They were largely derived from the wooden utensils of the countryside, such as the *kovsh* and the *charka*. They were plain silver and gold objects, engraved and adorned with single precious stones or bands of pearls.

About the middle of the century the decoration becomes richer. In enamel there is more frequent use of *cloisonné* and arabesque forms are used to make a polychrome covering of the whole surface of a piece. Towards the end of the century bird, flower, and berry themes are more in evidence, partly chased, partly painted in enamel—the latter especially in Solvychegodsk. Figure subjects, engraved or painted, have fore-runners in the Old Russian *lubok* picture sheets. Piscator's illustrated Bible too provided many models.

It is noteworthy that in the second half of the century interest in allegories and emblems was particularly strong. Books were published about them with illustrations and explanatory verses.[1] At the same time heraldry was a subject attracting much attention, though in Russia, by contrast with Western Europe, it lacked the tradition of the Crusades.

It was in 1672, however, that for the first time a Book of Armoury, the so-called *Titulyarnik*, was first drawn up at the command of the Tsar Alexey Mikhaylovich, containing the coats of arms of the Tsar, the Princes, and the States (or Provinces). Under Peter I all questions on coats of arms became the responsibility of the Master Herald's College which he had set up and from 1797 was additionally regulated by the Universal Arms Book *(Obshchiy gerbovnik)*.[2]

18th Century

Allegories and emblems, which throughout the century were mostly engraved or embossed on gold objects, were from 1720 onwards copied from a volume published in Amsterdam in 1705.[3] This book appeared in St. Petersburg in 1788, edited by

Nestor Maksimovich Ambodik under the title *Emblemy i simvoly izbrannye*, and was reprinted in 1811.

In style the masters at first often follow 17th-century German examples. From 1740 onward, however, they produced a specifically Russian, ponderous rococo style, which to some extent held its own till 1780 and then slowly gave way to classicism.

There has been much discussion of the problem how far art in Russia, after the reforms of Peter the Great, was still really Russian. It is well known how this Emperor recruited craftsmen from Western Europe to settle in Russia. Statistics of the period 1714 to 1800 show that the ratio of goldsmiths in the guilds was 609 foreign to 39 Russian masters.[4] For example the masters who made gold snuff-boxes in St. Petersburg were without exception of non-Russian birth. And yet if we turn our attention from the legal classifications of state or national affiliations to the actual art or craft objects made by these masters in the 18th century, we find that they are unmistakably Russian. Not only goldsmiths like Pauzié or Scharff, who had served their apprenticeships in Russia, but also those like Ador, for instance, who were immigrants, immediately adapted themselves to Russian realities and their customers' taste. The special characteristics of this change are in most cases a preference for large sizes and a certain ponderousness and colourfulness.

It can be argued that the whole concept of 'Russian' gold boxes is meaningless because of the foreign origin of their makers.[5] But the boxes by Ador, Bouddé, or Keibel cannot be considered Swiss, French, or German either: all the more so since the court style in Europe was in its totality moulded in Paris.

19th Century

French influence continued right up to the beginning of the 19th century, even during the Napoleonic wars. The *'Empire'* style of Alexander I, with its gold-ornamented sphinxes, bay wreaths, and classical emblems formed the artistic background to the wars of liberation which brought glory to Russia.

With Nicholas I, who pursued a policy of friendship towards Germany (his wife was the daughter of the King of Prussia), we have German-style romanticism together with Biedermeier as influences on the applied arts. Revivalist uses were found for Gothic, Renaissance, and later Baroque stylistic forms.

With the rise of nationalism historicism too appeared in Russian guise, the decorative and formal themes of its 16th and 17th centuries being copied and revived. This Russian historicism, which had affinities with Pan-Slavism, reached its peak at the All-Russian Exhibition of 1882 in Moscow.

Paralleling this development, which found adherents especially among the wealthy mercantile community in Moscow, and in parallel too with the first French- and then English-styled artistic trends at the Court in St. Petersburg, we find objects of the goldsmith's craft which must be regarded as specific and original Russian products. They comprise naturalistic forms of animals and fruits featured in articles of use and ornament which reflect the convivial, nature-loving life of provincial country estates.

Around 1900 historicism and nationalism were overtaken by Art nouveau. Unlike Western Europe, Russia accorded only limited success to this ornamental style with its reliance on vegetable structures. There was a popular mixture of Art nouveau with Old Russian stylistic elements, especially insofar as these too built on plant-like and arabesque structures. They are particularly evident in the *cloisonné* enamels of Fedor Rückert or Mariya Semenova.

An opposite pole to this style was presented by the *Mir iskusstva* ('World of Art') movement, founded in 1898, which attempted to find new possibilities in a union of international with historical currents of art. Adherents of this movement made particular studies of the 18th and early 19th centuries. Fabergé is considered a typical representative of *Mir iskusstva* ideas in the applied arts.[6]

Notes

1 Nilsson, N.A., *Russian Heraldic Virši from the 17th Century*, Acta Universitatis Stockholmiensis 10, Uppsala, 1964.
2 Loukomsky, L., 'L'art héraldique en Russie' (Russian), in *Starye gody*, 1911, II, p. 5-35.
3 *Symbola et Emblemata, iussu Czaris Petri Alexeidis excusa*, Amsterdam, 1705 (quoted after D. de la Feuilles, *Devises et Emblèmes*).
4 Bäcksbacka, *St. Petersburgs Juvelerare, passim*.
5 Corbeiller, Clare le, *Alte Tabaksdosen*, p. 64.
6 Habsburg-Lothringen/Solodkoff: *Fabergé*, p. 41; cf. Snowman, A. Kenneth, *The Art of Fabergé*, London, 1953, p. 95.

Materials, Techniques and Typical Objects

Basma

Basma is the technique of impressing thin silver or gold foil with regular patterns. For this purpose a matrix of stone, wood, or iron was made and engraved with an ornament in relief. A silver or gold foil was placed on the relief and pieces of lead over that. With a wooden mallet the soft lead could be manipulated in such a way as to impress the matrix ornament on the foil. Identical ornaments were then strung together in a repeating strip. Owing to the thinness of the metal in this technique it could be used only for the superficial decoration of an object, mostly icons, but also book bindings.

The *basma* technique is very ancient in Russia and was already in use before the period of Tatar rule. It is often found in 17th-century icons. During the 18th century it went out of use.[1]

Bratina

A *bratina* (loving-cup) is a round bombé vessel for drinks, with a short foot, and sometimes with a domed cover. *Bratiny* were made of gold or silver, also of coconut shell, stone, or horn in settings of precious metal. There is generally an inscription engraved below the rim, sometimes in *niello* or simply chased. The inscriptions either name the owner, record a presentation, or quote a drinking motto. The *bratina* was used for the drink of welcome. They were also placed on the graves of the dead, filled with *syta* (honey dissolved in water).

While *bratiny* are described in documents as early as the 16th century, the earliest ones to survive come from the 17th century. Then they were produced in considerable numbers in Germany, especially Hamburg, for the Russian market. Towards the close of the 19th century they were produced, in the vogue for historicism, by all the major firms.

Chara

A *chara* is a vessel for spirits, round and low in shape, with a horizontally attached flat handle at the side, current in the 16th and 17th century and later still in use as a kitchen container. In the 18th century the *chara* became smaller in size and was then called *charka*.

Charka

Charka is sometimes translated as vodka cup.

In the course of the 18th century various fashionable shapes appeared such as a globular or bulbous tumbler with octagonal rim, less often cylindrical, dating from 1730 to 1750. They are mostly smooth, with engraved decoration. From 1750 onwards the quatrefoil *charka* was popular, embossed with rocaille patterns.

In the 18th century *charki* with inlaid coins or tokens were produced, generally while the coins were still in circulation.

A curious development was the production of *charki* during the Seven Years' War (1756-62) incorporating conquered enemy coins. In those days gold and silver coins contained a high enough percentage of precious metal to ensure their acceptance in either camp.

Around 1800 the production of *charki* became less frequent since glasses were by now being used for vodka. But about 1900 there was again more frequent production of silver or golden *charki*.

Easter eggs

In Russia the Easter Feast was not only regarded as the supreme celebration of the Church, but, since it came at the end of the tedious months of winter it was observed with rejoicing as the first sign of spring. After the night service in church it was customary to meet for an Easter breakfast at which the guests gave one another eggs. The simple notion of colouring and decorating boiled hen's eggs goes back to the 13th century.

Besides these edible presents it soon became customary to make Easter eggs of *papier maché*, stone, and metal. Such objects are found from the 18th century onwards.

As Pauzié relates in his *Memoirs*, on his return from his visit to Geneva in 1751 he offered the Empress Elizabeth a patch box in the form of an egg. 'She seemed to me quite astonished to see before her such a small egg, so artistically worked. Her name was on it in small diamonds, together with a double eagle and her cypher. The egg opened at the touch of a button and served as a patch box.' This egg is still in the

Hermitage, where it is kept with other such eggs. About 1770 a goldsmith of French origin, Jean Jacques Duc, made for Catherine II a perfume pan in the form of an egg. It is enamelled and has a scene of sacrifice in *grisaille*, with crowds in classical costume doing homage to the Empress.

The series of examples can be continued in the 19th century. For Alexander II the goldsmith Joseph Nordberg made a silver egg with the enamelled monogram of the Emperor. It was originally kept in the palace of Tsarskoye Selo.

From 1883 onward Fabergé became famous for his Imperial easter eggs, which he used to make every year as the Emperor's present for the Empress and later also for the Empress-Dowager. Of the 57 which he made altogether 42 are known.

Fabergé was also the goldsmith who made miniature Easter eggs popular as pendants for necklaces and bracelets, although he was far from being their inventor, as Easter eggs of this kind were known already in the 18th century. In the 19th century all the larger firms produced these pendants. They occur in silver and in gold, with enamel and precious stones, and also as gold-mounted eggs of semi-precious stone. They vary in size from 0.8 to 2.5 cm.

Besides Fabergé his competitors, as for instance Britzin, Astreyden, and the 3rd Artel, made these Easter eggs. They were given by the hundred at Easter and chains of 30 egg pendants were quite usual.

Enamel

Enamel is a form of glass flux made from siliceous sand and coloured with metal oxides. The more lead the glass contains the easier it is to melt. After the glass flux has been heated a hard, shining mass of glass emerges. Enamel can be transparent or milky, the latter effect being due to the addition of tin, potash, or kaolin. The metal oxides yield the following colours: tin—white; iron—yellow or deep blue; copper—turquoise; magnesium—violet; gold—red; iridium—grey and black; silver—yellow. The pieces of raw enamel are coarsely pounded in metal mortars and then ground and pulverized in a mortar of stone.

The actual enamelling of an object is carried out as follows. First a drawing is made on the metal object, which is then filled out or covered with powdered enamel. This is done by moistening the enamel dust with water and applying it with a brush or a sort of spoon. Then the object is heated until the enamel melts and adheres to the metal base. In principle several layers of enamel are applied, and the use of layers of translucent enamels produces colour effects. Finally the enamel is ground with soft sandstone or pumice dust followed by a softwood wheel and last of all polished to a shine with a leather. Enamel holds best on a gold base, because the melting point of gold is so much higher than that of enamel. Because of the softness of this metal, however, strains may be set up, causing the enamel to spring away from the base. For this reason gold surfaces are often enamelled on both sides.

While silver is harder than gold, there are difficulties about enamelling on silver because its melting point is close to that of enamel. For this reason opaque enamels that melt more easily are preferred on silver.

The techniques listed below, apart from the artistic possibilities of ornament in painted enamel, often arise from the attempt to attach the enamel better to its metal base. The different techniques may be grouped in three main categories: incised enamel, *cloisonné* and painted enamel. The technique of enamelling an incised surface is among the oldest and takes the following three forms: firstly *champlevé* (or 'cavity fusion') enamel. Here depressions are dug out of a relatively thick metal base which together compose an artistic design, without having individually artistic shapes. The graphic framework consists of those portions of metal which have not been dug out. The depressions are filled with coloured—mostly opaque—enamel, so that the base forms a single plane with the enamel. The *champlevé* technique reached one of its highest points in the 12th and 13th centuries in the areas of the Rhine, Meuse, and Moselle. In the Renaissance in Italy and later in Germany it was taken up for engraved and enamelled twining ornaments and grotesques. In Russia *champlevé* enamel does not occur until the 19th century.

In the *basse-taille* technique translucent enamel is laid in excavated depressions each of which is itself an artistic low relief. The varying depth of the depressions gives the enamel different shades of colour. *Basse-taille* enamel occurs predominantly in gold snuff-boxes of the 18th century.

In the third process, *guilloché*, a metal surface is incised by machine in such a manner that a pattern of parallel, intertwined, concentric, or circular lines is formed to emerge in wave-like, ray-like, or zig-zag fashion. The surface thus treated is fired with translucent enamel so that the engraved pattern remains visible as gradations of colour, often comparable with a *moiré* textile. The *guillochage* requires a rose-engine, a special tool which was invented in the 18th century and used, principally in Paris, for snuff-boxes. In Russia *guilloché* enamel re-emerged towards the end of the 19th century with Fabergé and his competitors.

As for *cloisonné* (or 'compartment') enamel, there are three variants of this technique which are often treated as equivalent, but differ in their preparation.

'Ridge' enamel occurs predominantly in gold objects. In this gold 'ridges' are soldered on to a gold plate in such a way as to outline the drawing and form compartments (*cloisons*) to be filled with enamel. The ridges consist of very thin gold strips which are extremely complicated to solder edge-on. Often the metal plate is incised beforehand, so as to facilitate soldering on the raised parts of the surface. Ridge enamel was a speciality of Byzantine art which attained its highest development in the 10th and 11th centuries. The technique was introduced to Russia and Georgia from Constantinople by so-called 'Greek' craftsmen. In the 12th and 13th centuries we find enamelware under Byzantine influence in Kievan Rus.

Cloisonné ('hairnet', or filigree) enamel is the technique also called *Russian cloisonné*. The first step is forming a cellular pattern with soldered wire. The compartments are

47 Enamelled gold *bratina* with precious stones and pearls, Moscow about 1640, 27 cm high. (Formerly in the Secular Treasury, now in the Kunsthistorisches Museum, Vienna)
Bowl and cover of the *bratina* are chased with flutes, overlaid with a lavish enamel design in opaque white, light and dark blue, with translucent green. The gemstones, rubies and sapphires, also smaller emeralds, are partly cut, partly *en cabochon* or in their natural state. The finial of the cover is a white enamelled Polish eagle with the cypher W R on its breast while black enamelled inscription lines run round the rim, giving the name and various titles of the Tsar Mikhail Fedorovich. This Tsar, the first of the house of Romanov, ruled from 1613 to 1645. He had sent the *bratina* in 1637 to the Polish King Wladislas IV on the occasion of his wedding with the Archduchess Caecilia Renata, the daughter of the Emperor Ferdinand II, together with other presents.
The *bratina*, made in the enamel style typical of the Kremlin workshops, was recorded in the 1750 inventory of the Vienna treasury. (Cf. A. Ilg, *Album von Objecten aus der Sammlung kunstindustrieller Gegenstände des A.H. Kaiserhauses. Arbeiten der Goldschmiede- und Steinschlifftechnik*, Vienna 1895, p. 16)

48-9　Enamelled silver bowl, the central medallion fully painted with a swan and its young swimming on a lake, the sides with polychrome flowers—narcissi, tulips, and asters—in surface enamel. The exterior of the bowl (Pl. 49) shows similar flowers, which there, however, appear on areas of bare silver left unenamelled within the large compartments edged with silver wire. On the base the central medallion has its flowers on white enamel. The work is typical of Solvychegodsk, end of the 17th century, diameter 14 cm.

50　Enamelled silver coffee-pot of tapering form with detachable domed cover and wooden handle. The pot is chased and engraved with bowmen (Cupids?) within round foliage cartouches surrounded by scrollwork on a plain ground of blue enamel. Master's initials of Yakov Popov (220), Solvychegodsk, about 1750, 17 cm high. This enamel technique is typical of Solvychegodsk and found also with a white enamel ground.

51　Silver-gilt enamelled tankard built up architecturally in the form of a tower, decorated in brilliant colours with scrolling foliage, the base internally with a *plique-à-jour* rosette enclosing a crowned double eagle, Imperial Warrant mark of Pavel Ovchinnikov (174), Moscow, end of 19th century, 22 cm high.

52　(left) Cream-jug with shaded polychrome enamel flowers, master's initials of Mariya Semenova (150), Moscow 1899-1908, 4.2 cm high;

(middle) Cream-jug with a band of blue scrolls on a cream-coloured ground, by O. Kurlyukov (165), Moscow 1899-1908, 7.2 cm high;
(right) *Bonbonnière*, the lid with a medallion of flowers painted *en plein* on a pink ground, master's initials of Ivan Saltykov (98), Moscow, end of 19th century, 7 cm diameter.

53　Three enamel objects by Gustav Klingert (278) with predominantly turquoise decoration and spirals of silver wire:
(left) Cream-jug, 8.2 cm high;
(middle) Sugar-bowl, 10 cm in diameter;
(right) Tea-glass holder, 8.9 cm high.
All these pieces Moscow, late 19th century.

54　Rectangular enamelled silver casket, the lid with an *en plein* enamel painting, 'The Boyar's Wedding' after Constantin Makovsky, the casket signed by Fedor Rückert (207), Moscow about 1900, 16.2 cm wide. Rückert frequently used historicizing paintings by Russian 19th-century masters—as for instance, to take another example, Viktor Vasnetsov—as originals for the decoration of his enamel pieces. In the scene shown here silver articles from the 17th century are set up in the background. The *cloisonné* enamel decoration, characteristic of Rückert, is shown in detail in Pl. 73.

55　Silver-gilt *cloisonné* enamel service with coffee-pot, cream-jug, sugar-bowl, and sugar-tongs, decorated with stylized flowers on a cream ground, by Pavel Ovchinnikov (174), Moscow,

end of 19th century, the coffee-pot 17 cm high.

56　Enamelled casket with predominantly blue and turquoise decoration, the base with P. Ovchinnikov's mark, the lid with the initials (Cyrillic) AiPO (13), Moscow 1884, 18.6 cm.

57　Silver-gilt *cloisonné* enamel objects:
(left) Pitcher with green rosettes and blue and white scrolls, marks defaced, Moscow 1891, 9 cm high;
(middle) Sugar-bowl in predominantly blue shades, master's initials of N. Alexeyev (156, 157), Moscow 1896, 13.3 cm diameter;
(right) Sugar-bowl on ball feet, master's initials (Cyrillic) by Gustav Klingert (63), Moscow 1888-1908, 9.8 cm diameter.

58　(left) Silver-gilt *plique-à-jour* enamel liqueur cup, the foot with *cloisonné* flowers, Moscow 1892, 9.8 cm high;
(middle) Champagne cup of *plique-à-jour* enamel, P. Ovchinnikov (174), Moscow, 10.8 cm high;
(right) *Plique-à-jour* enamel beaker, master's initials T.I., 6.4 cm high.

59　Silver objects with lacquer painting on a red lacquer ground depicting rustic *troika* scenes:
(left) Cylindrical beaker, master's initials (Cyrillic) SP, Moscow 1908-17, 9.6 cm high;
(middle) Sugar-bowl with swing handle, master's initials IKA, St. Petersburg 1908-17, 13.5 cm diameter;
(right) Milk-jug from the same service, 10 cm high.

first produced in various shapes, mostly leaves or circles, and soldered to the smooth surface of the object. Then the compartments are filled with the enamel which, in contrast with the other methods, is not polished, as in this case the filigree wires stand proud of the enamel surface. Often circular compartments are filled with enamel in such a way that the enamel stands out in a hemisphere resembling a bead. In other cases the compartments are relatively large and filled with painted enamels.

This technique is employed principally on silver objects. It was well known among popular handicrafts in Eastern Europe, in Hungary and Greece, for example, and since 1900 has enjoyed special popularity among Russian silversmiths.

Plique-à-jour or 'window' enamel is a technique with affinities to filigree enamel but demands still greater artistic dexterity. The silversmith makes a filigree object out of silver wire, the strands of which are soldered together at the intersections and points of contact as in a net freely constructed without a metal base. The openings between the strands are filled with transparent enamel, the method being to introduce the enamel powder, plentifully mixed with water, drop by drop. After firing, tensions may occur between the metal and the enamel, causing the enamel cells to break or fall out, so that the enamelling process must be repeated several times.

Objects made by this method achieve their effect, like Gothic stained glass windows, by the light shining through. They were produced in Russia and also in Norway from the 19th century onward. A similar technique was used with fretwork ornaments. Here a metal surface was pierced here and there and the holes filled with translucent enamel.

In *painted enamel* the different colours are applied, singly or mixed, in an artistic picture or design. For this purpose the enamel powder is not mixed with water but with oils and applied to the object like oil-paint before being fired. While with other methods the individual colours are joined together in a desired pattern, which through the drawing on the metal emerges as a picture or as arabesques, in the painting method the picture is formed by the mixing of colours and their—temporarily—fluid arrangement.

In *émail en plein* (surface painting) the picture is produced on a metal surface which is completely covered with enamel. In firing there is a risk that tensions may be set up between enamel and metal, and these are counteracted by the enamelling of the reverse of the metal surface.

In *émail en ronde bosse* (encrusted enamel—enamel on a relief or sculpture) the artist first had to prepare a suitable sculptural base. This could be cast in metal or embossed. The relief was then painted with coloured enamel. As the enamel flux ran off the more prominent parts of the relief during the firing the process had to be repeated several times and demanded great experience and technical skill on the part of the artist. Encrusted enamel is found principally on gold. The history of enamel-work in Russia is best considered as falling into two periods, first, its emergence and flowering in the 16th to 18th centuries, and secondly, its revival in the 19th to 20th centuries.

16th to 18th Century: Moscow

During the first half of the 17th century the enameller's art in Moscow was still closely linked with the artistic tradition of the 16th century.[1] It was in this century that *cloisonné* enamel, which had suffered a total eclipse under Tatar rule, had its heyday. The style was characterized by particular definition and clarity in drawing and fineness of artwork in the filigree, with delicate leaves and flowers. Gradually this austerity gave way to a tendency to stronger enamelling, which spread over the metal base. Colours became stronger, such colours as emerald green, blue, light blue, and white predominating, with semi-precious stones being more frequently used for decoration. The foliage ornaments became thicker, enamelled in relief style. The leafy tendrils were longer and more intertwined, and strict symmetry was replaced by a more naturally scrolling decoration. A typical decorative method in the *cloisonné* of the early 16th century was that in which tiny metal pellets set in the molten enamel afterwards stood out like dots from the foliage. The effects of painting with enamel are often reminiscent of Indian or Persian enamel paintings. Understandably so, since in the 17th century there were commercial contacts between Moscow and Near and Far Eastern countries which often had an effect on the arts.

Cloisonné also came to be put to more varied uses around this period. It was employed not only on objects of special value for the Tsar's or Patriarch's Courts but also with more common objects, buttons, earrings, chains, and saddle ornaments.

In the course of the 17th century a new form of enamelling besides *cloisonné* evolved among the goldsmiths and silversmiths of Moscow, the combination of enamel on chased and engraved reliefs with painted enamel. Both these techniques were at the same time widespread also in Western Europe, especially in Germany.

Through the increased commercial and cultural exchanges between Moscow and Western Europe the most varied enamel objects reached Russia in the form of diplomatic gifts and in other ways. At this period German and other West European craftsmen, as well as Oriental ones, were working with Russian masters in the Tsar's Court workshops in the Kremlin.[2] The mixture of nationalities produced a distinctive style of Moscow enamelware.

This was a relief enamel in which a surface of chased decorations and figures was covered with enamel. The relief was first covered with a monotone enamel coating, mostly opaque, which was then enamelled in polychrome. Reserved areas of metal were engraved with ornaments and themes incorporated in the total design, and these were then often coated with transparent enamel. It could also be that different enamelling techniques were employed simultaneously and the work then decorated with coloured precious stones and pearls. One striking point is that the height of the reliefs steadily increased up to the end of the 17th century.

While *cloisonné* had become widespread, encrusted enamel, which was in principle confined to a gold base, remained a technique reserved for special commissions by the Tsar or Patriarch. The articles in question could be practical objects, even church utensils, or *oklady* for icons. Among the earliest commissioned work of this kind was the making of the *bolshoy naryad*—the Imperial regalia, crown, orb, sceptre, bow and quiver—in the years 1627-8 to the order of Tsar Mikhail Fedorovich Romanov.

Solvychegodsk

The *cloisonné* enamel technique developed in Moscow in the 16th century soon spread to northern Russia, where the colours of enamel used were preponderantly dark blue and green. In Solvychegodsk towards the end of the 16th century silversmiths were already beginning to combine the *cloisonné* technique with painted enamel and thus to evolve a typical style of their own.[3] Solvychegodsk, a town which in the 15th century was still called Usolsk—which is why the enamel too is often called Usolsk enamel—lay on the Archangel-Siberia trade route and had become a wealthy commercial centre. This was principally due to the activities of the merchant family of the Stroganovs, at whose hands not only trade but art and culture too attained a high level of prosperity throughout the region. They engaged their own artists and supplied them with commissions. The Stroganov school of icon-painting became famous and in the 17th century was itself not without influence on the Moscow school of icon-painting. Enamel too was among the fields of art which this wealthy merchant family promoted.

In enamel objects from Solvychegodsk the *cloisonné* technique is diluted to such an extent by the enlargement of the compartments enclosed by the filigree that the end result is often no more than a surface enamel with filigree interruptions. And in the last quarter of the 17th century the masters did in fact move over to surface enamel. The elements of Solvychegodsk enamel may be characterized as follows. A ground of white enamel is laid over the whole surface, on which exuberant drawings are painted with fine strokes in black, mostly of large tulips, camellias, cornflowers, and sunflowers. These are coloured in with liquid enamel in yellow, red, blue, and pinkish violet.

Flowers, however, are not the only subjects; there are also animals and birds which include the swan, the pelican, the lion, the bear, the stag, the fox, and the sheep. Later come human subjects, biblical scenes (David and Goliath, Samson in the lions' den), allegorical scenes, creatures from legend. Scenes representing the seasons, the five senses, and the signs of the zodiac were specially popular.

The objects thus decorated were also various—bowls, *charki*, cups, boxes, cutlery, buttons—and, once more, church utensils.

While flower-painting is often characterized by the exuberance of the drawing and painting—fixed patterns occur only rarely—the other subjects, especially those with human figures, are often painted in precise detail. For this class of painted enamel links can be established with the early Russian miniature painting of such artists as Grigoriy Mussikiysky or Andrey Ovsov at the beginning of the

60 A selection of pill-, cigarette- and other boxes, a spoon, and an icon of St. Catherine; silver-gilt and enamel; by various masters; 5-7 cm.

61 Silver-gilt enamelled service consisting of sugar-bowl, cream-jug, and six spoons, decorated with polychrome painted *cloisonné* enamel with turquoise pellet borders. The sugar-bowl by Mariya Semenova (150), Moscow 1899-1908, the other pieces by the 11th Artel, Moscow 1908-17, in an oak case with the stamp of the I.E. Morozov firm, St. Petersburg. This service with case is documentary evidence that the bigger businesses often had pieces made by different artists and then sold them under their own brand name.

62 Tapering beaker in *plique-à-jour* enamel with Chinese figure subjects and scrolling foliage and rosettes. Engraved signature under the foot rim (Cyrillic) Pavel Ovchinnikov & Sons, late 19th century, 13.5 cm high.

63 Enamelled silver-gilt vase in Oriental style with floral decoration, the foot, neck, and handle in transparent *plique-à-jour* enamel, by Grachev, St. Petersburg, end of 19th century, 29.2 cm high.

64 *Cloisonné* enamel *kovsh* decorated with birds and flowering scrolls on a cream-coloured ground with a border of turquoise enamel, by Dmitriy Nikolayev (80), Moscow 1899-1908, 23.5 cm long.

65 Silver-gilt *cloisonné* enamel *kovsh* decorated with polychrome geometrical patterns and scrolling foliage with silver beads, 8th Artel, Moscow 1908-17, 22.5 cm long.

67

68

66 Large silver-gilt enamelled vase with three handles, decorated with shaded flowers in pastel colours on a cream-coloured ground and set with cabochon citrines, amethysts, and tourmalines, by Pavel Ovchinnikov, Moscow 1899-1908, 27.5 cm high.

67 Oval bowl on stand with shaded *cloisonné* enamel in blue, violet, cream and yellow, decorated with flowers, birds and sheaves of corn. Signed by O. Kurlyukov (166), Moscow 1899-1908, 40 cm high.

68 Silver-gilt *cloisonné* enamel tea service of an unusual rectangular shape, with flowers and scrolling foliage in pastel colours, on an artificially blackened oxydized ground, Imperial Warrant mark of Pavel Ovchinnikov (174), Moscow 1899-1908, the tea-pot 16 cm high.

69 Three enamel objects from the workshop of Fedor Rückert (207), Moscow:
(left) Small *kovsh* with rosettes and flowers on a grey and brown ground, 1908-17, 11.2 cm long;
(middle) Case with a view of the Moscow Kremlin on the lid enamelled *en plein*, surrounded by stylized flowers and geometrical patterns, the sides similarly enamelled. The wires of the *cloisons* have been subsequently picked out with gilding. The Rückert mark has been subsequently overstamped by Fabergé, who sold the piece in his shop. Moscow 1908-17, 10 cm long;
(right) *Kovsh* with fleur-de-lys handle, enamelled with scrolling foliage and a harpy, Moscow 1899-1908, 15.5 cm long.

70 Silver-gilt *cloisonné* enamel tea and coffee service with shaded flowering foliage on a granulated gilt ground, the covers with mother-of-pearl finials, master's initials of Mariya Semenova (150), Moscow 1899-1908, the coffee-pot 16.5 cm high. This service was sold in a case having inside it the house stamp of *Maison Boucheron, 9 Pont des Maréchaux, Moscou – 2a Place Vendôme, Paris*.

18th century. In flower-painting tulips were especially popular, as indeed they were in the rest of Europe in the 17th century for their decorative character. For this reason too the enamel objects may be compared with those from Augsburg. For subjects with figures use was often made of well-known models, such as Piscator's illustrated Bible or the cosmographies which circulated also in Western Europe.

Painted enamel in Solvychegodsk reached its peak towards the end of the 17th century. From the beginning of the 18th it had a rapid decline, because of the deterioration in the city's commercial position, for which the opening of a trade fair at Irbit and the diversion of Siberian trade through Velikiy Ustyug were largely responsible. It is from now on that enamel was applied to copper objects.

The enamelware of Solvychegodsk, however, had its influence on other centres of the art. Some of its masters were already working in the Kremlin workshops in Moscow in the 17th century, and later in the 18th century the enamelware of Ustyug was influenced by craftsmen from Solvychegodsk. No marks or signatures are known on enamel objects from Solvychegodsk.

16th to 18th Centuries: Velikiy Ustyug

At Velikiy Ustyug, besides its famous *niello* production, there was an extensive output of enamelware. Ustyug enamelware uses surface enamel on copper (sometimes silver) with inlay in silver relief. Only three colours of enamel occur: white, blue, and greenish turquoise, in each case opaque. The enamel was applied in several coats to a shallowly embossed copper object, with counter-enamelling. Silver reliefs were worked into the final coat, setting fast in the enamel when it was fused. The silver relief ornaments were stamped on with a die and rechased, and showed flowers with rocaille patterns, animals and people, scenes and landscapes.

Enamel objects of this kind were produced in great numbers between 1760 and 1790, especially by the Factory for Enamelware and Nielloware of the brothers Afanasiy and Stepan Popov, founded in 1761. In this period there was evidently a regular fashion for white enamel objects. The explanation must be that owing to their resemblance to porcelain, which was still extremely expensive, the enamel equivalents were regarded as a decorative substitute.[4]

In St. Petersburg in the 18th century the main production was of gold snuff-boxes (q.v.) in the French style.

19th Century

At the beginning of the 19th century enamelware production was predominantly of enamel miniatures, which often served as plaquettes for the decoration of goldsmiths' objects. In this respect there was hardly any distinction between Russian handicrafts and those of Western Europe: it was an undistinguished period in the history of the craft. From the middle of the century onwards, with the growth of historicism, the enameller's art rose once more to a new peak. The return to traditional craft forms caused a revival of the Moscow *cloisonné* enamel of the 16th and 17th centuries. F. Mishukov for instance produced copies of two 16th-century gospel bindings.[5]

There arose a fashion for *cloisonné* enamelware, which appealed principally to the conservative mercantile society of Moscow and lasted until the Revolution. The spread of the fashion was largely due to the manufacturing activities of the Ovchinnikov firm. This firm owed its leading position not only to its large-scale production but also to the quality of its pieces. As early as in 1865 the firm won a gold medal at the Moscow Exhibition of Manufactures. In connection with the All-Russian Exhibition of 1882 contemporaries observed that the Ovchinnikov firm 'had the honourable task of making this important artistic technique known not only among ourselves but also in Europe'.[6] And in fact this firm with others did from now on exhibit *cloisonné* enamel at a succession of world fairs.

Cloisonné enamel can often have a ponderous effect owing to its arabesque riot of colour. At the Chicago World Fair of 1893 the opinion was expressed that the technique, owing to its too frequent use of the same decorative elements, quickly became monotonous.[7] Later Art nouveau influence brought about a curious mixture of historicizing and Art nouveau themes, particularly well illustrated by objects from the Rückert workshop or those of the 11th and 20th Artels.

Contrasting with the Moscow *cloisonné* style is the enamelware evolved towards the end of the 19th century in St. Petersburg, though here too there were some firms producing *cloisonné*, especially Grachev. But in St. Petersburg, with its western orientation, the fashion was for *guilloché* enamel. This type of surface enamel had already been perfected in the 18th century by the Paris craftsmen who specialized in gold snuff-boxes. It was Fabergé who was to become the outstanding representative of the technique. His pieces were being bought in Russia from 1884 onwards and from 1900 throughout the world. Yet Fabergé was not the only one to practise it. Other makers of *guilloché* enamel objects, especially Hahn, Britzin, and Sumin, often surprise us by the quality of their work, yet in the last analysis do not approach the smooth elegance of Fabergé.

Notes

1 Suslov, 'Moskovskaya emal' XVII v.', pp. 208ff.
2 Postnikova-Loseva, 'Zolotye... izdeliya', p. 148 (names of masters) and p. 152.
3 Cf. Pomerantsev, 'Finift usol'skogo dela', p. 104; Platonova, 'Usol'skaya emal'', p. 56.
4 Cf. Pushkarev, V. (ed.), *Russian Applied Art*, p. 45.
5 Pisarskaya, Platonova, Ulyanova, *Russkiye emali*, p. 218.
6 *Otchet Vserossiyskoy khudozhestvenno-promyshlennoy vystavki 1882 goda*, vol. III, pp. 3-5, quoted from Pisarskaya, Platonova, Ulyanova, *Russkiye emali*, p. 208.
7 Krantz, *Exposition Internationale de Chicago 1893*, p. 33.

71 Silver-gilt enamelled tea service with tea-pot, sugar-bowl, and cream-jug with polychrome flower and rosette decoration, Imperial Warrant mark of Pavel Ovchinnikov (174), Moscow 1889-91, the tea-pot 13 cm high.

72 Enamelled, silver-gilt tea service consisting of tea-pot, sugar-bowl, cream-jug, sugar-tongs, tea-strainer, fork and spoon, Imperial Warrant mark of the Pavel Ovchinnikov (174) firm, Moscow 1908-17. This service was the first prize in a competition at the Cannes Golf Club, of which Grand Duke Mikhail Mikhaylovich was president.

73 Two examples of different *cloisonné* enamel techniques: (above) by Mariya Semenova; (below) by Fedor Rückert. In the upper example the wires soldered on to the base as a frame for enamel compartments are easily recognizable. Between these *cloisons*, which are fully painted out with variously coloured, shaded enamel, the matt gilt ground appears. In the lower example the enamel technique typical of Rückert is clear. The whole decorated surface has a covering of enamel from which the wires stand out only slightly. They are subsequently gilded or silvered over, giving more brilliance to the mostly pastel-coloured surfaces.

74 Enamelled silver-gilt service of knife, fork, spoon, salt-cellar and salt-spoon, and napkin ring, by Grachev, St. Petersburg 1895. The service was a christening present from the Russian Empress.
(lower row) Tapering enamelled beaker with the turquoise enamel typical of Gustav Klingert's work, master's initials GK (278), Moscow 1895, 7.3 cm high, sold in an original case with the Morozov stamp.

Endova

Vessel in the form of a large *bratina* with a beak-formed spout at the top rim. The *endova* was used for pouring wine, beer, mead, and other drinks into smaller drinking vessels. There were various sizes of *endova*, which were made of silver up to the end of the 17th century, and of copper still in the 19th century.

Filigree

Filigree is the technique of soldering together an open pattern of silver or gold wire diversified with tiny balls or beads. The wire used for this purpose was made of relatively pure metal, as being more suitable for forging or drawing and then for forming into an ornamental shape because of its softness. Also several wires could be braided together into a sort of plait. There were two ways of using wire as a filigree, one the open, net-like way, the other as ornament soldered to a base. In this latter form filigree was a first step to the *cloisonné* enamelling technique, as the spaces between the wires were often filled with enamel.

The filigree technique is very ancient in Russia, the earliest objects of the kind being of the 9th-10th centuries. It reached its peak in the 15th and 16th centuries with the cities of Novgorod and Moscow as centres, as well as in Velikiy Ustyug, Solvychegodsk, and Vologda.

In Moscow it was a very early step to filling the filigree with enamel, and one that was taken above all in the 17th century. Probably the most important masters for filigree here in that century were Larion Afanasev (1661-92), Vasiliy Ivanov (1658-80), and Luka Murmiya (1682-1700). In the 18th century, by contrast, we find open filigrees characterized by a four-petalled flower pattern with *zern'* beads as centres. An outstanding master of this type was Stepan Kalashnikov. It is found on the most varied objects, either open or with a heavy background. Frequently, too, *nielloed* medallions were inserted in the filigree network.

During the early 19th century the following application of the technique was developed: a framework of relatively thick wires or strips, mostly in the form of vertical bands, was soldered together and its open spaces then filled with a flower pattern in fine filigree. Also the Old Russian technique of spiral filigree was revived in the 19th century: the most frequently occurring pieces of this sort are rather small open-work caskets.

Towards the end of the 19th century the filigree technique was adopted principally for *cloisonné* enamel. Yet we do find quite a number of icon *oklady* in open filigree from this period. Here too in the late period the great firms, Ovchinnikov, Khlebnikov, and Kurlyukov in Moscow, and Grachev in St. Petersburg, were very active.

75 Silver-gilt and red lacquer tea-pot, sugar-bowl, tongs, and pickle-fork, with foliage reliefs, the covers with naturalistically cast lizard and tortoise, Imperial Warrant mark of Pavel Ovchinnikov, Moscow 1899–1908, the tea-pot 10 cm high.

76 Jewel casket in the form of a reliquary shrine enamelled all over in *champlevé* with foliage, geometrical bands, and birds of paradise. On each of the main sides back and front is a medallion framing a peasant girl in Russian national costume while on each end is a similar design of a peasant lad making music. Ovchinnikov's Imperial Warrant mark, Moscow 1876, 91 *zolotniki*, 17.3 cm long.

77 Large silver bowl with *champlevé* enamel, together with stand and spoon *en suite*. The geometrical decoration with confronted barnyard cocks echoes the style of peasant textile embroideries. Imperial Warrant mark of Pavel Ovchinnikov, Moscow 1878, the stand 38 cm in diameter.

78 Silver-gilt cigarette-cases with various kinds of decoration in *cloisonné* enamel:
(first row from left) Master's initials of Ivan Saltykov (98), Moscow 1891, 8.2 cm long; same master, Moscow 1892, 9 cm long; another Ivan Saltykov, Moscow, 8.2 cm long;
(second row) Master's initials of I. Khlebnikov (99), Moscow 1908-17, 11.3 cm long; master's mark defaced, Moscow 1895, 10 cm long; mark of the 11th Artel, Moscow 1908-17, 10.5 cm long;
(third row) With medallion in painted enamel *en plein*, master's initials (Cyrillic) V.L., Moscow 1908-17, 11.4 cm long; mark of the 20th Artel (333), Moscow 1908-17, 10 cm long; master's mark of Fedor Rückert with the stamp of the firm O. Kurlyukov, end of 19th century, 10.5 cm long.

The stamping of filigree objects, because of the thinness of the wire, was only rarely possible. Thus only a small number of the masters who worked in the technique are known.

Literature

M.M. Postnikova-Loseva & N.G. Platonova, *Russkoye khudozhestvennoye serebro*, Moscow 1959 (with a list of the filigree masters, pp. 38-47); M.M. Postnikova-Loseva, *Russkoye yuvelirnoye iskusstvo*, pp. 203 ff.

Jewellery

Russia was famous for the richness and splendour of its jewellery. This was very largely due to the fact that its territories were in close contact with the classic lands of precious stones, India and China, whose Europe-bound caravans also supplied the Court in Moscow. Over and above that the Grand Dukes and Tsars, some of whom, notably Ivan the Terrible, had the reputation of being mad about precious stones, also bought jewels in Western Europe. In a letter to the Queen of England, Elizabeth I, in 1567 Ivan IV mentioned sapphires and rubies which were to be bought for him by his ambassador in England.[1] The rich deposits in Russia itself were not on the whole completely exploited until the 19th century.

In the 17th century and earlier precious stones were mainly used in the ecclesiastical domain for the adornment of robes and utensils and in the secular world for vessels and other items. Jewelled ornament for the purpose of display and enriching one's personal appearance, without being exclusively a badge of rank, did not appear until the 18th century. In this the Russians were following Western fashions. Generally speaking, it must of course be granted that this century was the first in which gem-cutting techniques were far enough developed to allow some improvement on the polished (*cabochon*) or at best rose-cut stones available till then. In the last quarter of the 17th century and also at the beginning of the 18th there was particularly frequent mention in Russia of 'diamonds of Greek cut'.[2] These stones had rectangular or square tables with obliquely cut sides and ended in a pyramid below. In the middle of the 18th century the poly-faceted 'old brilliant' cut became established.

There is one general problem in giving any step by step account of the jeweller's art. It is that gemstones are always being re-set as fashions change, so that old original pieces, from the 18th century for instance, are very rare. Moreover, jewellery can only rarely be attributed to a particular master. Jewellery or ornaments involving gemstones were exempt in Russia, as generally in Europe, from any stamping obligation. In the 19th century jewel *étuis* marked with the jeweller's name are valuable in identifying the maker of a piece.

The most important collection of Russian jewellery is now to be found in Moscow. This is the Old Crown Treasure, containing—apart from the Dresden Green Vault—probably the most comprehensive collection of gemstone jewellery of the 18th century. During the Revolution the entire jewellery of the Russian Imperial family was preserved under seal. In 1925-6 there was a comprehensive publication of the collection, a document of great interest.[3] All the more so, as in 1927 some of the crown jewels were sold by the Soviet state as a means of procuring foreign currency.

After the Revolution a great mass of jewellery left the country with the emigrants. But only a small part of this was preserved since the jewels were needed for the owners' subsistence and sold piece by piece or broken up.

18th Century

At the beginning of the century, during the reign of Tsar Peter I, jewellery was produced only in small quantities. But the Empresses Anna Ioannovna (1730-40) and Elizabeth (1741-61) laid the foundations of Russia's fame in jewellery.

A particularly valuable source for this period is provided by the memoirs of the Court jeweller Jérémie Pauzié. He tells for instance of caravans bringing from China and the Far East precious stones, especially rubies, in the raw state to St. Petersburg. The Empress Anna Ioannovna had these stones cut for her by the Court jeweller Gravero, to whom Pauzié was apprenticed.[4]

In another passage Pauzié's business methods are clearly set out. 'Shortly after Elizabeth's accession I had the opportunity of seeing her. The Prince of Saxony (Karl-Christian Joseph), her godson, came to St. Petersburg with the purpose of asking her for the dukedom of Courland, which he indeed obtained. She conferred on him the Order of St. Andrew. Her lord-in-waiting and favourite, Ivan Ivanovich Shuvalov, who thought very highly of me, being informed by her that she wanted the star of the Order set with diamonds, sent for me and asked if I was able to accept this commission from the Empress, to whom he had recommended me. I thanked him for his kindness and told him that I flattered myself with the hope of doing the work no worse than any Greek or Armenian. After I had negotiated a good profit for the work I determined without fail, before actually starting it, to make a wax model and arrange the diamonds on it just as they would be arranged on the real star when it was finished. The Empress had never yet seen such models, since it was a custom not in use among the jewellers ordinarily working for her. I asked Shuvalov what sum it pleased her majesty to spend? He told me, about 15,000 roubles.' The commission was then executed to the Empress's complete satisfaction, and thereafter she regularly ordered from him jewellery and *objets de vertu*, especially presents for diplomats.[5]

The style of the jewellery between 1730 and 1760 was baroque: it was then the period of fireworks and masquerades. Asymmetry and polychromy predominated in all the jewels. Gems of different sizes were set irregularly in flower sprays, bouquets, and rococo ornament.

Especially popular around 1750 were coloured stones, with emeralds and sapphires in the lead. These were combined also with coloured semi-precious stones. Another technique often used about this time was that of backing diamonds with foil, so as to give these rather cold stones a light shimmer of colour, pink, yellow, or green.

In the choice of jewellery at that time chief attention was paid to the whole effect of clothing and accessories. The head was adorned with hairpins, ear-rings, and *aigrettes*. Tiaras, like necklaces, were on the whole unknown. Clothes were fitted out with brooches and clasps, their buttons often consisted of jewels. Hems were trimmed with jewelled braid.

On the incredible lavishness of jewellery in St. Petersburg Pauzié writes: 'The clothing of the ladies was very rich, as were their golden jewels. The ladies of the Court wore amazing quantities of diamonds. Ladies of comparatively low rank may be wearing as much as ten to twelve thousand roubles worth of diamonds.' For this reason the relatives of Peter III who had come to Russia for his coronation in 1762 had jewellery made for them by Pauzié of imitation stones. The poverty of these Holstein princes would otherwise have made too poor an impression in Russia.[6]

This imitation jewellery is said to have been indistinguishable from the real thing, according to Pauzié. In this he was at least at the very forefront of jewellers' technique, for in 1758 the jeweller Joseph Strasser had made the '*strass*' (paste) named after him all the rage in Paris. *Strass* was made of lead-containing glass, coloured with various metal oxides.

Besides Pauzié we know the names of other jewellers working in St. Petersburg around 1760: Auroté, Duval, Loubier, and Pfisterer. The last of these in 1764 engraved his name on a spinel *parure* among the crown jewels.[7]

From about 1760 onwards diamonds became increasingly popular and at the same time the foiling of diamonds went out of fashion. More value was put on the natural qualities of these stones and their fire. This was a consequence also of the considerable improvement in cutting techniques. Diamonds were now being given their full effect by the 'old brilliant' cut.

Like most European ruling houses the Russian Court was seized by a regular mania for diamonds. A splendid array of diamonds was viewed as inseparable from the claims of power and rank. Catherine II wrote to Voltaire on 1 September 1772 that after buying the Crozat collection of paintings she was negotiating the purchase of a '*diamant de la grosseur d'un œuf*'.[8] This stone, however, which has passed into diamond history under the name Orlov, was actually presented to her on her name day in 1773 by Prince Orlov.[9] Two other favourites of the Empress, Zubov and Potemkin, are said to have carried brilliants about with them in their waistcoat pockets in order to look at them from time to time and enjoy their glitter. Moreover, it is said to have been usual at Court to play games of cards for diamonds.[10]

The richness of the jewellery at the Court of St. Petersburg again and again astounded foreign travellers. Thus in 1784 W. Coxe writes: 'Among the manifold

79 Silver-gilt *kovchik* on three lion feet, exterior decorated with a relief of medallions with the double eagle, a lion, and a unicorn within scrolls, above them engraved the owner's inscription with a drinking motto: 'Kovchik of Vasiliy and Ivan Semenovich Maslennikov—drink to your health and ease', Novgorod, 17th century, 13.4 cm long.
Kovshi and *kovchiki* from Novgorod are distinguished by the fact that their sides are often very high. Moreover they often stand on the backs of lions or griffons.

80 Parcel-gilt presentation *kovsh* with double-eagle decoration and the engraved inscription recording the presentation of the *kovsh* by the Tsars Ivan and Peter to the merchant Abram Filimonov in the year 1688. Unmarked, 27 cm long.

81

82

83

91

92

81 Detail of parcel-gilt *kovsh* with engraved dedicatory inscription showing that it was a present by Peter the Great to the Astrakhan merchant Ivan Artemev for increasing the revenue in 1698 and 1699. Dated 1701, Moscow, 40 cm long. The round cartouche contains the beginning of the dedication with the tsar's title: 'In the year 1701, on 14th March, the Great Sovereign, Tsar and [Grand Prince]...' In the 17th and early 18th centuries engraved inscriptions in cartouches were so arranged that the ruler's name and title were distributed over four opposing, usually round cartouches, while the rest of the dedication with the recipient's name and services ran continuously across four other cartouches.

82-3 Details of an Imperial presentation *kovsh* given by Empress Anna Ioannovna to the ataman Ivan Ivanov Frolov for services rendered on 1st April 1734:
(left) The handle is decorated with an engraved portrait in profile of the Empress in an oval medallion beneath a crown. The portrait was probably copied from a coin.
(right) An engraved cartouche showing part of the dedicatory inscription with the date when the service was rendered. Beneath: the engraved signature: 'made by Larion Artemev'.

84 Large silver-gilt *kovsh* of shallow form with threefold Imperial Eagle decoration, 35.4 cm long, early 18th century. Gift of Peter the Great on 30 May 1707 to Andrey Zhdanov, citizen of Solikamsk and tax inspector for the duties on alcohol in Yakutsk in Siberia from 12 June 1698 until 1 November 1704.

85 (left) Rare silver-gilt presentation *kovsh* of Peter II (1727-30) with high straight sides, interior chased with the double eagle, exterior engraved with the presentation inscription at the sides and the Emperor's portrait in front, the handle with the monogram P A in a cartouche under a crown. The inscription says that the *kovsh* had been presented on 17 February 1728 by the Emperor Peter II to Timofey Gavrilov, ataman of the Zimovaya stanitsa of the Don Cossacks, for long and faithful service. 25.5 cm long, second quarter of the 18th century.
(right) Massive silver-gilt *kovsh*, interior applied with a cast and chased double eagle, the handle decorated with festoons of fruit surmounted by a medallion with the monogram of Catherine II, the finial shaped as a large chased double eagle. The exterior is decorated with a *nielloed* inscription inside rococo cartouches. 32 cm long, weight 1.340 grammes. The *kovsh* was presented by the Empress Catherine II to Alexey Ivanovich Osorgin, a merchant of the first corporation of Moscow and member of the guild.

86 Parcel-gilt Imperial presentation *kovsh* with chased and engraved decoration, the sides with engraved medallions containing the Emperor's names and titles, along the rim the presentation inscription in *vyaz'*, 30 cm long, unstamped, end of the 17th century. The presentation inscription says that the *kovsh* was presented by the Tsar Peter I in 1690 to Mikhail Ksenofontov, collector of the tax on spirits in Solikamsk.

87 Parcel-gilt presentation *kovsh* with double eagle decoration, engraved on the exterior with scrolling foliage and the presentation inscription. The *kovsh* was presented at the command of the Empress (Catherine II) by the Senate to the mayor of Yadrinsk, Andrey Petrovich Ovchinnikov, on 14 October 1774. He had distinguished himself in the operations against the Pugachev insurrection. Master's initials of Christoph Friedrich Wegener (255), assay-master Yevgraf Borovshchikov (181), St. Petersburg 1774, 29 cm long.

88 Large presentation *kovsh* with double-eagle decoration and unusual engraving of fruit and scrolling filled in with *niello*. On the outside is the presentation inscription referring to the gift of the *kovsh* by Peter the Great to a merchant for tax collections. Unmarked, dated 1701 in the inscription, 36 cm long.

89 Silver-gilt *nielloed* presentation *kovsh* of the Emperor Alexander I with the usual double eagle decoration but without the normal presentation inscription. This *kovsh* is among the latest examples of the tradition of *kovsh*-giving, then drawing towards its close, master Vasiliy Popov (52), Moscow 1819, 21.5 cm long.

90 Interior view of a presentation *kovsh* of the Empress Catherine II, with the double eagle arms and the sovereign's cypher, master Andrey Andreyev, Moscow 1776, 27.5 cm long. The engraved inscription records the gift of the *kovsh* on the 1 June 1776 to the Cossack ataman Mikhail Afanasevich Barabanshchikov.

91 Silver-gilt box for the Imperial Seal, which accompanied presentations or patents of nobility, chased with the Imperials Arms in a bay wreath, St. Petersburg 1786, 14.2 cm diameter.

92 Silver-gilt round box for the Imperial Seal of the Empress Elizabeth, the lid chased with the double eagle in a bay wreath, assay-master's initials of Ivan Frolov, St. Petersburg, 1743. Boxes of this kind accompanied all important patents of nobility and deeds of gift involving the Imperial Seal.

signs of wealth which distinguish the Russian nobility there is none more likely to impress the foreigner than the abundance of diamonds and precious stones which glitter everywhere. In this the gentlemen rival the ladies—many of the nobles are literally covered with diamonds.'[11]

As may often be seen on 18th-century portraits, the insignia of Orders constituted in the broadest sense an important category of jewellery. All the important personalities wore rich diamond-set insignia. It was even usual to have an Order privately embellished with precious stones. Such independent initiatives of display were expressly forbidden by Paul I in the Order Statutes of 1797. A famous figure of the period just before that was the 'diamond prince' Alexander Borisovich Kurakin, who liked to appear in public and be painted in all the splendour of his treasure of diamond-set Orders.

It is of interest too that foreign ambassadors usually received diamond rings as presents. This is reported by Pauzié of the Austrian ambassador Count Esterházy, who at his farewell audience in 1761 received from the Empress Elizabeth a 'ring with a brilliant worth 12,000 roubles'.[12] Only towards the end of the 18th century was this form of present superseded by the gift of snuff-boxes.

In Russia as elsewhere the influence of classicism was responsible from about 1780 onwards for the symmetrical arrangement of the elements in a piece of jewellery. Paris was the centre from which such decrees of fashion emanated. The case was just the same with the *mode à l'antique* of the Directoire in the 1790s and into the early years of the 19th century. The ladies wore light high-waisted classicizing dresses on which jewellery, apart from bangles and combs, was scarcely in evidence.

19th Century

With the emergence of the Empire style about 1804 gemstone jewellery began to be treated with more respect, though it was now freely combined with semi-precious stone pieces. The passion for antiquity had made cameos and intaglios popular and these were now made of semi-precious stones, such as for instance the popular cornelian, and used with diamond-set frames for brooches, bracelets, and diadems. Turquoise, opal, and coral became fashionable in about 1820.

This was the period in which the *parure* (which has remained classical to this day, consisting of tiara, necklace, and ear-rings) established itself. One reason for this no doubt is to be seen in the new technique of *à-jour* setting of stones, which substantially reduced the weight of the ornaments. Whereas in the 18th century pieces of jewellery were mostly assembled on a solid foundation gems were now inserted in open settings.

A certain Christian Müller in his book *Tableau de Pétersbourg ou lettres sur la Russie écrites en 1810, 11, 12* (Paris and Mainz, 1814, pp. 353 ff.) has given an informative account of jewellery in Russia at the beginning of the 19th century. Of particular interest is his account of the jewels reaching Russia through French emigrants, among them the Comte de Provence, the future Louis XVIII, who had settled temporarily in Mitau in what was then the Russian Baltic. 'In Germany there is an incorrect idea that in St. Petersburg there is an unending quantity of wonderful diamonds. Their number, if you will have it so, is indeed fairly large, especially in splendid Moscow—but it is not, and this must be said, infinite. At the time of the French Revolution émigrés brought pearls, splendid jewels, etc. with them from France and sold them in Russia, either because they needed the money or because they enjoyed speculating. In what other state could such valuable treasures be bought and sold if not in Russia, which was at the height of its political power, military strength, and economic prosperity. Thus the best and most valuable diamonds were acquired by the Russian princes and rulers of the day. The quantity of diamonds at this time at Catherine's glittering Court was really tremendous. Yet after the Peace of Tilsit a great part of these riches returned to France, by the very same way it had come there. At one of the last Leipzig fairs the mass of diamonds offered for sale from Russia was so great that their price fell by 30 per cent.

'The most valuable stones in Russia are to be found on the Icon of the Mother of God at Kazan. This icon is bedecked with the largest and most valuable sapphires, emeralds, and diamonds. They were mounted with great art by the master jeweller Tenner, a German, who is regarded by the whole of St. Petersburg, and also abroad, as a talented artist with fine artistic taste. The general public estimates the value of the jewels on the Icon of the Mother of God at Kazan together with the gold at 1,800,000 roubles. Herr Tenner, however, has convinced me that their value does not exceed 300,000 roubles.

'After these the best and most valuable diamonds in Russia are those which I saw a few months ago at the consecration of Kazan Cathedral on the wonderful head of the Empress Yelizaveta Alexeyevna. They belong to a diadem of leaves which surrounds the whole head like a crown. Each leaf consists of a single large brilliant in an *à-jour* setting of wonderfully fine work by which each is surrounded, with smaller stones composing the base of the leaf. Over the forehead itself the diamonds and leaves become bigger and a very large sapphire of fabulous fire joins the ends of the leaf stalks. At the same ceremony the Empress Mariya Fedorovna, the Emperor's mother, likewise wore a wonderful *parure* of precious stones—bracelets, ear-rings, and a necklace.

'Some ladies of the highest society also own valuable diamonds. Among them I particularly admired the jewels worn by the wife of the Lord Chamberlain (Naryshkin).

'Valuable diamonds are worn also by the merchants' wives, whose pride and joy it is to wear national costume on holidays. Ear-rings and finger-rings are very much in fashion with them and they are sometimes decked out with quantities of pearls.'

The production of jewellery in general received great impetus from the discovery of the Russian gemstone deposits at the beginning of the 19th century. In the Urals and in Siberia emeralds, amethysts, aquamarines, topazes, siberite, turquoise, and alexandrite were discovered. The last stone, a form of chrysoberyl, fascinated people by its changes of colour between green and red, according to the way the light struck it. It was called after the heir to the throne, later Alexander II, on whose birthday in the year 1830 it was first discovered.

In the 1820s the tide of Romanticism swept the symbolism of stones into the forefront of attention. The movement was broadly based on Russia's wealth of precious and semi-precious stones. Another custom was to put semi-precious stones together in such a way that the initials of their names spelt another name or a saying.

While the 'Gothic' style made its entrance into the decorative arts of Russia as into the whole of Europe, the emergence of historicism under Nicholas I gave a Russian national tendency to the art of personal adornment.

This Tsar had imposed on the ladies as Court dress a form of the Russian national costume—a white silk dress with red velvet sleeves and trains trimmed with gold, together with the *kokoshnik* head-dress. This was in velvet sewn with jewels. The form, however, soon became established for diamond tiaras, which were often built up from straight bands of diamonds side by side in semicircular arrays like bursts of light.

Since the beginning of the 19th century in Russia the larger coloured gems, especially emeralds and spinels, were set in such a way as to be surrounded by diamonds, but yet so that the real setting was formed of a row of closely packed (pavé-set) rose-cut diamonds hugging the stone. This form of setting can often be evidence of Russian provenance in a piece of jewellery.[13]

From about 1840 onwards an extensive production began of jewellery combining gold, enamel, and precious stones. The pieces of this period often give a ponderous and inelegant impression. In diamond pieces greater attention was often paid to effect than to the purity and colour of the stone.

At the Great Exhibition of 1851 in London several pieces were exhibited by Bolin & Jahn and Kaemmerer & Zaeftigen featuring turquoises with a diamond setting.[14] This form of combining semi-precious with precious stones enjoyed lasting popularity in Russia.

Among the reports of the Chicago World Fair of 1893 there was one interesting observation: 'As jewellers the Russians formerly enjoyed a great reputation for the finish of their mounts and the perfection of their settings. Their *bijouterie* and *petite orfèvrerie* is finely done and good to look at.'[15]

The three most important firms of jewellers in Russia at the end of the 19th century were Bolin, Hahn and Fabergé. They all had the Imperial Warrant and all received extensive commissions from the Imperial family.

It was Bolin who made the wedding present of Alexander II to his daughter Mariya Alexandrovna when she married the Duke of Edinburgh in 1874. It was a particularly splendid *parure* of rubies and diamonds.

The Hahn firm in 1896 received the commission to make one of the so-called small Imperial crowns. The original of this crown had been made by Duval towards the end of the reign of Paul I and had been worn since then by the empresses. For the coronation ceremony of Nicholas II in 1896 this crown had been assigned to the Empress-Dowager Mariya Fedorovna, but the *Cabinet de Sa Majesté* had meanwhile ordered a replica from Hahn, and this was then worn by the Empress Alexandra Fedorovna.[16]

The Fabergé firm, which did not specialize in gemstone jewellery, had likewise supplied the Court with important pieces, as for instance in 1895 a rather unusual *parure* with tiara and brooch of turquoises and diamonds.[17] One of Fabergé's workmasters, Erik Kollin, was a specialist in gold jewellery. In the 1880s he had copied the Scythian gold treasures from Kerch and created pieces of jewellery resembling those of Giuliano and Castellani in style.

About 1900 there was competition with these firms from French jewellers, as for instance Cartier and Boucheron, who, in the international French-speaking circles of the St. Petersburg Court, could always count on a substantial clientèle.

Notes

1 Postnikova-Loseva, *Russkoe yuvelirnoye iskusstvo*, p. 20.
2 Postnikova-Loseva, op. cit., p. 20, note 3.
3 Fersman, *Les Joyaux de Russie*, and Christie's auction catalogue of 16 March 1927: *Catalogue of an Important Assemblage of Magnificent Jewellery.*
4 Pauzié, 'Zapiski', p. 79.
5 Pauzié, op. cit., pp. 91-3.
6 Pauzié, op. cit., pp. 210 ff.
7 Rybakov (ed.), *Sokrovishcha Almaznogo Fonda SSSR*, Pl. 7.
8 Voltaire, *Œuvres complètes*, Paris 1785, vol. 67, p. 216.
9 Prince Lobkovicz to Prince Kaunitz, 7 December 1773, *S.I.R.I.O.*, vol. 125, p. 293.
10 Martynova, *Precious Stones*, p. 39.
11 Coxe, W., *Travels into Poland, Russia, Sweden and Denmark*, London, 1784.
12 Pauzié, op. cit., p. 102.
13 Hinks, *19th Century Jewellery*, p. 33.
14 *Great Exhibition of the Works of Industry of all Nations*, catalogue, vol. III, nos. 322, 376.
15 Krantz, *Exposition Internationale de Chicago*, p. 33.
16 Fersman, *Les Joyaux de Russie*, vol. III, no. 82, p. 29; Pl. I, 1.
17 Fersman, *Les Joyaux de Russie*, Vol. IV, nos. 153, 154; Pl. LXXXI.

Kovchik

A *kovchik* is a small, usually oval *kovsh* on a raised foot with a flat side-handle. The *kovchik* is double-walled, with chased decoration on both walls, inside and out. In the middle is a round, dished plaque, the 'bowl' (Russian *mishen'*), which may be decorated with chased designs or the sculptured figure of a bird. Along the rim there is frequently an engraved inscription with the owner's name or a drinking slogan. *Kovchiki* mainly date from the 17th century.

Kovsh

An oval drinking vessel with side handle, similar to a ladle or 'dipper'.

In old Russian handicrafts the *kovsh* was carved in wood, in the form of a swimming duck or goose whose head and bill constituted the handle. Vessels similar to the Russian *kovsh* were made in Scandinavia, called *kåsa* in Sweden and *sölvgass* (silver goose) in Norway.

The *kovsh* made of metal appeared in Russia in the middle of the 14th century, and the term *kovsh* also became established at about that time. The original name was probably *chum*, as can be gathered from earlier sources (Ignatiev Chronicle for the year 1250).

The first illustration of a *kovsh* to reach us is in the 14th-century manuscript *Legends of St. Boris and St. Gleb* (published by Sreznevsky, St. Petersburg, 1860, p. 125). Here on the table of Prince Izyaslav Yaroslavich *kovshi* are shown of a rather rounder shape with a high handle.

The first metal *kovshi* were probably made in Novgorod. The oldest preserved silver *kovsh* dates from the first half of the 15th century and was made for the Mayor (*posadnik*) of Novgorod, Grigoriy Kirillovich Posakhno.[1] Among the gifts received by the Grand Duke Ivan Vasilevich in December 1476 at a banquet with the *posadnik* of Novgorod the Chronicle lists a *kovsh* of 2 *grivennik* gold weight.

Kovshi of different sizes had varying uses. They were ladles, containers or drinking vessels. When the smaller size of *kovsh* was used as a drinking cup, of silver or gold, the drink was principally mead: wine was normally drunk from beakers. In historical sources from the 10th century onwards, from the time of Prince Vladimir, mead is mentioned as an indispensable accompaniment of banquets at a grand-ducal table, especially at wedding celebrations. There were different kinds of mead—honey dissolved in water, or on a foundation of fruit syrup, spiced with nutmeg and cinnamon, with cloves, ginger, and all kinds of herbs and then fermented. At a celebration by the Patriarch in the Kremlin Palace of the Cross in 1667 the *stolniki* or lord high stewards of the Tsar served wine in silver beakers, but red or white mead in gold or silver *kovshi*. From the end of the 16th century onwards the traditional draught of welcome which would have been previously offered in the *chara* or *bratina* was offered in the *kovsh*.

Quite early on, special names came into use for the different sorts of *kovsh*. There were *piti*, drinking *kovshi*, one to each guest; *vynosnye*, larger *kovshi* for several persons; *khoromnye*, which belonged to the Imperial Court and bore an appropriate inscription.

But the most important and best-known form of *kovshi* were the *zhalovannye*, or presentation *kovshi* which from the 16th century onwards were given by tsars and emperors for services rendered. After the conquest of Kazan in 1552 Ivan the Terrible presented the returning boyars not only with furs, brocades, and horses but also with golden *kovshi*. Towards the end of the 16th century persons close to the Court received *kovshi* as a reward of service, and most of these were drawn directly from the Imperial Treasury. In the 17th century the *kovsh* was used as the preferred gift of honour for all kinds of service, whether military or civil.

In the 16th century and the first third of the 17th the *kovshi* were still given personally by the tsar or at any rate in his presence, usually on the occasion of a meal. After the middle of the 17th century there is no record of the tsar being personally involved in the presentation. All we find is an order on the Treasury for the issue of a *kovsh* or an order for the making of a *kovsh* in the Silver Palace at the Kremlin. Finally in the 18th century all that remains is a reference to the provision of a sum of money.

From the middle of the 17th century onwards the following decoration had become customary on a presentation *kovsh*: on the shallow central part—the so-called *mishen'*—a Russian double eagle; the same also often on the handle and crowning the spout. An engraved inscription—often in *niello*—encircled the rim of the *kovsh* in a band, containing the tsar's name and full title together with the name and services of the recipient. The size of the *kovsh* depended on the rank of the recipient and the importance of his services.

The actual form of the *kovsh* had meanwhile undergone changes. While the *kovsh* carved of wood as a ladle was originally more rounded and high-walled—and the early metal *kovshi* of Novgorod retained this style—in the 16th century the shape began to change after a fashion which was only to find its completion in the 18th. The so-called Moscow style of *kovsh* emerged as a more oblong oval with shallow side walls, often no deeper than the band of the inscription was wide. Hammered relatively thin and thus light in weight, these *kovshi* had lost their function of drinking vessels and from the end of the 17th century on were simply ornamental objects used as official gifts of honour. The importance of the double eagle emblem and the inscription, which was handled with ever-increasing artistic freedom, was correspondingly increased. After the beginning of the 17th century the raised end of the *kovsh* opposite the handle is likely to have as finial a cast and chased double eagle, or a pine cone, or a mask. The inscription band was partitioned into cartouches, at first baroque in style, then later rococo. Even the script itself is now ornamental in purpose. Whereas the letters were earlier more or less round and singly spaced, by 1700 we are more likely to find them narrowly vertical and with contractions *(vyaz')*, making them extremely difficult to read. In some rarer examples we find on the exterior an engraved portrait of the ruler of the time in a cartouche.

From the second half of the 17th century onwards only two categories of person can be identified as recipients of presentation *kovshi*. On the evidence of their inscriptions the *kovshi* were presented either to tax-collectors or to Cossack *hetmans*.

The first category received their *kovshi* according to the inscription, *za pribor*, for tax-collections. Apart from commercial taxes the duties on beverages were among the most important state revenues. These were collected by authorized tax-collectors who were not officials in the modern sense but private persons, themselves trades-men. Thus any favouritism or misappropriation of taxes for private purposes endan-gered the public revenues. But whenever the tax receipts equalled or exceeded the estimates, the tax-collectors were rewarded not only with textiles and furs but also with silver *kovshi*. The first *kovshi* of this sort were presented in 1621-3, mostly to merchants.[2]

From the second half of the 17th century onwards the recipients often included more ordinary townspeople (*posadskiye lyudi*) as well, and not only merchants of a recognized class organization. In the year 1718 the *Kammerkollegium* was established and took over the collection of taxes, for which a stricter administration was set up, and some public recognition of the tax-collector's function in particular became overdue. The consequence was that around the middle of the 18th century *kovshi za pribor* became less frequent. In the Historical Museum in Moscow the period is represented by only two examples, dated 1754 and 1774, which were both awarded to merchants of the First Corporation.

The other group of recipients were the Cossack *hetmans* and heads of families, who received their *kovshi* 'for faithful service' (*za vernye sluzhby*). The reasons for the awards were in such cases the consolidation of the state organization among the Cossacks on the Don and Volga, who were partly still nomadic. This attempt at consolidation had already begun on the Don in the 16th century under the Moscow princes, who tried to attach these warlike people to their rule by gifts and patents. Their efforts were continued right into the 18th century. The *starshiny*, or local chieftains, who visited the Court in Moscow and later in St. Petersburg to demon-strate their attachment to the Russian Empire each received from the Tsar a *kovsh*. By a number of such gestures of submission on the part of a Cossack group quite a collection of presentation *kovshi* could be accumulated by a single family. The *hetman* Frola Minayev for instance owned more than twenty. Often the recipient got money to make his own *kovsh*, with the corresponding inscription.

All these Cossack *kovshi* were made in Moscow. In many cases the date of the maker's stamp shows that they had been manufactured some time before the inscription, also dated, was engraved.

In the last quarter of the 18th century, after the Peace of Kuchuk-Kainardzhi (1774) and the incorporation of the Crimea into Russia, the Cossack communities were incorporated in the Empire. The once wild Cossacks became regular military units, with appropriate military ranks, from 1798 onwards. There was thus no longer any reason for the award of *kovshi*, though the custom did not cease overnight. The latest known presentation *kovsh* (Historical Museum, Moscow) is dated 1821.

The presentation of *kovshi* to tax-collectors and Cossacks can thus be regarded as a peculiar phenomenon of Russian history, for both these two groups were economically and politically important in the social development of Russia. In one case it was a question of the involvement of the burgher class—the *bourgeoisie*—in the affairs of state, by the devolution of tax collection to merchants, in the other of the attachment of a nomadic people to the Empire. In both developments the gift *kovshi* played their part, until tax collection on the one hand was regularized by the administrative reforms of Peter the Great, while the Cossacks on the other were integrated with the Russian Empire by a transfer of power.

As awards of honour the *kovshi* had a special position in the history of Russian state distinctions, a peculiarly Russian one in that these two different groups each required an award of its own, the merchants and *posadskiye lyudi* because an organized bourgeoisie was lacking, the Cossacks because they scarcely yet belonged to the state. There was no question in this case of conferring an Order or decoration, such things being reserved for the nobility.

As a border-line case in the development of form and style among *kovshi* an example illustrated here will serve. It is an Imperial presentation *kovsh* of Alexander I dated 1819, of traditional form. This *kovsh*, however, no longer has any inscription to indicate giver and recipient more precisely. It thus seems to bring the development of the presentation *kovshi* to an end, showing that the *kovsh* was by then regarded only as an object of ornament, without either any practical use or concrete function as an award of honour. Almost all the 19th-century *kovshi* can be classed in this category.

From the middle of the 19th century hardly an example is known, but with the growth of historicism in the latter half the *kovsh* as ornament enjoyed a special return to popularity. At the All-Russian Exhibition in Moscow in 1882 Tsar Alexander III gave his special blessing to the historicizing style, which in the sphere of politics of course had a particular affinity with the Pan-Slav movement. In reaching back so extensively to Old Russian forms of the 16th and 17th centuries the practitioners of ornamental art surrendered to historicizing influences. *Kovshi* were now for the most part richly decorated with *cloisonné* enamel: here Ovchinnikov and Khlebnikov were the most important craftsmen. By the end of the 19th century the *kovsh* could be described as an object of historical curiosity which in its jumble of every style, even Art nouveau, and variety of materials conveys only a distant reminder of its original function.[3]

Notes

1 Now in the Zagorsk Museum; cf. Svirin, *Yuvelirnoye iskusstvo drevney Rusi*, Pl. 35.
2 Postnikova-Loseva, *Russkie serebryanye i zolotye kovshi*, p. 24.
3 Habsburg-Lothringen/Solodkoff, *Fabergé*, p. 32; Pls. 39, 40, 43, 44.

Kovshik

Kovshik means a small *kovsh*, the difference being only one of size. It is rare to find a *kovshik* with an inscription.

Lacquer

The art of lacquering, under Chinese influence, had been practised in Russia since the 18th century. Lacquer was mainly painted on wooden or *papier-maché* objects. In the 19th century, besides other smaller firms, there were two big ones which became particularly famous: Vishnyakov and Lukutin. The firm of Vishnyakov had been founded in 1785 by Filipp Nikitin Vishnyakov, while that of Lukutin had its origin in a business built up in about 1785 by the merchant P.I. Korobov and directed from 1824 by Petr V. Lukutin. Both firms, Vishnyakov and Lukutin, remained in family ownership till the beginning of the 20th century. They were famous for their miniature lacquer paintings, especially those with peasant scenes, landscapes, and also portraits. In 1867 Lukutin exhibited a series of lacquer objects, principally boxes, at the Paris World Exhibition. From this time, the culmination from an artistic point of view of what was more of a folk craft, people began to be interested in transferring the technique of lacquer painting to silver objects. At the All-Russian Exhibition of 1882 pieces of this kind by Ovchinnikov attracted special notice. From then on up to 1917 we find lacquer-painted silver objects.

The technique consisted of applying to the piece several coats of lacquer, beginning with one or more opaque coats and so on to transparent ones, letting each dry out in its turn. The last coat was polished to a high gloss. The difference from enamel is that lacquer is put on cold. The most plentifully occurring objects are those with lacquer paintings on a red ground: rustic troika scenes and other folk subjects are among the most frequent.

In pieces by the Ovchinnikov firm the lacquer is used as follows. The silver article is decorated with a gilt figured or floral relief over a ground with a glossy red lacquer covering. The gilt relief elements thus stand out with peculiar effect from the coloured background.

The following is a list of firms and makers of lacquer items:
1. Master with the initials IKA, St. Petersburg, 1908-17.
2. Morozov (St. Petersburg), end of 19th century.
   Workmaster with the initials HK, who in particular produced lacquer views of the city of St. Petersburg.
3. Ovchinnikov (Moscow), about 1880 to 1917. (Gilt reliefs on red lacquer.)
4. Master with the initials (Russian) SP, Moscow, *c.*1900-17, working for the firm V. Gordon.
5. Master with the initials TN, St. Petersburg, end of 19th century.

6. Fuld, Alexander Iosifovich, Moscow, 1862-1917 (no. 34).
7. **3** K, St. Petersburg, end of 19th century.
8. P B, Moscow?, 1908-17.
9. (Russian) G S, Moscow, 1908-17.
10. J.K., St. Petersburg, 1908-17.

Literature

Pisarskaya, L., Platonova, N. and B. Ulyanova, *Russkiye emali, XI-XIX vv.*, Moscow 1974, p. 210, Pl. 112.
Ukhanova, I.N., *Russkiye laki v Sobranii Ermitazha*, Leningrad, 1964 (lacquer in general).

Medals and their makers

Medals in memory of an important event or in honour of some person were struck in Russia with special frequency from the time of Peter the Great onwards. They were popular as art objects for collections or as illustrations of history throughout the 18th century.

Such medals usually show on one side a portrait (in profile) of the sovereign of the day or of some other person and on the reverse an allegorical design with a surrounding legend referring to some important event. The medals were struck in larger numbers in bronze, fewer in silver, with only a few examples in gold, mostly for the Court.

While the medal-maker's art is often regarded as a branch of numismatics, it has two important links with the goldsmith's and silversmith's art. It is remarkable that in Russia, especially from the middle of the 18th century onwards, medals were used to decorate gold and silver boxes. Here there were two techniques for their re-use. First, an original medal could be worked into the lid of a snuff-box. Such a use perhaps had less artistic independence, yet it did show, particularly in the case of medals in relief, the great esteem in which they were held. Alternatively medals could be split or used as one-sided plaques. Even an outstanding artist such as Ador did not hesitate to work other artists' medals into his boxes.[1]

The other way of using medals was to make a cast of a medal design and so transfer the design to another object. Thus it was frequently the sovereign's profile which was taken without the circumscription. Perhaps the most important examples of this are the boxes by Pauzié with the profile of the Empress Elizabeth. However, the technique of casting a medal in the form of a relatively thin plaque was often employed on silver boxes as well.

A further point of contact with the goldsmith's art was that the medal-makers, being highly qualified craftsmen in chasing and engraving metal, could employ their skills on other art objects also. It was quite common for a goldsmith specializing in engravings to be employed on making medals or conversely for a medal-maker to be diverted to a gold box. Though such things are often difficult to prove, the following examples can be quoted:

In the Admiralty Mint, founded in Moscow in 1701, there worked a Dutchman called Yuriy Frobus who had come to Russia as early as the 1660s, and who was described as 'master goldsmith and coin engraver'.

In the second half of the 18th century we encounter a goldsmith whose work was distinguished by special excellence—Johann Balthasar Gass, who in 1760 was Master and member of the Guild. In 1773 he was awarded the title of 'Imperial medal-maker'. Besides a series of gold boxes distinguished for their excellent engraving Gass made medals, of which 21 are known.

Timofey Ivanov, a master goldsmith known from 1770 onward, may have been identical with the well-known medal-maker of the same name. Mention can be made also of Johann Caspar Eger (Jaeger), a medal-maker who also cut precious stones. From him we have two profile portraits of Catherine II engraved on emeralds.

In the 19th century too the medallist's art was further cultivated. The pieces, however, were no longer baroque show medals but more classical reliefs under French *Empire* influence. The Napoleonic wars supplied opportunity enough for the production of memorial pieces.

About the middle of the 19th century medals were often worked into the sides of large silver beakers or handled cups. This technique was later revived by Fabergé. However, he used almost exclusively 18th-century medals and coins.

Note

1 Troinitsky, 'Medal'nyya tabakerki', in *Starye gody*, 1915, vol. VI, p. 41.

Niello

Niello (Italian, from the Latin *nigellus*, 'blackish', Russian *chern'*) was a black to grey-black substance used as a filling for engraved decoration.

Niello is an alloy of silver, copper (or zinc), lead, and sulphur. The proportions of the mixture vary from one silversmith to another. An example might be 1 part silver, 2 parts copper, 3 parts lead, to some sulphur. The durability and colour of the *niello* depend on the proportions of these ingredients.

After cooling the alloy is ground to a fine powder and then moistened with a boracic solution. The resultant paste is applied to a silver or, less often, gold surface carved in low relief and fired in a furnace so that the *niello* melts and adheres to the metal. After grinding off and polishing of the whole surface the *niello* appears only as a black design in the recesses.

Niello was already known in Egyptian and ancient Roman art. Pliny mentions a recipe for its preparation. The *niello* technique was cultivated in Italy in the 15th and 16th centuries and a formula of those times has been handed down by Benvenuto Cellini. It was also used in the east (in India and Persia) and by Byzantine silversmiths and those of Germany, as for instance in Augsburg. In the 19th century *nielloed* objects were produced in Vienna also.

In Russia *niello* was known already in the 10th century. Excavations have brought to light *nielloed* objects from the 12th and 13th centuries, not only in the main cities of the Russian principalities—Kiev, Chernigov, Vladimir, and Ryazan—but also in smaller townships and hill graves in the country. *Niello* in these cases was used for the decoration of ear-rings, finger rings, bracelets, and pectoral ornaments.

In the 14th century and the first half of the 15th, *niello* was generally used as a ground for cast, chased, or engraved designs and ornaments. In the second half of the 16th century *nielloed* decorations and ornaments have more the effect of blotches or broad strokes reminiscent of paint-brush strokes.

The Russian *niello* craft reached its peak in the 16th century. Moscow masters at that time achieved a special perfection in the ornamentation of gold objects. In such cases the *niello* technique was used rather differently, the whole surface of the metal being overlaid with a thin coating of *niello* and then decorated with plant-like ornaments and arabesques.

At the beginning of the 17th century we more often find objects with *niello* in clear, fine strokes, no longer drawn on the plain ground of an object as in the 16th century but on a decorated ground. The development of *niello* technique in Moscow was considerably influenced by Greek jewellers, who came to Moscow from Constantinople between 1662 and 1664. They worked in the workshops of the Kremlin and passed on their special knowledge to Russian silversmiths. Their *niello* technique was called Turkish *(turskaya chern')*. In the last quarter of the 17th century silver objects may have *nielloed* plant and flower patterns serving as a background for engraved and gilt ornaments of flowers, fruits, and animals. The more or less stylized ornaments are based on the fan, pomegranate, cypress, and various flowers as well as subjects from Oriental and Ukrainian folk art.

At the beginning of the 18th century Moscow remained the chief centre of *niello* technique, and one of the most important Moscow masters of that century was Alexey Ratkov (1777-1821).

In St. Petersburg *niello* was not widely used: the art there was mainly under the influence of masters who had come in from Velikiy Ustyug. The technique reached its period of greatest success in northern Russia—in Velikiy Ustyug, Vologda, and Vyatka—after the middle of the 18th century. Its typical products were snuff-boxes with maps of town and country and town views transferred to metal from copper prints.

93-4   *Nielloed charka* with floral decoration, on three ball-and-claw feet, the reverse with the *Levok* mark which was in use from 1685-94, beside it the year mark for 1692-3, Moscow, 9 cm long.

95-6   Silver-gilt *nielloed charka* with two pierced handles. Master's initials of Petr Ivanov (171), Moscow 1703, diameter 6.5 cm.

97   Silver-gilt *nielloed* tankard on three ball-and-claw feet, decorated with biblical scenes in cartouches: Joseph and Potiphar's wife, Samson and Delilah, Judith and Holophernes. The cartouches and flowering scrolls are set off against a stippled *niello* ground. Engraved inscription 'Tankard of Vasiliy Vasilevich Kochubey', unmarked, about 1700, 18.6 cm high.

98   Silver-gilt *nielloed* tankard on three ball-and-claw feet, decorated with festoons of flowers and fruits, unmarked, engraved with its weight, 4 *funti*, 18 *loti*, 30 *zolotniki* (1718 grams), about 1700, 18 cm high. The form is a counterpart of the Balto-Scandinavian tankard of the second half of the 17th century.

99   Silver-gilt *nielloed charka* in the form of a peach, the handle modelled as the stalk with leaves, the bowl decorated with a hunting scene and on the reverse with the arms of the governor of Siberia, Denis Ivanovich Chicherin, Tobolsk about 1775, 9 cm long.

100   Back view of the beaker of Pl. 112 with the escutcheon of Denis Ivanovich Chicherin in a *rocaille* cartouche.

101   (left and right) A pair of silver-gilt, *nielloed* beakers on ball-and-claw feet, the body engraved with flower swags on a *nielloed* ground, Moscow 1692, 7.5 cm high;

(middle) Silver-gilt and *nielloed* belt buckle decorated with a high priest before a seven-branched candle and an Old Testament scene within a rococo frame, unmarked, about 1780, 11.8 cm high.

102   (left) Silver-gilt *nielloed charka*, the handle in the form of a branch, engraved with the year 1791 and the coroneted cypher JE in *rocaille* cartouches, unmarked, probably Tobolsk, about 1791, 6.5 cm high;
(middle) Silver-gilt *nielloed* cream-jug on three claw feet, decorated with architectural motifs in oval medallions, unmarked, probably Moscow, about 1780;
(right) Silver-gilt *nielloed charka*, the handle in the form of a branch and decorated with flowers, Tobolsk about 1785, 5.5 cm high.

103   (left) Silver-gilt and *nielloed charka*, decorated with landscape scenes in rococo cartouches on an engraved ground, with chased handle, no marks, length 8.7 cm, about 1770;
(right) Round silver-gilt *nielloed* box, the lid with pastoral scenes in *rocaille* panels, diameter 11 cm, about 1770.

104   Silver-gilt and *nielloed* snuff-box in cartouche form, decorated with reliefs of allegorical subjects and trophies, surrounded with *nielloed rocaille* ornaments on a granulated ground, the push-piece chased with *rocaille* curves, Vologda, about 1765, length about 14 cm. (Louvre, Paris)

105   Silver-gilt *nielloed* snuff-box decorated with classical deities and figures, the lid with thumb-piece in the form of a shell and waved borders, unmarked, probably Velikiy Ustyug, about 1780, 8.7 cm long.

106   (left) Silver-gilt *nielloed* round box, the lid decorated with an ancient temple ruin within a *rocaille* frame, the base with the cypher A P, the sides encircled by a seascape, assay-master A. Torlov (33), Velikiy Ustyug, 1779, 8.7 cm diameter; (right) Silver-gilt *nielloed* round box with architectural landscapes on a sun-burst ground, assay-master A. Torlov, Velikiy Ustyug 1785, 8.7 cm diameter.

107   *Nielloed* silver boxes of the 19th century: (upper row from left to right) Engraved hunting scene, by I. Kaltykov (89), assay-master N. Dubrovin (158), Moscow 1830, 7.5 cm long;
View of the Kremlin, Moscow 1846, 6.4 cm long;
Russian officers with a Turkish prisoner of war, by I. Kaltykov, Moscow about 1830, 7.2 cm long;
(second row from left to right) Cigarette-case with a *troyka* in a cartouche on *nielloed* scrolling foliage, master's mark P.A., Moscow 1896, 9 cm long;
Silver box *nielloed* with the Monument of Peter the Great, assay-master Viktor Savinkov, Moscow 1856, 6.8 cm long;
Engraved mythological scene with Venus, Amor, and Mars, Moscow about 1800, 9.3 cm long;
(third row from left to right) *Nielloed* scene of a military exercise with an officer on horseback and infantry, master's initials I.O., Moscow 1818, 8 cm long;
Nielloed allegory on the *Pax Europaea*, with Alexander I led by Pax, surmounted by an eagle with wreaths of victory, master's initials I.O., Moscow 1818, 8.2 cm long;
The Memorial to Minin and Pozharsky in Moscow, with trophies in the background, assay-master M. Karpinsky, Moscow 1819, 9.3 cm long.

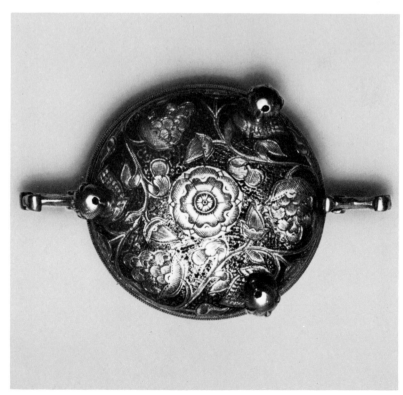

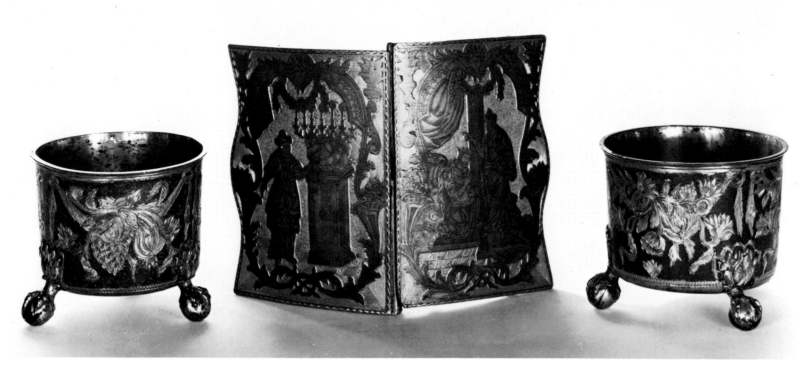

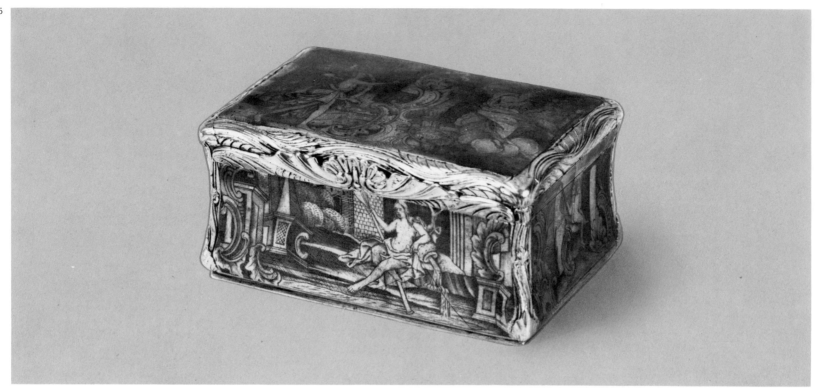

109

110

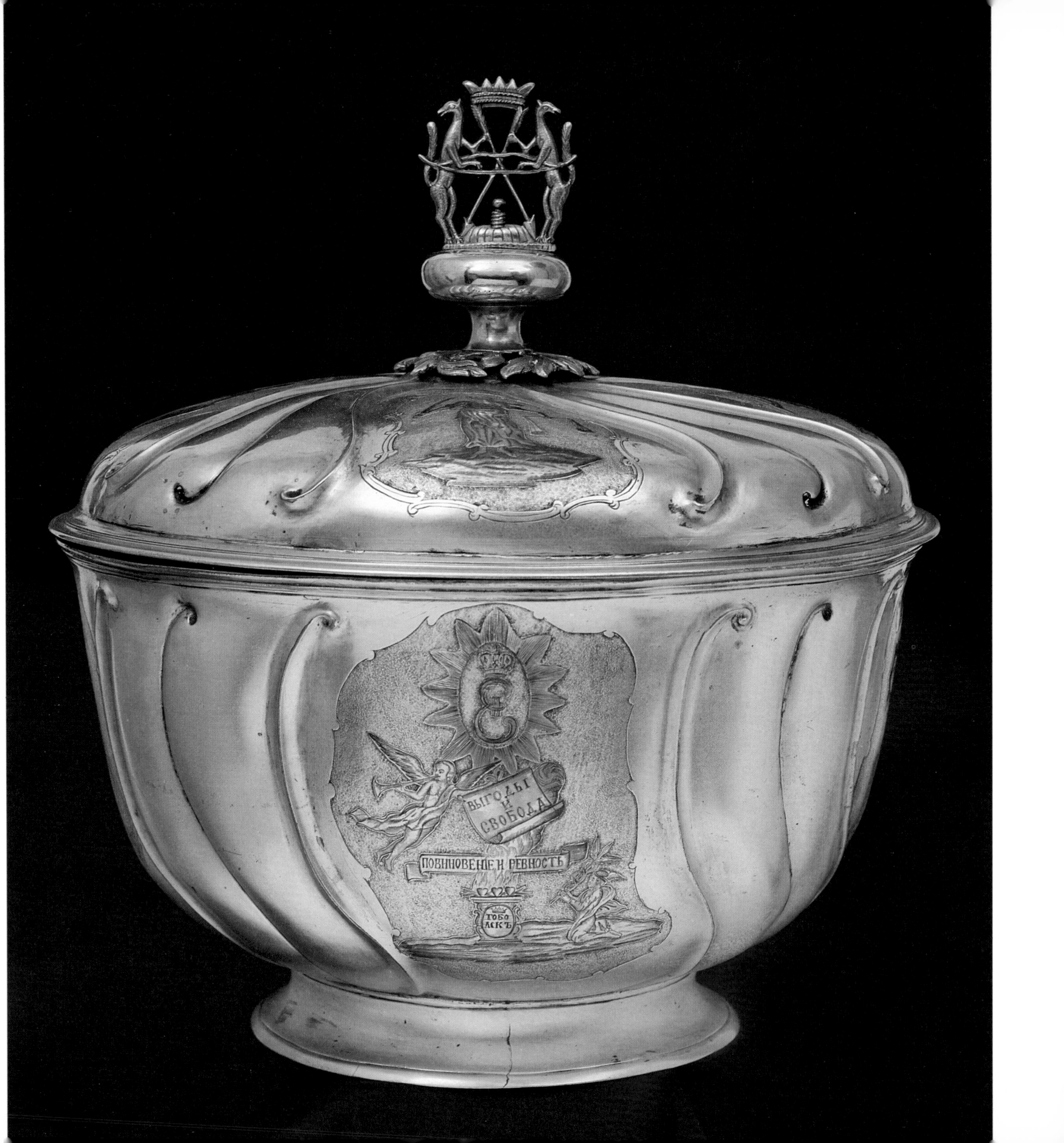
ВЫГОДЫ И СВОБОДА
ПОВИНОВЕНИЕ И РЕВНОСТЬ
ТОБО ЛКЪ

112

113

108 *Nielloed* snuff-boxes:
(top) With a view of the Kremlin, master's initials (Cyrillic) A.S., Moscow 1869, 6.9 cm long;
(second row, left) With view of Kremlin, master's initials (Cyrillic) G.B., Moscow 1869, 7.8 cm long;
(right) With scrolling foliage, master's initials ee, Moscow about 1850, 8.2 cm long;
(middle) *Nielloed* box in the form of a shoe with the superscription *Kavkaz*, Novocherkassk about 1860, 10 cm long;
(fourth row, left) View of Kremlin, master's initials N.K., Moscow 1882, 8.7 cm long;
(right) Monument to Peter the Great in St. Petersburg, master's initials (Cyrillic) O.B., Moscow 1847, 8.2 cm long;
(bottom) Monument to Peter the Great in St. Petersburg, master's initials (Cyrillic) O.B., Moscow 1842.

109 A pair of parcel-gilt *nielloed* plates, engraved and gilded each with three stylized tulips, the edges decorated with scrolling foliage and a coat of arms, later deleted, on a *niello* ground with meticulously engraved flowers, unmarked, towards the end of the 17th century. Diameter 21.4 cm.

110 (left) Silver-gilt *nielloed* beaker, engraved and gilded with sunflowers, asters, and narcissi on a *niello* ground with intertwined scrollwork, the rim engraved 'Beaker of stolnik Ivan Ivanovich Kaysarov', the bottom engraved with three flowers and the Cyrillic initials D. and I.G. Ivan Kaysarov was *stolnik* (steward) at the Tsar's court from 1676 to 1692. Unmarked, late 17th century, 18 cm high;

(right) A pair of silver-gilt *nielloed* beakers decorated with engraved tulips and sunflowers with scrolling foliage on a *nielloed* ground with scrollwork in spirals, unmarked, late 17th century, 11 cm high. The *niello* ground with spiral scrolls, most of which are dotted, is typical of *niello* production in the second half of the 17th century.

111 Large parcel-gilt *nielloed* tureen, the cover with the arms of Siberia as finial, on the sides four allegorical subjects with inscriptions, one with the date 10th July 1775, on the front (see illustration) an altar of sacrifice with the designation Tobolsk and on it burning hearts, surmounted by banners with the slogans 'Obedience and Zeal' and 'Benefits and Freedom' and the crowned cypher of the Empress Catherine II. On the cover are figures representing Justice, Mercury, Ceres and Mars. Master's initials (Cyrillic) M.P. Sh. (147), assay-master Lev Vlasov (128), Tobolsk 1774, diameter 29.5 cm, weight 2,750 gr, engraved inventory number 249.

112 (left) Silver-gilt *nielloed* snuff-box, the lid *nielloed* with a lady and a gentleman making music within a rococo frame on an engraved gilt ground, the sides *nielloed* with mythological scenes, probably in the factory of the brothers Afanasiy and Stepan Popov in Velikiy Ustyug (194, 195), assay-master Mikhail Gavrilovich Okonishnikov (143), dated 1766, 5.2 cm long;
(middle) Silver-gilt *nielloed* beaker chased with wave-bands, *nielloed* with the coroneted cypher D.Ch. of the governor of Siberia, Denis Ivano-

vich Chicherin, surrounded by *rocaille* ornaments, the reverse with the governor's arms (cf. illustration 100), Tobolsk about 1775, 10.2 cm high;
(right) Silver-gilt *nielloed* snuff-box, the lid *nielloed* with a harbour scene, the sides with genre scenes, the interior of the lid has an oil miniature in *bleu camaieu* of Justice with a Cupid, the underside of the box has in a *nielloed* cartouche the initials of the Popov brothers (nos 194, 195), Velikiy Ustyug, assay-master's initials A.T. (33), 1768, 8 cm long.

113 Large *nielloed* silver-gilt table snuff-box decorated with scenes within *rocaille* frames, the lid with waved edge and swung thumb-piece. Like almost all *nielloed* boxes this splendid piece is unsigned, probably Velikiy Ustyug, about 1770, 11.5 cm long.

114 Silver-gilt *nielloed* service by Semen Petrovich Kuzov, Moscow 1798-1799, consisting of: 14 dessert plates with pierced borders and *nielloed* rosettes, diameter 24 cm; a tureen in the form of an urn applied at the sides with lion's heads with ring handles, the cover with flower finial and engraved with a scene of bathers, the tureen body with mythological scenes of Poseidon and Hera (?) and of Aphrodite with Tritons, 43.4 cm long, weight 5.035 kg. A pair of dishes in the same style as the tureen decorated with pastoral scenes, 38 cm long. Additionally every piece is engraved with a coat of arms which was borne simultaneously by Count Sheremetev and by Konovnitsyn.

115 Round *nielloed* box with the inscription 'It's a queer world' in a panel of toys, emblems of war and art, and putti, the underside with the inscription 'That's how the world goes' in (Cyrillic) letters formed out of Russian folk types. Unstamped, about 1820, 10 cm diameter.

116 *Nielloed* round box with maps of the eastern parts of Siberia together with the islands in the Arctic Ocean, the sides with folkloristic types, among them an 'American', Tobolsk about 1770, diameter 10 cm. The box is of similar style to those which Governor D.I. Chicherin of Siberia sent back to St. Petersburg with his account of the newly discovered Aleutian Islands. On the underside of this box (right) the Aleutians are specially picked out by an inscription.

117 Silver-gilt *nielloed* snuff-box, the lid with a map of Vologda province and a distance table of different cities in *versts*, the sides with city arms, and the underside with a population table totalling 299,801, master's initials (Cyrillic) of Aleksandr Zhilin (9), assay-master M.I. Igumnov (161), Velikiy Ustyug, 1824, 8.7 cm long.

118 Silver-gilt *nielloed* box with a scoring table for a card game and the initials A P in a *rocaille* frame, about 1840, 10 cm long.

119 Silver-gilt *nielloed* case decorated with the map of Vologda province and a distance table, the reverse with a map of Archangel province, master I.M. Zuyev (88), Vologda 1837, 13 cm long.

120 Parcel-gilt *nielloed* case engraved with a map of the province (*guberniya*) of Archangel, the reverse with a map of the province of Vologda,

master's mark of Ivan Zuyev (87), the cover with a panoramic view of Velikiy Ustyug, beginning of the 19th century, 14.8 cm long.

121 (left) Silver-gilt *nielloed* snuff-box with an allegory upon Alexander I, Moscow about 1820, 8 cm long;
(middle) Silver-gilt *nielloed* snuff-box with the Monument to Peter the Great in St. Petersburg, Moscow 1826, 7.8 cm long;
(right) Box with allegorical scene in *rocaille* frame, Moscow about 1820, 8.7 cm long.

122 Three *nielloed* cigar-boxes with Moscow city marks:
(left) with the Minin and Pozharsky Monument, master's mark AS, about 1840, 13.5 cm long;
(middle) with the Monument to Peter the Great in St. Petersburg, 12 cm long;
(right) with the Alexander Column on the Palace Square in St. Petersburg, about 1850, 12 cm long.

123 Silver-gilt *nielloed* tea-pot, the sides with a view of the Kremlin, ebonized wood handle, master's initials (Cyrillic) P.S., perhaps for Pavel Sazikov, Moscow 1835, 10.2 cm high.

124 (left) Silver-gilt *nielloed* beaker with architectural views in medallions, master's initials (Cyrillic) of V. Semenov (57-60), Moscow 1859, 8.5 cm high;
(middle) Parcel-gilt *nielloed* cup and cover, decorated with a medallion in scrolling foliage, master's initials AK, Moscow 1842, 15 cm high;
(right) Silver-gilt *nielloed* beaker with the Minin and Pozharsky Monument in Moscow, master's initials (Cyrillic) NG, Moscow 1840, 8.5 cm high.

125 (left and right) A pair of silver-gilt *nielloed* cups and covers decorated with trophies within medallions, master's initials (Cyrillic) I.K., Moscow 1857, 15 cm high;
(middle) A pair of silver-gilt *nielloed* champagne flutes with scrollwork in wavy bands, master's initials AK, Moscow about 1850, about 18 cm high.

126 Three parcel-gilt *nielloed* champagne flutes, Moscow about 1845, 17.5 cm high, and one parcel-gilt champagne flute applied with a band in relief of dancing maenads. Master's initials of M. Borodulin (133), St. Petersburg 1835, 21 cm high.

127 Parcel-gilt *nielloed* tea and coffee service, consisting of tea-pot, coffee-pot, sugar-bowl, milk-jug, sugar-tongs and tray, decorated with townscapes of Moscow in oval medallions, surrounded by a scroll pattern, by Khlebnikov, with grand-ducal warrant mark, Moscow 1875-6, the tray with the master's initials of Dmitriy Nikolayev (80), Moscow 1885.

128 Two silver-gilt *nielloed* beakers on ball feet, engraved with scrollwork, the rim with drinking mottos;
(left) with master's initials of V. Semenov (57-60), Moscow 1867, 6.6 cm high;
(right) with master's mark ee, Moscow 1855;
(centre) Rectangular tea-box with views of the Kremlin, master's initials P.A., Moscow about 1850, 13 cm high.

129 *Nielloed* service with tea-pot, coffee-pot, sugar-bowl and cream-jug, decorated with views of Moscow within medallions on scrollwork, master's initials (Cyrillic) of V. Semenov (57-60), assay-master Savinkov, Moscow 1885, the coffee-pot 18 cm high.

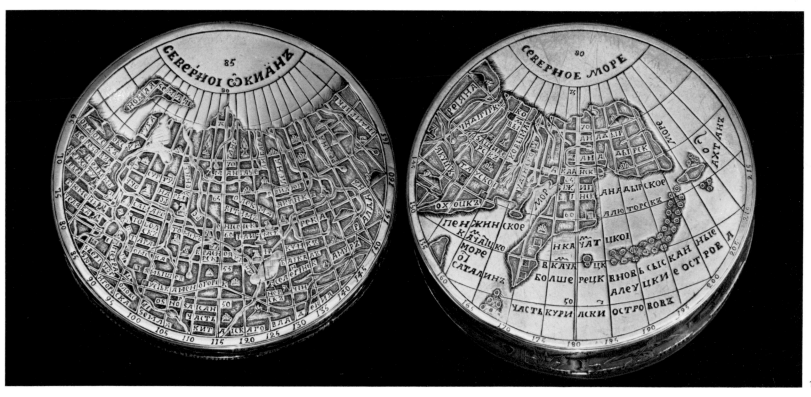

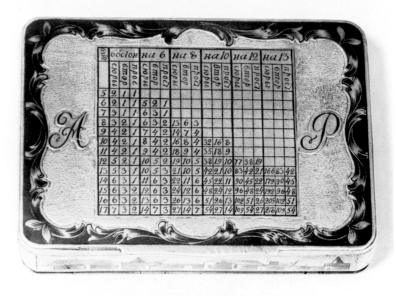

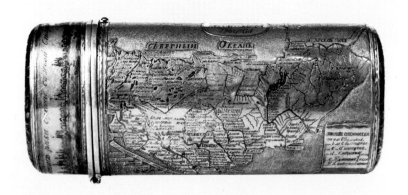

123

124

It was obviously from Velikiy Ustyug that *niello* spread to Siberia. It was developed in Irkutsk, Tomsk, and Yakutsk but especially at the big centre of Tobolsk. In small quantities *niello* was also produced in Kaluga, Kostroma, Ryazan, and Rostov-on-Don.

Nielloed products by the masters Zuyev (1810-44) and Skripitsyn (1837-44) of Vologda were known in the 19th century for their high quality. In Moscow in the 19th century the production was mostly of small snuff-boxes, often with town views and allegories of the wars of liberation against Napoleon. All the larger workshops and factories of Moscow and St. Petersburg, except that of Fabergé, towards the end of the 19th century were producing *nielloed* articles.

Niello is often wrongly called 'Tula work' or 'Tula-ed silver' after Tula, the city south of Moscow. Silver production in Tula was actually of no consequence and only one *nielloed* snuff-box is known, by the master Sobinin in the first half of the 19th century (it is now in the Moscow Armoury). This expression is based on a mistake. Tula was the centre of the Russian iron and steel industry and from 1712 onwards of the arms industry in particular. In Tula there was also a production of decorative parcel-gilt steel articles in which the gilt parts are set off against the blue-black metal.

Literature

Rosenberg, M., *Geschichte der Goldschmiedekunst auf technischer Grundlage, Niello*, Darmstadt, 1907.
Postnikova-Loseva, M.M., *Russkoye yuvelirnoye iskusstvo*, Moscow, 1974, pp. 205 ff.
Postnikova-Loseva, M.M., Platonova, N.G. and B.L. Ulyanova, *Russkoye chernevoye iskusstvo*, Moscow, 1972.

130 Silver-gilt and *nielloed* medallions and plaquettes with representations of saints from the end of the 18th century. Only the two rectangular plaquettes in the bottom row are stamped;
(left) Silver-gilt, *nielloed* icon with St. Antony, St. John, and St. Eustace, surmounted in clouds by Christ Pantokrator, Velikiy Ustyug, assay-master A. Torlov, 1769, 10.3 cm high;
(right) Silver-gilt *nielloed* icon of St. Procopius and St. John standing in front of a church, surmounted in a band by the inscription 'The miracle-working saints of Ustyug', Christ Pantokrator in the clouds, Velikiy Ustyug, about 1770, 10.1 cm high.

Objets de fantaisie

In the 18th century the German word *galanterie* had come to indicate a kind of article which can only be described as a 'luxury object'. Among these objects were all sorts of cases (*étuis*) which seldom had any specific use. The St. Petersburg goldsmiths' guild had accordingly introduced a distinction between gold- and silversmiths on the one hand, then jewellers, and finally 'masters of *galanterie*'. It follows that in respect of technical ability and also fertility of ideas the master of *galanterie* stood out from the others.

In the early 19th century it seems that less in the way of *galanterie* was produced, and the production of snuff-boxes also declined. Large-sized silver pieces and services from the *Magasin anglais* were fashionable around 1840. The jewellery produced at this time was predominantly of heavy gold jewels, scarcely even elegant, set with disproportionately large gems. With historicism and the revival of the old Russian *cloisonné* enamel technique, gold boxes with *guilloché* enamel or miniature painting (themselves influenced, it is true, by French originals) were forgotten.

The subsequent revival of the idea of *galanterie*, with reference back to 18th-century objects, was essentially due to Carl Fabergé. Such luxury articles, which from about 1870 to 1890 were made mostly in a baroque style, were then called *objets de fantaisie*. Fabergé's principal concern from then on was less with the production of ostentatious pieces set with large diamonds than with that of more elegant confections in gold and enamel set with semi-precious stones. The use of rose-cut diamonds was especially popular and had parallels in Russian jewellery of the time in which larger stones were typically framed with tiny *pavé*-set diamonds.

Fabergé's work seems to have been extensively explored, although the existing archive material in Leningrad has evidently been published only selectively. In contrast, concrete evidence about the masters in competition with him at the time is not easy to find. Since Fabergé represented the pinnacle of achievement in Russia technically, artistically, and also quantitatively, it is understandable that all other workshops are judged relatively to his.

Before listing these individually in order of importance, it seems necessary to refer to one master who began work as a master goldsmith in 1845 long before Carl Fabergé and was still working up to 1890. This was Samuel Arnd, who occasionally produced pieces for Nicholls & Plincke and in his ideas above all can be regarded as a forerunner of Fabergé. There is the evidence, for example, of his making stirrup cups in the form of realistic silver animals. But there is his early work, too, in *guilloché* enamel and mounted semi-precious stones.

Between 1870 and 1917 Ivan Savelevich Britzin (Britsyn) had a workshop which exported articles to Western Europe and America. It specialized in *guilloché* enamel and produced in particular picture frames, clocks and watches, cigarette-cases, and powder boxes, mostly mounted in silver. Very few examples of gold work by Britzin are known. His palette in enamel was simpler than that of Fabergé, being confined mostly to pastel shades of light blue, violet, and grey, with white also. It has been suggested but not proved that Britzin was apprenticed to Fabergé or worked for him.[1]

While Britzin seems to have been Fabergé's leading competitor in quantity of production, in quality it was the jeweller Hahn. Karl Karlovich Hahn (Russian: Gan) was a Court jeweller whose workshop also produced *objets de fantaisie*. Among his workmasters at one time or another were Alexander Tillander and also the outstanding goldsmith known only by the initials C B. Enamel was often used on gold at Hahn's and his pieces are more ponderous than Fabergé's. Gemstone embellishments and in particular brilliant cut diamonds are characteristic of Hahn.

The firm of Tillander, in existence from 1860 onwards, like Hahn specialized in jewellery.[2] In Alexander Tillander however, the son of the founder Alexander Edvard, the firm had a master goldsmith specializing in *objets*. Apart from *étuis* and

131 Gold beaker and cover with tray, the bell-shaped beaker on raised foot, chased with decoration of *rocaille* bands, the cover with rococo finial, the tray with *rocaille* border on three chased feet. Beaker and tray are engraved with the arms of Count Petr Borisovich Sheremetev (1713-87) appearing on the Cross of the Polish Order of the White Eagle. The Order had been conferred on the Count in 1758. On the 30th August, the annually celebrated Day of Alexander Nevsky, in 1760 he was appointed adjutant-general. This was probably the occasion on which he received the beaker as a present from the Empress Elizabeth. Master's initials of Johan Henrik Hopper (294), St. Petersburg 1760. Beaker: 14.5 cm high; tray: 16.5 cm wide.

132 Vase of two-coloured gold with blue enamel, the cover with two putti holding a cypher on shield with the initials of Grigoriy Grigorevich Orlov. The vase is decorated with enamel plaques, one on either side, both in grisaille, one of a flower-pouring Flora with putti, the other of Ceres with corn sheaves and putti. The handles are lion's heads with rings, the octagonal foot is applied with rams. On the lower edge of the vase is the engraved signature *Ador à St. Petersbourg*. The stamps are as follows: the city mark 1768, assay-master Ivan Frolov (101), master's mark I A within a crown (286). 28.5 cm high.

This vase, which belonged to Prince Orlov and was probably a present from Catherine II, is interesting since the city mark (1768) proves that Ador was working in St. Petersburg before 1770. Stylistically it is an early example of Louis XVI style in Russia.

(Walters Art Gallery, Baltimore)

136

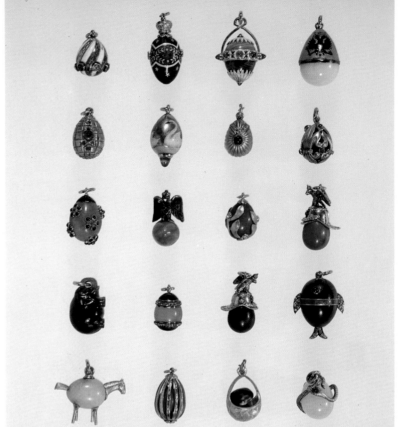

137

138

139

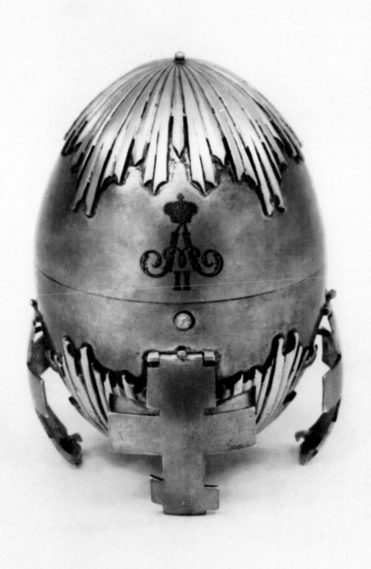

133 The Romanov Jubilee Easter egg, a present from Nicholas II to the Empress Alexandra Fedorovna in 1913. The gold egg is enamelled in opalescent white and set with miniatures of the Romanov sovereigns framed with chased double eagles and crowns. It is supported by a gold double eagle standing on a purpurine plinth. Inside is a parcel-gilt steel globe showing the frontiers of the Russian Empire in 1613 and 1913. Fabergé, workmaster Henrik Wigström (285), St. Petersburg 1913, 18.6 cm high. (Armoury Museum, Moscow)

134 Easter egg with the model of the cruiser *Pamyat' Azova*, a present of Alexander III to Mariya Fedorovna in the year 1891 (?). The egg is carved from a block of bloodstone (heliotrope) and mounted in Louis Quinze style in gold. Inside is a model of the cruiser in gold, mounted on an aquamarine. The Tsarevich in 1890-1 went on a world voyage on board this cruiser (cf. Pl. 142).
Signed by Fabergé (197), workmaster Mikhail Perchin (145), St. Petersburg, 9.8 cm long. (Armoury Museum, Moscow)

135 Miniature table in Louis XVI style of gold, enamel, and semi-precious stone, the 'wood' in *guilloché* enamel simulating the grain, the flower festoons in multi-coloured gold, the table-top of nephrite, signed Fabergé, workmaster Mikhail Perchin (146), St. Petersburg, 1899-1908, 8.5 cm wide. This *objet de fantaisie* is a typical product of the Fabergé firm and exhibits in outstanding quality various gold-working techniques. An almost identical miniature table, from the collection of the late H.M. Queen Mary, differs in the use of mother-of-pearl instead of nephrite. It was a matter of principle with Fabergé not to produce any of his pieces in identical series.

136-9 Miniature Easter eggs of gold and silver with enamel and precious or semi-precious stones by Fabergé and his competitors, end of the 19th and beginning of the 20th century. Sizes varying from 1.5 to 2.5 cm.

140 Cigarette-cases by Fabergé's competitors:
Above:
Three silver cigarette-cases with *guilloché* enamel in the light blue colour typical of Ivan Britzin:
(left) With opalescent white enamel between light blue bands, 1908-17, 8.5 cm long;
(middle) With waved *guilloché* ground and gold bay-leaf bands, 1908-17, 10.5 cm long;
(right) 1908-17, with English import marks for 1910, 9.2 cm long.
Below:
(left) Cigarette-case with blue *guilloché* enamel and opaque white stripes, in the style of I. Britzin (44), St. Petersburg 1908-17, 8 cm long;
(middle) Square cigarette-case with pale mauve enamel on a waved *guilloché* ground applied with a lattice-work of silver-gilt bay wreaths, with cabochon sapphire push-piece, master's initials (Cyrillic) A G, St. Petersburg 1908-17, 9 cm long;
(right) Gold cigarette-case with royal blue enamel on *guilloché* ground, applied with a gold double eagle and a cabochon moonstone push-piece, master's initials (Cyrillic) S V (183), St. Petersburg, end of the 19th century. This master worked for the Hahn firm. 8.5 cm long.

141 Parcel-gilt Imperial Easter egg. The plain silver egg is decorated above and below with a gilt sunburst pattern, and on the upper half, in blue *basse-taille* enamel, is the cypher of Alexander II (1855-81). The egg stands on four folding Russian crosses, it can be opened to reveal inside, in the upper half, a painted icon of the Vladim-irskaya Virgin, and behind that a compartment for a 'surprise', with a similar compartment in the lower half, master's initials of Joseph Nordberg (299), who was at work from 1848 to 1887, St. Petersburg before 1881, 10.9 cm high.
This Easter egg, which up to the Revolution was in the Alexander Palace in Tsarskoye Selo, is an interesting example of the well-loved Russian tradition of Easter presents of this kind. Hitherto it was assumed that Carl Fabergé had the idea originally of supplying the Emperor Alexander III with Easter egg surprises for his Empress Mariya Fedorovna. Although the Easter egg here illustrated does not show the mastery of Fabergé's mostly golden eggs, of which he produced the famous series of 57 examples, it can none the less be included among the prototypes of the idea otherwise attributed to Fabergé.

142 Gold vase, supported by three double eagles and decorated with a band of translucent red enamel over a *guilloché* ground in which is an engraving of the cruiser *Pamyat' Azova*. The enamel is framed with two rows of turquoises.
Signed by K. Hahn (120), workmaster A. Tillander (237), St. Petersburg, end of the 19th century, 10 cm high.
The vase was a present of the Crown Prince to Prince George of Greece, together with whom he made a voyage around the world on the cruiser in 1890-1891.

143 Collection of enamelled gold railway badges, predominantly by Alexander Tillander. The badges bear the crests of the different railway companies on whose lines the holders were carried free. End of the 19th, beginning of the 20th century, about 3 cm high.

charki, all kinds of *jetons* and badges are typical of Tillander. His enamel colours are often dark blue and red. As a technical speciality we often find *guilloché* surfaces additionally engraved with devices or scenes and subsequently enamelled.

Notes

1 Ross, *The Art of Fabergé*, Oklahoma, 1965, p. 92.
2 'A Short History of the Firm of Tillander', in *Carl Fabergé and his Contemporaries*, exhibition catalogue, Helsinki, 1980, p. 62.

Oklad

Oklad is the adornment of icons with a silver, silver-gilt, or more rarely gold frame which covers everything but the face and hands of the painting. The *oklad* serves not only to adorn but also to protect the sacred picture and in the 17th and 18th centuries was made subsequently to the icon itself. Thus the date of an icon-painting and that of its *oklad* are not necessarily the same and the two arts do not have the same chronology. Not until the second half of the 19th century, when icons were mass-produced, did it become customary to sell the icon complete with *oklad*.

Oklady were either made entire in silver repoussé work or put together from the following parts, which can also be used on their own: the frame (*rama*) covers the outer edges of the icon and in the 16th to 17th centuries was made by the *basma* technique (q.v.); the *riza* covers the clothing of the figure: it first appeared in the 17th century; the *venets* is the adornment of the nimbus painted around the head of the sacred figure. In the 17th century the *venets* (translated 'wreath', 'crown') was often surmounted by an additional crown of leaves, which was called *koruna*.

Tsata is an icon decoration in the form of a pendant half-moon which is hung from the lower side of the nimbus. The ornamentation of the *oklad* itself occurs in all shapes and techniques, the use of cloisonné enamel being especially popular, and much used in the 19th century. A rarer type of *oklad* is that in which the *riza* is embroidered with river-pearls or made of filigree. In this latter case it is backed with silver foil.

Orders and decorations

Orders played an important part in Russian life. Their relatively large number and their division into different classes was a reflection of the ranking system introduced by Peter the Great. Some of the Orders were reserved for the Imperial family or the higher aristocracy; with others, an Order conferred lifelong or hereditary nobility. A detailed hierarchy of Orders evolved which lasted until 1917.

144 (left) St. Sergey, folding icon painted on silver, Fabergé's (125) Imperial Warrant mark, Moscow 1908-17, 6 cm high;
(right) Enamelled icon of the Crucifixion with the Mother of God and St. John before a townscape. The icon is a relief chased in gold and fully painted in enamel. The haloes and the frame are set with rubies. Moscow, end of the 17th century, 7 cm high.

145 Miniature icon of the Kazanskaya Virgin, the silver-gilt *riza* richly decorated with *cloisonné* enamel, the robes in river pearls, unmarked, probably by P. Ovchinnikov, about 1890, 11.5 cm high.

146 The Vladimirskaya Virgin with silver-gilt *oklad*, the robes in silver filigree, the upper corners with enamel spandrels, by P. Ovchinnikov, Moscow 1889, 31.5 cm high.

147 Icon miniatures with silver *oklady*:
(first row, from left) Christ Pantokrator, the outer frame with *champlevé* enamel, master's initials (Cyrillic) S E, St. Petersburg, late 19th century, 8.3 cm high;
Virgin with a kneeling believer, silver-gilt *riza*, master's initials (Cyrillic) I E, 1899-1908, 9.3 cm. high;
Christ Pantokrator, *oklad* by Sazikov, 8.9 cm high;
(second row) Vernicle, the frame St. Petersburg 1908-17, 3.7 cm high;
St. Vasiliy, St. Grigoriy, and St. Ioann with silver-gilt *riza*, 1883, 5 cm high;
(third row) Archangel Michael, with silver frame, master's initials (Cyrillic) N K, 1899-1908, 7 cm high;
The Virgin with silver-gilt *riza*, master's initials AMM, 1899-1908, 6.7 cm high;
St. Sergey of Radonezh with silver-gilt *riza*, Moscow 1908-17, 7 cm high;
(fourth row) The Tikhvinskaya Virgin, with oval, silver-gilt *riza*, master's initials of Ivan Zaytsev, 10 cm high;
Christ Pantokrator with silver *riza*, the halo with *champlevé* enamel, by P. Ovchinnikov, 9 cm high;
The Iverskaya Virgin with parcel-gilt *riza*, by G. Sbitnev, 11.2 cm high.

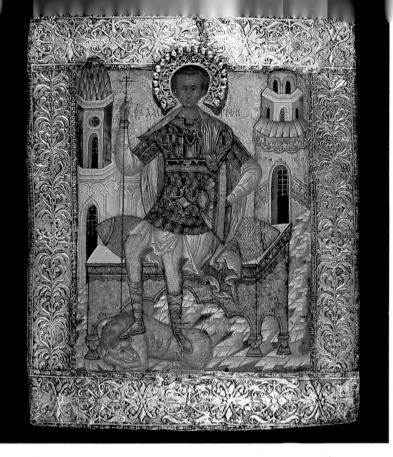

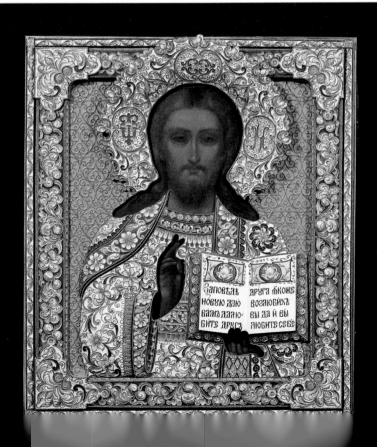

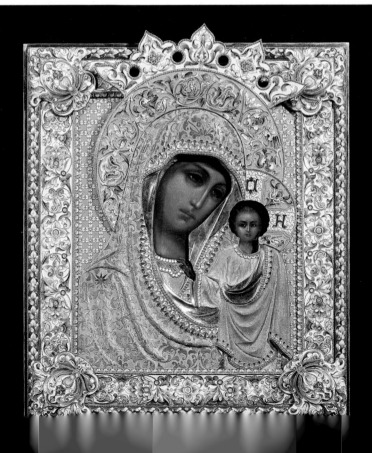

162

164

163

148   Icon of St. Demetrius of Thessalonika, Moscow School, 16th century, the outer frame with a silver band nailed on, stamped in the *basma* technique with rosettes and foliage, the halo in *cloisonné* enamel. The silver decoration was made in the 17th century. Height of the icon 32.6 cm.

149   Icon of the Presentation of the Virgin in the Temple, the silver-gilt *oklad* entirely covered with *cloisonné* enamel. An unusual feature is the decoration of the clothes with enamel, so that the wires forming the *cloisons* mark the folds of the draperies. The colours are in brilliant green, orange, and violet, with cream and olive-green for the architectural background, the outer frame with shaded flowering scrolls on a green ground, the corners with angels' heads, master's initials of Fedor Rückert (207), Moscow 1899-1908, 51.5 cm high.

150   (left) Christ Pantokrator, the silver-gilt *oklad* with polychrome *cloisonné* enamel, the background turquoise-coloured, the volume of the gospels painted *en plein*, by O. Kurlyukov (166), Moscow 1899-1908, 31.5 cm high;
(right) The Kazanskaya Virgin, the *oklad* with silver-gilt, chased and engraved, clothing decorated additionally with *cloisonné* enamel, by I. Khlebnikov, workmaster's mark (Cyrillic) D S, Moscow 1899-1908, 31.5 cm high.

151   Enamelled golden Collar and Badge of the Order of St. Andrew on seventeen alternating badges, seven with the double eagle, six with the St. Andrew's Cross on a rosette with the initials SAPR, and four with the crowned reversed cypher of Peter I on trophies, Keibel's (305) Imperial Warrant mark, St. Petersburg 1868;
(middle, left) Parcel-gilt and enamelled silver Star of the St. Andrew's Order, unmarked; the Cyrillic letter I is incorrectly written, suggesting that the star was made outside Russia to make up a set;
(middle, right) Enamelled gold Badge of the Order of the White Eagle, by Keibel, initials A K (20), St. Petersburg about 1890.

152   Cross of the Order of St. Catherine, with the central enamel medallion of the saint, set with diamonds, about 1870.

153   Star of the Order of St. Catherine with diamonds, about 1870.

154   Badge of the Order of St. Andrew in gold, silver and enamel, set with diamonds, enamelled also on the reverse, about 1765, 11.5 cm long. This Order was probably conferred on Frederik V of Denmark by Catherine II. The occasion was the conclusion of peace between Russia and Denmark in 1765, leading to the Treaty of Exchange of 1767, according to which King Frederik received the possessions of the Duke of Gottorp, Schleswig-Holstein, in exchange for the counties of Oldenburg and Delmenhorst, which had been acquired for Russia by Peter III.
The Badge of the Order was first mentioned in the inventory of the Danish crown jewels of 1784. In style it could be attributed to Pauzié. (Rosenborg Castle Collection, Copenhagen)

155   Star and Grand Cross of the Order of St. Alexander Nevsky, silver, gold, and red enamel set with diamond-cut paste, master's initials (Cyrillic) I L, St. Petersburg about 1890.

156   Grand Crosses and Stars for personages of non-Christian faith with the Russian double eagle instead of the saint's picture in the central medallion:
(top, left) Cross of the Order of St. Stanislaus, by Edvard, 4.9 cm high;
(top, right) Cross of the Order of St. Anne, signed Keibel;
(bottom, left) Star of the Order of the White Eagle, signed Keibel, 9 cm diameter;
(bottom, right) Star of the Order of St. Anne, signed Keibel, 9 cm diameter.

157   (above) Cross of the Order of St. Anne, gold and red enamel, master's initials of Keibel, about 1890;

(middle) Star of the Order of St. Anne in parcel-gilt silver with red enamel, about 1900;
(below) Cross of the Order of St. Stanislaus 3rd Class, gold with red enamel on a *guilloché* ground, master's initials of Keibel under the double eagle, about 1900.

158   Cross of the Order of St. Vladimir 3rd Class with swords. Gold and red enamel, about 1900.

159   Cross of the Order of St. George 4th Class with the rare superscription '25 Years'. Gold and white enamel, about 1850.

160   Star of the Order of St. Vladimir in parcel-gilt silver with enamelled centre-piece and the motto of the Order, 'Advantage, Honour, and Fame', signed Edvard (210), about 1900.

161   Star of the Order of St. George in parcel-gilt silver with enamelled centre-piece and the motto of the Order, 'For Duty and Valour', signed Edvard (210), about 1890.

162   Silver box with medal portrait of Peter the Great on an engraved lozenge-pattern ground with flowers, unmarked, about 1790, 7.2 cm diameter.

163   Parcel-gilt *nielloed* silver box applied with a medal by J. G. Waechter for the wedding of Grand Duke Pavel Petrovich and Marie Dorothea von Württemberg on 26 September 1776, master's marks S.B. and M.N.A., Moscow 1782, 9.4 cm diameter.

164   Parcel-gilt silver box, the lid applied with a portrait medal of the Empress Elizabeth by V. Klimentov (on the occasion of her death and the accession of Peter III) on a ground engraved with the Star of an Order, unmarked, about 1780, 10 cm diameter.

The importance of the Orders is demonstrated by the fact that the insignia were as a matter of principle carefully worked in gold, with enamel and precious stones. They are often high-quality examples of the goldsmith's and jeweller's art. Beyond that the emblems of the Orders were used also in heraldry and to ornament *objets d'art*.

The history of Russian Orders begins with the foundation of the Order of St. Andrew by Peter I in 1698. A systematization and legal classification was carried out by Paul I in the Order Statutes of 1797.

Especially in the 18th century Orders were set with diamonds as pieces of jewellery. In such cases the knights of an Order themselves often went so far as to have their decorations adorned with gems. Paul I in 1797 put an end to this practice by reserving to the Sovereign's Imperial award the right of adorning an Order with diamonds. However, whenever an Order was awarded 'with diamonds' the recipient had the choice of taking it either in this form or with paste, and in the latter case the value of the diamonds was paid out in cash. The reason for this custom is no doubt to be found in the fact that so many Orders 'with diamonds', as also in the case of snuff-boxes, were broken up soon after receipt.

Other important enamel workshops were those of Sumin, who worked in the same way as Britzin, of Astreyden, and of the 3rd Artel, which may be compared with Fabergé in regard to gold objects in particular.

These firms had a fairly considerable output until 1917, but smaller firms also sought to have a part in the market for *objets de fantaisie*. For example, there are enamel frames by Edvard, a workshop that specialized in Orders. In addition foreign firms such as Cartier, Boucheron and Lacloche sold such objects in Russia.

Decorations

The chamberlains, or gentlemen-in-waiting, had a special position at Court, with immediate access to the Sovereign. As a badge of office they wore a golden key, of which the bow, in the form of a double eagle, was worked with the Emperor's monogram. One of the earliest mentions of such a key is in a bill from Libmann of 5th July 1728, demanding payment of 2,500 roubles for a chamberlain's key in gold and diamonds made for Prince Ivan Alexeyevich Dolgorukiy.[1] Pauzié mentions in his memoirs the making of such a key in the year 1762, to be handed to the Senior Chamberlain Count Sheremetev by Catherine II.[2]

In the 18th century, in personal recognition of military services, the Emperor might award a dagger with a golden hilt, often set with diamonds. During the 19th century a dagger with the badge of an Order could be awarded as a preliminary step to the award of the Order itself.

For services rendered to the Emperor personally a medal might be awarded, bearing a miniature (often painted) of the Emperor surrounded with a bay wreath and with his crown set in diamonds. This form of decoration was introduced by Peter the Great himself. From the 19th century medals are known with several portraits of successive emperors. Similar medals were worn by ladies-in-waiting.

The ladies-in-waiting and maids-of-honour (*freileiny*) received as a badge of office a crowned monogram of the Empress set in diamonds (*chiffre*), which were worn on a bright blue ribbon. Ladies-in-waiting who served the Empress and the Empress-Dowager simultaneously wore their crowned initials intertwined. The earliest known lady-in-waiting *chiffre* dates from the end of the 18th century.

The makers of Orders and decorations

No 18th-century decoration is known with a maker's signature. The reason probably is that the insignia of Orders were usually enamelled all over (or often set with precious stones like pieces of jewellery) and thus not subject to stamping requirements. Pauzié in his memoirs several times mentions receiving a commission for an Order. In 1758 he had to make a diamond-set star of the Order of St. Andrew for Prince Karl Christian Joseph of Saxony and another in 1763 for Count Stanislaus Poniatowski, later King of Poland. Not until the beginning of the 19th century do we learn the names of goldsmiths who were occupied more or less exclusively with the making of insignia for Orders. They are as follows:

Kämmerer, Heinrich Wilhelm, 1806-54, associated with Keibel in the production of Orders from 1836 to 1846.

Pannasch, Emanuel Georg, 1809-37, specialized in Orders, 1821-33.

Master with the initials I P (Collar of the Order of St. Andrew, St. Petersburg 1828, presented to the 6th Duke of Devonshire, Chatsworth). (no. 113)

Keibel, Johann Wilhelm, 1812-62, Imperial Warrant. From 1836 to 1846 he worked under commission from the Chapters of the Orders in association with Kämmerer. Keibel's workshop was still in business at the beginning of the 20th century. The majority of the insignia of Russian Orders are signed: Keibel. (nos 20, 305)

Edvard, firm of goldsmiths specializing in Orders, end of 19th, beginning of 20th centuries. Workmasters with the Cyrillic initials I L, 1899-1908, (Cyrillic) V D, 1908-17. (no. 210)

Zhivago, made insignia of Orders at the end of the 19th century.

Notes

1 *S.I.R.I.O.*, vol. 84, p. 47.
2 Pauzié, 'Zapiski', pp. 220f.
3 Pauzié, 'Zapiski', pp. 91, 236.

Literature

Andolenko, S., and R. Werlich, *Badges of Imperial Russia*, Washington, 1972.
Gritzner, M., *Handbuch der Ritter- und Verdienstorden aller Kulturstaaten der Welt innerhalb des XIX. Jahrhunderts*, Leipzig, 1893.
Mericka, V., *Orden und Auszeichnungen*, Prague, 1966.
Quadrie, V., and Konarjevsky, *Ordres russes, Abrégé historique, extrait des statuts*, St. Petersburg, 1901.
Spassky, I.G., *Inostrannye i russkiye ordena do 1917 goda*, Leningrad, 1963 (with detailed bibliography).

Platinum

Platinum was discovered in Russia in 1819 and from 1825 onwards was produced especially by the Demidov mines. The state owned the monopoly for dealing in platinum but issued licences for its production.

In 1828 the first platinum coins were minted, pieces of 12, 6 and 3 roubles, which were in circulation from 1830 to 1845. The suspension of the platinum coins and their withdrawal from circulation in 1846 can be attributed to the fact that there had been an enormous fall in the price of the metal; this was endangering the Russian monetary system. Before the Revolution the world consumption of platinum was amply covered by the discoveries in Siberia and the Urals. Not until 1900 did the price again rise, but even then it remained a long way behind that of gold.

While it is well known that platinum was already being used by goldsmiths in Paris in 1785/1786—Marc Etienne Janety (Maître 1777), for instance, was famous for snuff-boxes of platinum.[1] In Russia the first attempts to use this metal artistically began about 1830. The first goldsmith to do so there was Jean Berel (Index of marks no. 242), a French immigrant, who in 1841 delivered parts of a hunting service for the Court in platinum.[2] Keibel too worked in platinum and a snuff-box of the 1830's by him is preserved in the Treasury at the Hermitage.

With the fall in price around 1845 goldsmiths became less interested in using platinum. Hardly any platinum objects were produced in the second half of the 19th century. Not until 1900, when the price of platinum began to rise, do we again meet with objects in this metal; Fabergé, for instance, besides one Imperial Easter egg (1910), made necklaces, bracelets, and watch chains.[3] Jewellery settings, however, continued to be predominantly in gold or silver.

Plate-marks for platinum did not exist in Russia any more than they did in any other European country.

Notes

1 Nocq, H., *Le poinçon de Paris*, vol. II, Paris, 1927, p. 353.
2 Bäcksbacka, *St. Petersburg Juvelerare*, p. 289.
3 Habsburg-Lothringen/Solodkoff, *Fabergé*, p. 63 and n. 19.

Literature

MacDonald, D., *A History of Platinum*, London, 1960, p. 156 (with Bibliography).

Podstakannik

Podstakannik means a tea-glass holder, cylindrical in form with a side handle. They were not made until late in the 19th century.

Samorodok

Samorodok (Russian for 'native', 'pure' metal), technical term for the preparation of a silver or gold surface in such a way that it resembles that of a natural nugget. It is achieved by the rapid cooling of an almost molten mass of metal. The crust which forms is cratered like a lunar landscape. Cases with a *samorodok* finish were particularly fashionable around 1900.

Samovar

A *samovar* is a vessel for heating water for tea. In contrast to West European samovars, which were simple water containers, the Russian samovar had a vertical tube in the centre to hold glowing coals. The tea was always prepared separately in a pot as an extract and diluted with hot water from the samovar. The first silver samovars are not found till the second half of the 18th century.

Snuff-boxes and gold boxes

The fashion for snuff-boxes which lasted throughout the 18th century must be seen first of all in connection with the fashion for taking snuff. In Russia this was known at an early date, as Olearius in 1647 confirms: 'Tobacco was formerly so widespread there as to be universally enjoyed, whether smoked or as powder.' It was said that the poorer people spent so much on it that in 1634 the sale and consumption of snuff was forbidden.[1]

Early 18th Century

Though it must be supposed that tobacco boxes were already in use at this time, no examples are known, the earliest being from the time of Peter the Great in the early 18th century. Peter I, with his foundation of St. Petersburg in 1703 and the removal there of the Court, introduced western ways of life and art to Russia. His particular model was the maritime nation Holland, which was copied in the sphere of technology (shipbuilding) and also of art. A typical example is the snuff-box which Peter I personally is said to have used. It is made of walnut in the likeness of a schooner's hull, with a gold mount.[2]

As so often with Russian 18th-century art we cannot determine where this object comes from, Holland or Russia, or whether it was made in Russia by a foreign master.

A further example of the beginning of snuff-box manufacture is an oval box made in 1720 which also belonged to the Tsar. It is decorated on the lid with a miniature, a view of St. Petersburg (the SS. Peter and Paul Fortress), and on the inside of the lid has a portrait of the Tsarevich Peter Petrovich, who was born heir to the throne in 1715 but died when he was only four.[3]

The third and last known box of the Petrine age is a snuff-box which belonged to the Empress Catherine I and is frequently assigned to a later period. It is carved out of white quartz, and the lid is engraved with two dolphins and bears the word VIVE in gold, together with the double monogram IP and the letter C in a crowned cartouche.

What characterizes the Petrine snuff-boxes is on the one hand a certain heaviness of style, often comparable with the Dutch, and on the other the use of wood, tortoise-shell, and semi-precious stone, without much prominence of gold.

As in Western Europe the production of gold boxes did not begin till the 1720s. In Russia, however, it very soon became usual to embellish such boxes with diamonds and other gems.

This can be inferred for example from Peter II's instructions regarding the distribution of the effects of Peter the Great and Catherine I on 18 July 1727. With a number of valuable objects and mementoes are listed two silver boxes and in gold a 'round snuff-box with diamonds' and a 'snuff-box in the form of a book with diamonds'. Interesting in this context too is the bill sent to the Empress Anna Ioannovna by the merchant (and later Lord Commissioner of the Court) Isaac Libmann, dated 23 November 1733. He presents an account altogether for 12 gold boxes and 4 golden snuff-boxes with diamonds, all articles delivered within a year.[4]

Of the snuff-boxes preserved from this period it can be generally said that they are characteristically heavy gold boxes with chased ornamentation. The decoration is often so widely dispersed as to seem parsimonious. The diamond embellishment consisted partly of small stones incorporated in the gold decoration, or else of

138

specially big ones, which often seem rather pointlessly placed. Thus the effect is frequently austere or forbidding.

A snuff-box of this kind is mentioned in a letter by the French ambassador in St. Petersburg, the Marquis de la Chétardie, in 1741. The box was presented by the Duke of Brunswick, the husband of the Regent Anna Leopoldovna, to the Austrian ambassador, Graf Wilczek. Perhaps rather jealously, the Marquis writes: 'The box is completely ordinary and not new, and the stones set in the lid are so small and so widely dispersed that it would have been better to leave them out altogether.'[5]

This typically Russian fashion of embellishing a box persisted until the 1760s, especially with the pieces of master jeweller Pauzié. Parallels in Western European snuff-box work may be found in the boxes of Daniel Govaers (Gouers), who worked in Paris 1717-1748, though his are undoubtedly more elegant, or in the diamond-set hardstone boxes of Frederick the Great (mostly around 1760).

All the same it may be said that the Russian boxes of this period do possess a certain charm, perhaps precisely because of their heaviness. In the memoirs of the Court jeweller Pauzié there are some references to snuff-boxes which he had to make. 'Frequently rich snuff-boxes and rings were required as presents for foreign ministers when they were received for a farewell audience.'[6] Thus the Empress Elizabeth commanded 'the merchant Pauzié to make in his own workshop a big golden snuff-box with diamonds', which was to cost 1650 roubles. This unusually high price for a snuff-box, which would usually cost 300 to 700 roubles, was paid in 1759.[7]

It is worth noticing that in Russia, besides snuff-boxes, a quantity of boxes were produced which were certainly not intended for keeping snuff: *bonbonnières*, comfit-boxes, toilet boxes, and patch boxes. Possibly this has some connection with the fact that from 1725 to 1796 Russia was mainly ruled by women, the Empresses Catherine I, Anna, Elizabeth and Catherine II.

In 1750 Pauzié had brought back from a visit to Switzerland for the Empress Elizabeth 'snuff-boxes in a style unknown to Russia'; also the Empress 'was quite particularly amused by a small egg of artistic workmanship, on which the double eagle and her name were set in diamonds, and which opened with a spring catch and which could serve as a box for toilet articles or other small things.'[8]

The general popularity of snuff-boxes, which apart from their use for tobacco could often be regarded as nothing but decorative objects, can be judged from the great number of porcelain boxes produced in Russia from 1751 onwards. These boxes, frequently gold-mounted, in Russia assumed the special likeness of a packet or small wrapped parcel on which the names of addressee and sender were given, with a seal.

Porcelain boxes were mostly provided with gold mounts, which were partly enamelled, often too set with diamonds. These mounts, in the 1750s and 1760s, were made of Astrakhan gold in the Peterhof workshop. The director of the Porcelain Factory, Schlatter, entrusted the work to the masters Peter Botton, Petr Semenov, or 'Gakstein' (perhaps Erik Hagstedt).[9]

Reign of Catherine the Great

At the beginning of the reign of Catherine II in 1762 the influence of French culture and art was particularly strong. This Empress, who corresponded with French philosophers, bought art collections in Paris and in St. Petersburg gave presents of snuff-boxes made in Paris. One such, for instance, by Master G.J. Maillet, 1753, is preserved in the Geneva Museum. It bears an enamel representation of *sujets galants* and in its interior the engraved Russian inscription: 'Gift of Her Majesty the Empress Yekaterina Alexeyevna in the year (1)762 to A. Shishkin.' (It could often happen that French boxes were engraved or received other additions in Russia.)[10]

The importation of snuff-box art from Paris had its effects on the style of the Russian masters. The heaviness of the large diamond-laden gold boxes gave way to a certain elegance of form and decoration. This might be achieved after the French model by enamelling the gold surfaces—mostly transparent on a *guilloché* ground.

165 Rectangular gold box, the lid chased with a relief of Europa and the bull, surrounded with shells, festoons, and bands set with diamonds, the *bombé* sides chased with lattice-work and shells. Unmarked, 8.2 cm long, about 1745. The box can be attributed to Jérémie Pauzié. It was among the effects of Abraham Pavlovich Veselovsky who was for a time Russian minister at the Danish Court.

166 Round gold box (comfit box), the lid chased with the portrait of the Empress Elizabeth with architectural background, the sides with five pictures of important events of her reign, in front with an allegory on the birth of the Grand Duke Pavel Petrovich, whose initials appear on a shield. The underside shows an allegory on the might of Russia, with Minerva, Mercury, war trophies, and artistic emblems. The thumb-piece is set with diamonds. The box must be attributed to Pauzié. It resembles another box, also round, with the Empress's portrait, now in the Moscow Armoury, which is said to have been a present to Count Razumovsky and to have been made between 1757 and 1760. The Empress's portrait is based on a medal portrait, possibly by Hedlinger, which appears on another gold box, of the year 1757 by the Paris goldsmith Georges. The box here illustrated is probably to be dated between 1754 (year of the Grand Duke's birth) and 1761 (death of the Empress).
No marks or signature, diameter 10.3 cm.

167-8 The Esterházy Box, by Jérémie Pauzié, a present of the Empress Elizabeth to the Imperial ambassador, Count Nicholas Esterházy-Galantha.

The box is in four-coloured gold with views of St. Petersburg in *rocaille* panels chased with swags of flowers. The interior of the lid is inlaid with a miniature portrait of the Empress, signed Sampsoy, engraved on the flange *St. Petersburg*, no marks or signature, 1761, 9.3 cm long.

The views are based on copperplate originals after N. Makhayev which were published in 1753 and 1761. The lid shows the Palace of Tsarskoye Selo. *Maison de Plaisance de Sa Majesté Impériale de toutes les Russies &c &c &c à Sarskoye Selo, 25 Verstes de St. Petersbourg* was the title of the engraving as it appeared in 1761.

The remaining views were printed in 1753: in front, the Summer Palace; behind, the Stock Exchange; left side, the Fontanka Embankment; right side, the Admiralty; base, the Fortress of SS. Peter and Paul and the Neva (cf. Pl. 176).

The dating of the box can be inferred from the following points: 1761 was the year in which the view on the lid was published and in which the Empress died. Moreover, it was in October 1761 that Count Esterházy terminated his mission in St. Petersburg. The box was very probably a farewell present from the Empress.

The outstanding quality of the work in this box means that only Pauzié can be considered as master. As he writes in his memoirs, he was always the one entrusted by the Court with orders for snuff-boxes. He employed various techniques of treating the surfaces and was thus able to give the low relief of the views an astonishing depth of perspective. Apart from the combination of gold colours the box is chased, engraved, and granulated.

◀ 169-174

169-74 Stroganov box: details; see Pl. 175.

175 The Stroganov box, a gold snuff-box engraved and *nielloed* on all sides with amorous scenes and figures in hunting costume, no marks, about 1770, 9.2 cm long.

The box, a masterpiece of *niello* work, seems to be the only gold object to have been *nielloed* in 18th-century Russia. As with enamel, for technical reasons to do with the melting-point, the use of silver was preferred for *niello* work.

The snuff-box illustrated here is said to have been presented to Count Stroganov by Catherine II. This was Alexandr Sergeyevich Stroganov (1733-1811), famous for his collections and as a patron of the arts. He was one of the Empress's closest advisers, often accompanied her on her travels, and was usually her partner at the game of boston. Catherine II loved his free-thinking ideas and his distaste for politics.

176 The base of the Esterházy box, by Jérémie Pauzié, with a view of the Fortress of SS. Peter and Paul, see also Pls. 167-8.

177 The Orlov box. A present of Catherine II to Grigoriy Orlov. A gold box with enamel miniatures and diamond surround. The miniatures show scenes of the *coup d'état* and the accession of Catherine II, who on 28 June 1762, with the help of the Orlov brothers, had her husband Peter III arrested and herself proclaimed Empress. The particular scenes are as follows:
(left side) Alexey Orlov fetches the Grand Duchess from Monplaisir in Peterhof;
(front) The arrival in Kalinkin with the jubilant crowds and Grigoriy Orlov on horseback in the foreground. Below the hoof can be seen the signature *Kaestner pinx*;
(lid) Generals and military swear allegiance to the new Empress, who is illuminated by a divine light;
(right side) Arrival at Kazan Cathedral;
(back) Soldiers in front of the Winter Palace;
(underside) Allegory on Catherine II, with Fama floating in the clouds beside a pyramid with an Imperial cypher, in the background the SS. Peter and Paul Fortress.
The box bears on its flange the engraved signature *Ador St. Petersbourg*, and the enamel minia-

tures were painted by J. C. Kaestner. Probably completed about 1765, 9 cm long, 5 cm high. (Smithsonian Institution, Washington, D.C., stolen 1979)

Joachim C. Kaestner had been known to Catherine II since her accession. She ordered from him drawings of scenes of the *coup d'état*, which were then used for this gold box. Later he worked as a porcelain painter in the Gardner factory. In the Russian Museum in Leningrad there are pieces of porcelain painted by him; a solitaire breakfast set with allegorical scenes is signed *J. C. Kaestner inv. et fec. 1775*.

There is a close technical affinity between the painting of enamel and of porcelain miniatures. The artist Andrey Chernov also painted in both techniques (cf. Pl. 186).

Grigoriy Orlov, as illustrated on the box, took a decisive part in the *coup* of 1762. He became Catherine II's favourite, and she wanted to marry him but was prevented for political reasons by the chancellor, Count Vorontsov. Orlov had a son by the Empress, Count Bobrinskoy, and a daughter Sofiya Grigorevna Alexeyeva.

Orlov was made count and later prince, and as a special favour received a miniature portrait of the Empress in a frame set with exceptionally large diamonds. In 1722 this portrait was taken away from him and presented to Potemkin in token of Orlov's fall from grace.

Orlov's love of display and his wealth of diamonds is well enough attested. In the context of snuff-boxes, there is a copperplate engraving extant, which shows the prince catching a man in the act of picking his pocket. It bears the title: 'Barrington detected picking the pocket of Prince Orlow in the Front Boxes at Covent Garden Theatre; of a Snuff Box set with Diamonds supposed to be worth £ 30,000. Published as the Act directs, October 6th 1790 by G. Kearsley Fleet Street, Etch^d by Barlon.'

178 Diamond-set and enamelled gold box with miniatures in *camaïeu rose* and green enamel of putti playing in landscapes of ruins, the thumb-piece with diamond-set foliage and a large diamond. Signed *Ador à St. Petersbourg*, about 1775, 8.7 cm long.
(Musée d'Art et d'Histoire, Geneva)

179 Oval enamelled gold box decorated with miniatures of *en plein* enamel painting with pictures and allegories of the sea battle of Chesmé Bay, when in 1770 the Turkish fleet was virtually annihilated by the Russian under the command of Count Alexey Orlov(-Chesmensky). The lid shows the battle, on the sides are scenes of the reception of Turkish delegations together with maps of Majorca and southern Greece, and on the base an allegory of Victory. On the edge the engraved signature *Ador à St. Petersbourg*, St. Petersburg about 1772, 8.7 cm long. A box conceived on much the same lines is in the Hermitage. It is also signed by Ador, and dated 24 June 1771.

180 Oval enamelled gold box, the lid with enamel miniature after the painting by Boucher *L'Hymen et l'Amour*, the sides with four miniatures of putti, the base with an allegorical scene of sacrifice, engraved signature *Bouddé à St. Petersbourg* and master's stamp (277), St. Petersburg 1773, 8.8 cm long. (Musée Cognacq-Jay, Paris)

181 Round enamelled gold box with the portrait of the prince regent of Portugal within a frame of blue and white enamel foliage and a lattice-work of rose diamonds on blue *guilloché* enamel, the outer border with an interlacing band and opalescent enamel beads, signed with the mark D R for David Rudolph (265), St. Petersburg 1785, diameter 8.8 cm.

The box was a present by the prince regent to Earl St. Vincent about 1806. It originally reached Portugal as a present from Catherine II to Queen Maria, and there the portrait was subsequently changed. The embellishment of enamel surfaces with narrow diamond lattices is typical of St. Petersburg gold boxes around 1780. Scharff's boxes are similar in style.

182 Oval enamelled gold box with a *grisaille* and pink miniature, surrounded with blue enamel panels and chased with wreaths, signed *Lajoye à Moscou*, Moscow about 1765, 8.2 cm long. One of the extremely rare examples of snuff-box production in Moscow.

183 Gold *bonbonnière*, the lid applied with a medal bearing the portrait of Catherine II by Waechter, the base with the reverse of the medal, an allegory on the Empress's accession to the throne on 28 June 1762, signed with the crowned initials IA (287), by J. P. Ador, St. Petersburg 1774, *zolotnik* mark 85, diameter 8.3 cm.

184 Diamond-set enamel box with green *guilloché* enamel and a sepia *grisaille* medallion with a picture *Le Ramoneur* ('The Chimney Sweep') after Jean-Baptiste Greuze, by J. G. Scharff, St. Petersburg 1781, 8.5 cm long. (Louvre, Paris)

185 Gold box enamelled *en plein* with amorous scenes, the lid with a picture of Susanna and the Elders with architectural background. Engraved on the rim *Ador St. Petersbourg*, St. Petersburg about 1770, 8.8 cm long. (Louvre, Paris)

186 Snuff-box with porcelain miniatures mounted *à cage*, the lid with the arms of Count Grigoriy Orlov outside and his portrait in a casual pose inside. The sides have hunting scenes, the golden mounts are enamelled a translucent blue. The miniature portrait is signed with the initials of Andrey Chernov, and the mount can be attributed to Ador, about 1765, 9 cm long.

187 Oblong octagonal gold box, the lid and underside with natural pyrites, the golden mount with opaquely enamelled rosettes and circles, master's initials of François-Claude Theremin (273), St. Petersburg 1808, 8.5 cm long. Belonged originally to the 6th Duke of Devonshire, who was a collector of minerals and in 1825 represented the British Crown at the coronation of Nicholas I. (Collection: The Trustees of the Chatsworth Settlement)

188 (Above) Enamelled gold box decorated with an oval miniature enamel painting of an amorous scene, with green and white bands and blue wreaths and flowers in *basse taille* enamel. Master's mark EH for Ephraim Hyppen, St. Petersburg about 1790, *zolotnik* mark 85, 8 cm long.
(Below) Rectangular gold box chased with scrolling foliage on a granulated ground, the lid with an oval cameo signed by Morelli. Probably by Keibel, assay-master Aleksandr Yashinov, St. Petersburg about 1820, 8.5 cm long.

189 Oval snuff-box of engraved steel with inlaid gold reliefs in three colours, the lid with a scene of putti with a goat in front of ruins, the sides with *capriccio* landscapes, together with putti, goats, and dogs, interior lined with gold. Engraved signature on the rim: *Kolbe à St. Petersbourg*, about 1765-75, 8.6 cm long. Members of the family Kolb or Kolbe were known in the 18th century as armourers and goldsmiths. They were scattered over the whole of Europe. A Johann Gottfried worked about 1740 as iron engraver in Suhl, Thuringia, a Johann Paul around 1775 as goldsmith in Vienna, a Friedrich Joseph Kolbe in St. Petersburg between 1806 and 1826. The present box cannot be immediately attributed to any of these, but it must be supposed that one of the Kolbes —perhaps Johann Paul—was for a time resident in St. Petersburg. The combination of blued steel and gold in boxes can generally be put down to Russian work. For works in steel the Tula workshops were specially famous, and decorative objects were manufactured there besides weapons.

190 Oblong octagonal gold box with the portraits in miniature of the Grand Dukes Aleksandr and Konstantin Pavlovich as children, master's mark F S (276), probably François Seguin, St. Petersburg about 1781. This snuff-box exactly matches in style those from France, from where Seguin had emigrated to Russia in 1779.

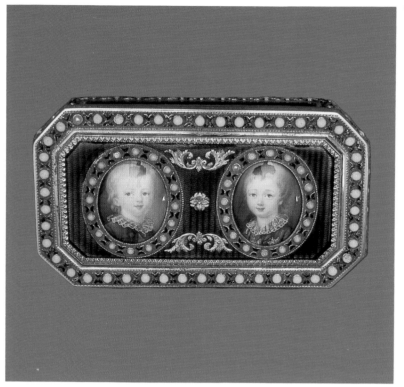

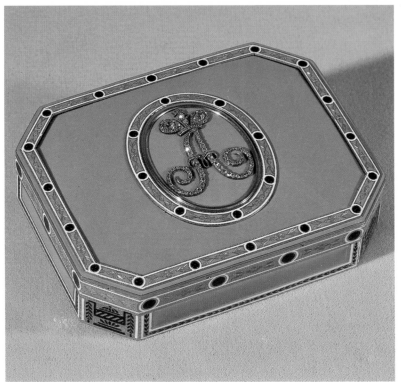

Yet the very Russian manner of lavish embellishment with diamonds was not so easily pushed aside. It is true the diamonds were no longer used in such baroque sizes as in Elizabeth's time but were now mostly applied to the enamel in fine lattices or rows. This was the method used in particular by the masters Scharff and Ador.

Ador is probably the best-known master for snuff-boxes in the time of Catherine II, whose Court jeweller he was. A Swiss by birth, he came to St. Petersburg at the beginning of the 1760s and worked there till his death in 1784.[11] Apart from enamelled snuff-boxes with diamonds or gold boxes *à quatre couleurs*, he seems to have preferred producing boxes with medallions of the Empress. These gold boxes, nearly all comfit-boxes with a removable lid and no hinge, were also much copied in silver in Russia.

191 Round gold snuff-box with enamelled miniature portraits of members of the Orlov family. The box is chased only with bands along the edges and has on the lid the portrait of Princess Yekaterina Orlov, née Zinoviev (1758-81). Grigoriy Orlov had married her in 1776, in scandalous circumstances, because she was his cousin. She was not immediately admitted to court but later became a lady-in-waiting and was decorated with the diamond-set *chiffre* of the Empress, which she is wearing in the portrait. During a journey through Europe in hope of a cure for consumption she died in 1781 in Lausanne. A monument to her was put up in the cathedral there by Orlov.

The box, which is said to have belonged to Grigoriy Orlov himself, contains in its lower half a fitted double interior. On the bottom and four sides of this inner lining are the portraits of the five brothers Orlov, respectively Fedor, Grigoriy, Alexey, Vladimir and Ivan.

The miniatures can be attributed to the painter G. Zharkov. The box is by Jean-Pierre Ador, St. Petersburg about 1781, diameter 8.3 cm. (Museo Nacional de Arte Decorativo, Buenos Aires)

192 Round enamelled gold box, the lid with the equestrian statue of Peter the Great by Falconet *en grisaille* on a simulated lapis lazuli ground with the date 6 August 1782 when the statue was unveiled, master's initials of François-Xavier Bouddé (277), St. Petersburg 1782, diameter 7.5 cm.

193 Diamond-set gold box, rectangular with chamfered edges, the lid with a miniature portrait of the Sultan Selim III (1789-1804), surrounded by diamonds on a blue *guilloché* enamel ground. The sides and base are also decorated with blue enamel, the bay-leaf bands and the fillets on the chamfered edges in *champlevé* enamel, master's initials of Pierre Theremin (317), assay-master Aleksandr Yashinov (38, 39), St. Petersburg 1797, gold standard 80 *zolotniki*, 9.5 cm long.

The box was a present from the Sultan to the British Admiral Lord Keith, who had helped the Turkish fleet with advice in the fighting against France. Among Lord Keith's letters (Bowood Archives, Calne, Wiltshire) there is one dated 22 June 1800 mentioning the box: 'A Turkish Aga arrived a few days ago with complimentary letters from the Sultan and a very handsome snuff-box set in diamonds, for which I have little use... I believe it valuable'

The question is why the Sultan chose to make a present of a *Russian* gold box. It is improbable that the box was specially ordered in St. Petersburg from Turkey. It is conceivable that it was originally a present of the Emperor Paul I to the Sultan himself on the occasion of his accession to the throne in 1796. The Sultan's portrait would then have been substituted for the Tsar's in Turkey. And in fact there are some notches in the framing of the miniature which could be so interpreted.

194 Enamelled octagonal presentation box with the diamond-set cypher of Alexander I on an opaque light blue enamel ground within a white and blue enamel foliage and rosette border. Signed with the initials of Pierre Theremin (317), St. Petersburg 1801.

195 Rectangular gold box with an enamel painting of a Swiss Alpine landscape with enamelled rosettes, the sides and base with translucent blue enamel—the enamel painting probably imported from Geneva, master's initials of Pierre Theremin (317), St. Petersburg 1800.

196 Oblong octagonal gold box with an oval portrait in miniature of Alexander I with a surround of foliage and scroll work in relief on a matt gilt ground and with blue enamelled edge, the sides similarly decorated—punched mark *Keibel*, by Otto Samuel Keibel, St. Petersburg about 1810, 9.6 cm long.

From the 1770s onwards there was a special cult of enamel painting on Russian snuff-boxes. Snuff-boxes with painted enamel plaquettes *montées à cage* are found, as are also those with enamel painting *en plein* on the gold ground of the boxes. At the same time portrait boxes also occur, adorned with a picture of the Empress or of other persons in enamel. These enamels were partly produced by the box makers themselves, partly ordered from other masters.

Russian enamel painting, which had already begun around 1700 in St. Petersburg with the miniaturists Mussikiysky and Ovsov, was taught from 1781 in the Academy of Arts in a 'Class for Miniature Painting on Enamel'. It was directed by Petr Gerasimovich Zharkov (1742-1802), who had a special reputation for portrait miniatures. Among his pupils was Dmitriy Yevreinov, who had been apprenticed to Sanson in Geneva. As a foreign enameller Charles-Jacques de Mailly is well known.[12]

Zharkov is frequently mentioned in the correspondence between Grimm and the Empress. On the 22 June 1790 she mentions in a letter to him 'a portrait, painted by Monsieur Garkoy (sic), who has done in enamel the same one that the Comte de Ségur has on his box'. The Comte de Ségur was the French ambassador in St. Petersburg whose snuff-box was adorned with the portrait of the Empress 'with fur-trimmed hat'—after the original by Shebanov.[13]

197   Oval gold box with blue enamel on *guilloché* ground, the lid with the cypher of Alexander I in rose-diamonds inside a paste-set medallion, St. Petersburg 1800, assay-master A. Yashinov, 9.3 cm long. Master's mark I B (288).

198   Gold box with an enamelled seascape, signed Richter, by Otto Samuel Keibel (305), St. Petersburg 1801, 8.9 cm long. The enamel miniature by the well-known Geneva enamel painter Richter was exported to Russia and there mounted on a box exactly conforming to the Geneva model.

199   Enamelled gold box, the lid with a view of a harbour in the manner of the Geneva enamel boxes. St. Petersburg 1800, assay-master A. Yashinov, 9.2 cm long.

200   Enamelled gold box with an allegorical picture in the Geneva style, by Pierre Theremin (317), St. Petersburg 1800, assay-master A. Yashinov (38), 8.5 cm long.

201   Rectangular box in two-coloured gold with a miniature portrait of Alexander I, St. Petersburg about 1810, 9 cm long.

202   Rectangular gold box with oval miniature portrait of Alexander I in oak-leaf surround, with rosettes and scrolling foliage on a matt gilt ground, by Keibel (305), St. Petersburg about 1813.

203   Box of gold *en quatre couleurs* with military trophies and a miniature of Prince Sergey Fedorovich Golitsyn (Galitzine, 1748-1810) within a paste surround, assay-master A. Yashinov, St. Petersburg about 1810, 9.8 cm long.

The prince in question distinguished himself in the wars against Turkey and in 1788 took part in the capture of Ochakov. Alexander I appointed him in 1801 governor of Estland and Courland. He had married a niece of Prince Potemkin. The box contained on the interior of the lid an inscription recording that the box was made from the gold of a sabre presented to the Prince after his capture of Ochakov.

204   Rectangular gold box with the portrait of Alexander I on a chased ground within blue, green, and black enamel borders, by Otto Samuel Keibel, St. Petersburg about 1801, 9.8 cm wide. This box was presented in traditional fashion by the Tsar to the British ambassador in St. Petersburg, Lord Granville Leveson Gower, when in 1804-5 he had been recalled because of a *'traité pratiquement inopérant'*.

In comparison with the splendid snuff-boxes which Catherine II gave as official presents, two examples may be quoted which have curiosity rather than monetary value owing to their personal character. One is the simple box with monogram in carved steel which the Empress gave to Princess Dashkova 'whilst making her toilet one day after some slight difference, or jealousy had occurred between them—in consequence of some playful allusion about sneezing mal à propos—the Empress offering her a pinch of snuff begged with a smile that she would keep the box'.[14]

Another personal present was the turned ivory box with her portrait which Catherine II sent to Voltaire in Geneva. She wrote of it in her letter of 6/17 December 1768: 'I would love to send you verses in exchange for yours. But if one is not clever enough to write good verses, it is better to work with one's hands. Here is how I practise what I preach. I have turned a snuff-box, which I beg you to accept. It bears the impress of the person who has the greatest respect for you. I need not name that person, whom you will easily recognize.'[15]

The popularity of snuff-boxes as official presents is documented by the fact that the Empress during her journey through the provinces in 1787 gave away as presents four hundred gold boxes with precious stones and enamel, apart from watches and finger-rings, all to an estimated total value of half a million roubles.[16]

As late as 1795 she presented Field Marshal Count Alexey Orlov-Chesmensky with a snuff-box on which was a view of the Memorial to his victories at sea in 1770, which had been erected in the park of Tsarskoye Selo. There is the interesting

205 Rectangular gold box *en quatre couleurs* applied with scrolling foliage in platinum, the lid with a platinum medal of Nicholas I, by Keibel, St. Petersburg about 1830.

206 Rectangular gold box, with symmetrical scrolling foliage in various gold colours; tips of leaves in platinum on granulated ground, stamped Keibel (305), otherwise unmarked, 8.8 cm long, about 1830.

207 Oval gold box with translucent blue enamel over a *guilloché* ground, decorated with bands and rosettes, master's initials W G (328), St. Petersburg about 1830, 8.7 cm long, *zolotnik* mark 72. (Victoria and Albert Museum, London)

208 Gold box in baroque form with the miniature portrait of Grand Duke Alexander Nikolaye-vich (later Emperor Alexander II), signed

W. Hau 1850, applied with the arms of Prince Vorontsov surrounded by the chain of the Order of St. Andrew. The lid is engraved inside with an inscription recording the presentation of the box by the Grand Duke and heir to the throne to Prince Mikhail Semenovich Vorontsov in the year 1850. Signed by Andreas Spiegel (235), St. Petersburg 1850, 8 cm long.

209 Rectangular gold box with the portrait of Alexander II, signed Rokshtul (Rockstuhl), surrounded by sixteen large diamonds in a design of foliage set with rose-cut diamonds.
The box was a present from the Emperor to Sir Roderick Murchison in recognition of his geological explorations in Russia. (Geological Museum, London)

210 Rectangular gold box with the oval portrait of Nicholas I, signed by Winberg, surrounded by diamond-cut paste on a granu-

lated ground chased with scrolling foliage, about 1840, 9 cm long.

211 Enamelled gold presentation box, the lid with the diamond-set double eagle on a translucent white enamelled medallion with blue-grey enamelled surround embellished with diamonds and rubies. Workshop of Karl Hahn (Gan), workmaster with the initials CB (183), St. Petersburg 1899-1908. 7 cm diameter. This box was a present of the Tsar to a Persian viceroy. It is technically quite the equal of Fabergé's productions, but the use of precious stones is typical of pieces from the jeweller Hahn's workshop.

212 Oval gold box with nephrite lid set with the crowned cypher of Nicholas II in a bay-wreath, the sides engraved with rosettes and bay-wreaths, master's initials of F. Köchli (275), 7.8 cm long.

addition in her own hand in the letter to Orlov: 'I have put snuff in the snuff-box from tobacco grown in my own garden but which I no longer take ... yet I fear it may dry up on the way'.[17]

While the aging Empress no longer took snuff perhaps for reasons of health, there is no doubt that as the 18th century came to a close snuff-taking went out of fashion. This was not the case, however, with snuff-boxes, which as gifts of honour rather than for use now assumed a position of their own. In the early 19th century they were correspondingly no longer called 'snuff-boxes' but *'boîtes en or'*—gold boxes.

From about 1790 the form of the boxes changed. While they had previously been mostly oval and relatively high, they were now rectangular and increasingly flat. Attention was now paid almost exclusively to the decoration of the correspondingly larger box lid. For these we have two main groups, enamel boxes and portrait boxes.

19th Century

After 1800 enamel became more and more popular, and it was much more easy to use on the flat, large-sized box lids. In keeping with the times we find many enamel paintings with classicist allegorical subjects. This was the style in which Pierre and François-Claude Theremin,[18] in particular, made boxes in St. Petersburg. This style of box-making was specially influenced by Swiss enamelware, the art of which was then at its peak in Geneva. Geneva enamelware was exported all over the world. One interesting example of the Swiss style is Otto Samuel Keibel's box into which is worked an enamel picture signed by a painter named Richter. This artist may have been the well-known Swiss enameller Jean-Louis Richter,[19] whose enamel painting would thus have been mounted later in St. Petersburg.

At the beginning of the 19th century Keibel's workshop, which was carried on after Otto Samuel's death in 1809 by his son Johann Wilhelm, specialized mainly in gold boxes. Often we find portrait boxes—gold boxes with classicist or Empire decoration on a matted ground, the lid adorned with a miniature. Apart from private orders the requirements of the Court had to be met. Alexander I, who reigned from 1801 to 1825, had to make countless diplomatic presents during the Napoleonic period both in war and in peace. Gold boxes were available for this purpose, adorned with the Imperial portrait in miniature and with more or fewer diamonds according to the importance of the recipient, as mementoes or gifts of honour. This kind of portrait box in Empire style retained its currency in Russia under Nicholas I as well, until about 1845.

Just as in Paris from the Empire onwards, Russian boxes were made of variously coloured gold with scrolling foliage and rosettes with the roughened and granulated ground giving the decoration a more sculptural appearance. Boxes of this kind too were made predominantly by Keibel. About 1830 uses were found for platinum as well as gold. A platinum box by Keibel with a symmetrical foliage decoration is in the Treasury at the Hermitage.

With the baroque revival the boxes changed their form . Their function however as official gifts of honour had become firmly established. In accord with the exuberant style of the baroque the decoration of the boxes became more lavish. The use of diamonds in imitation of the so-called Neuchâtel boxes increased steadily throughout the second half of the 19th century. Presentation boxes with diamond-set Imperial monograms were typical between 1860 and 1890.

Fabergé's great contribution, from about 1890 on, was to start once more producing boxes in enamel. In this period all kinds of cases made their appearance, and these began on the whole to take the place of the official presentation boxes. None the less it is remarkable that in Russia right up to 1917 a number of presentations in 'snuff-box' form were made by the Imperial family.

Stamping of gold boxes

Before 1760 gold snuff-boxes were only rarely marked: this applies both to assay marks and to master signatures. Pauzié for instance did not sign any of his boxes.

From the end of the 1760s makers began to have gold boxes also stamped with the usual assay marks with city arms and *zolotnik* number. However, the various masters, those working particularly for the Court for the most part, did not stamp their boxes with the usual master's marks but engraved their names in full on the inside edge of a snuff-box. A typical example is Ador's signature: *Ador à St. Pétersbourg.*

The French influence in snuff-box fashion becomes noticeable around 1780 even in stamping. Bouddé's boxes, for instance, have stamps (assay and master's marks) inside on every part: lid, underside, and side edge. Here it is obvious that the Paris stamping system is being copied, though clearly not because the special legal regulations of the *Maison Commune* and the *Fermiers* were applicable in Russia!

One still undeciphered mark on gold boxes of the period between 1770 and 1797 is a punched letter-like stamp which was obviously changed year by year (see chapter on Marks). This seems to have been a mark of the guild.

Notes

1 Quoted after Corbeiller, *Alte Tabaksdosen*, p. 10.
2 In the Hermitage, Leningrad; cf. Snowman, *Eighteenth Century Gold Boxes*, Pl. 599.
3 In the Hermitage, Leningrad; cf. *Les Trésors d'Art en Russie*, 1903, p. 30, Pl. p. 15.

4 S.I.R.I.O., vol. 69, p. 574, 106, pp. 579ff.

5 De la Chétardie to M. Amélot, 27th June 1741, S.I.R.I.O., vol. 96, p. 161.

6 Pauzié, 'Zapiski', p. 93.

7 Central National Archive, Moscow (TsGADA), Court papers, III, 115, no. 61749, quoted after Terekhova, A.M., *Zolotaya brilliantovaya tabakerka 18 v. v sobranii muzeyev Kremlya* (The 18th-century gold snuff-box in the Kremlin museum collection), Moscow, n.d., p. 166.

8 Pauzié, op. cit., p. 93.

9 Cf. Troinitsky, 'Farforovyya tabakerki', in *Starye gody*, 1913, XII, pp. 15 ff; Kaznakov, S.N., *Paketovyya tabakerki Imperatorskogo Farforogo Zavoda*, St. Petersburg, 1913.

10 Foelkersam, 'Novyi zal' in *Starye gody*, 1911, I, p. 31; cf. also Berry-Hill, *Antique Gold Boxes*, p., 203, for a Louis XVI box bearing the monogram of the Grand Duke Pavel Petrovich, about 1785.

11 For hitherto unpublished biographical data on Ador see pp. 160-3.

12 Postnikova-Loseva, *Russkoye yuvelirnoye iskusstvo*, p. 159. Other pupils included: P. Vardashevsky, P. Ivanov and P. de Rossi; cf. Wrangell, N., 'La miniature en Russie', in *Starye gody*, 1909, X, pp. 572f, providing a list of 140 miniaturists.

13 S.I.R.I.O., vol. 23, pp. 483, 499.

14 Description of collection inherited by Miss Martha Wilmot from Princess Dashkova; cf. auction catalogue, Christie's, Geneva, 8th May 1979, no. 51.

15 Voltaire, *Œuvres complètes*, Paris, 1785, vol. 67, p. 31; Troinitsky, 'Medal'nyya tabakerki'.

16 TsGADA, Fond 1239, no. 61791; after Martynova, p. 33.

17 Letter of 19th July 1795, S.I.R.I.O., vol. 1, p. 114.

18 For hitherto unpublished biographical notes on Pierre Theremin see p. 215.

19 Snowman, *Eighteenth Century Gold Boxes*, p. 114.

Stavets

A *stavets* or *stavchik* is a flattish cylindrical vessel for food, sometimes with a lid, comparable with a porringer or soup bowl. It has been known since the 17th century.

Watches and clocks

In the context of the goldsmith's art watches and clocks are of interest for their cases, often enough of silver or gold. It can be established, however, that neither the movements nor the cases of timepieces were often produced in Russia itself. They were predominantly imported. In so far as they were manufactured there they followed Swiss, French, or English models.

For the history of timepieces in Russia the following principal dates can be fixed:

From 1725 onward Swiss technicians were working in the Academy of Sciences.

In 1765 at the command of Catherine II an attempt was made to set up a watch and clock factory, but it failed.

In 1773 Jean Fazy from Geneva was working as clock-maker in St. Petersburg and continued for some years. Other masters included Sandoz-Basselier-Jurine and Michael Henrik Tiriong.

In about 1780 the clock-maker D.T. Musiard, St. Petersburg, signed a diamond-set pocket watch with chatelaine, a present from Catherine II.

In 1815 Paul Leopold Buhré (Bouret) from Le Locle set up shop in St. Petersburg. His son Paul later took over the business and received the Imperial Warrant. He opened a manufactory in Switzerland which was managed by Paul Girard, who in 1880 took over the firm. It remained in business till 1917, with shops in St. Petersburg and Moscow, and had a reputation for gold watches adorned with the Tsar's portrait in enamel or with the double eagle which were given as a present by the Tsars for services rendered.

In 1827 Henri Moser came from Le Locle to St. Petersburg to establish trading connections. The firm of Moser continued to deliver timepieces to Russia until 1917.

During the second half of the 19th century the better known firms of goldsmiths produced watch and clock cases of gold and silver. A report of the Swiss Consul in St. Petersburg of 1884, however, shows that practically all timepieces sold in Russia came from Switzerland.

After 1900 the firms of Fabergé and Britzin in particular were making watch and clock cases. The movements however came almost exclusively from Buhré or Moser.

The following Swiss manufactories were in business contact with Russia: Philippe Du Bois & Cie., Le Locle (1794); Robert & Courvoisier, La Chaux-de-Fonds (from 1815); Borel & Cie., Neuchâtel; Charles Tissot, Le Locle; Matthey-Tissot, Les Ponts-de-Martel.

Note

1 M. M. Post Collection, Hillwood, Washington D.C., Ross, p. 220, Pls. 70, 71.

Literature

Foelkersam, 'Inostrannye mastera...', pp. 109 ff.
Jacquet and Chapuis, *Technique and History of the Swiss Watch*, 2nd ed., London, 1970, pp. 70, 125 f.
Ross, M.C., *The Art of Carl Fabergé...*, Oklahoma, 1965.
Habsburg, G. von, 'Die Uhren des Peter Carl Fabergé', in *Alte Uhren*, I, 1981, pp. 12-26.

Vyaz'

Vyaz' (from Russian 'wickerwork') is a calligraphic Cyrillic script in the form of a frieze in which the Russian letters are partly ligatured, partly arranged over or under one another, thus resembling wickerwork. As a decorative element in the ornamentation of objects worked by goldsmiths the *vyaz'* script is found principally in the 17th century. *Bratiny* especially, and other drinking vessels, are often engraved with such friezes in script.

The *vyaz'* tradition disappeared in the 18th century but was revived in the 19th under the influence of historicism. In icon-painting, where it formed part of the composition, it always remained in uninterrupted use.

162

Marks on Russian Gold and Silver Objects

History of the marking system

The first statutory stamping regulation in Moscow was in the year 1613. The earliest marks which have been found on objects date from the year 1651/2. They show the arms of the Russian Tsars, the double eagle, in similar form to its appearance on coins. Until 1684 the mark could have various shapes—triangle, circle, oval, or rectangle. It could include dates indicated in the old Slavonic form, by letters. Between 1684 and 1700 the double eagle stamp was replaced by the 'Yefimok' or 'Levok' *titre* mark, with the addition of a stamp with the year in the Old Russian chronology.

Special marks were used for the Tsar's and the Patriarch's workshops in the Kremlin. Those of the former bear the double eagle in an especially well-executed and bold version with no date. Those of the Patriarch (indicating that he owned the object not that he guaranteed its quality) show a hand outstretched in blessing.

In the 17th century marks were used exclusively in Moscow. In the provinces there was no obligation to stamp. Yet a stamp on an article does not indicate that it was made in Moscow. On the contrary, at the great fairs and annual markets in Moscow the pieces brought by masters or dealers from the provinces were also stamped with control marks.

In 1700 Peter the Great began to reform the stamping of precious metal. By an *ukaz* of 13 February 1700 stamping was made a general obligation. Between 1700 and 1710 the double eagle with imperial orb and sceptre appears as the Moscow mark. Master marks also make their appearance from 1700.

Whereas the date stamp before 1700/1 was written out according to the Old Russian system of chronology, starting from the Creation of the World, from 1700 onwards the new European chronology was used, but until 1721 this date was written with letters in the old Slavonic manner. In the years 1716 and 1719 and afterwards from 1729 onward date stamps with Arabic numerals were used. The date too was to some extent combined with the double eagle in one stamp and it was not till 1729 that it became separate again.

From 1733-41 the city name MOCKBA appears under the double eagle. This is because at about this time there was more and more stamping in the provinces, where the double eagle mark was used with an abbreviation of the city's name. St. Petersburg had the letters СП and СПБ; Velikiy Novgorod BH; Velikiy Ustyug BY etc. The earliest mark of this kind for St. Petersburg dates from the year 1713/14.

With the year 1741 the city marks occur in the form of individual city arms, and this method of indicating the place of origin of objects persisted until 1899. By the same date at the latest the following marking system had become the rule:

1   The city mark (coat of arms).

2   The control mark with the assay-master's initials.
    The date appeared at first under the city arms, and then together with the assay-master's initials.

3   The master's mark with two or three initials, or else his name written out in full.

4   The *titre* mark with the number of *zolotniki* (per pound of precious metal).
    In the 18th century this mark was usually optional, since by the impression of the city and assay-master's marks the legal *titre* was already guaranteed. Not until 1 May 1798 did the stamping of the *zolotnik* mark (at least 84) become obligatory.

5a On articles of silver from *Moscow* there appears in the 18th century, besides the marks 1-3 (city mark, assay-master, master), the mark of the alderman (the 'president' of the guild, that is), who was required to supervise the quality of the objects produced. This mark was in the form of a heart or clover-leaf and had three Cyrillic letters:
    ААК Alexey Kosyrev (1762-91) (Index of marks, no. 3)
    АФП Fedor Petrov (1759-84) (nos 37, 40)
    АОВ unknown (1777-89) (nos 24, 25)
    АОП unknown (1775-1804) (no. 26)
    АФВ unknown (1796) (no. 36)

5b *In St. Petersburg*
    On 18th-century gold objects, especially snuff-boxes, there is frequently a mark in the form of a punched Russian letter. This letter used to be interpreted as a form of dating, giving the year, since numbers in the Cyrillic-Slavonic script were indicated by letters.[1] But closer examination shows no possible agreement between such a 'number' and the true date. The latter can be easily checked in almost all cases, since the St. Petersburg city mark is provided with the year number written out in full. Moreover the double dating of any such piece would

be unintelligible. So there must be another reason for these stamps, as for instance a quality control by the guild, which was just as influential in St. Petersburg as in Moscow. No archival material has yet been found to confirm this. The following letters are so far known, the accompanying dates being those given by the corresponding city marks. In the middle of the 18th century the Court Office stamped objects of gold, silver, or copper-gilt belonging to the Imperial collections with a die-stamp showing the double eagle in a small format. This mark, which can be described as a 'collection' stamp, is found in particular on gold boxes, whether of Russian, French, or English origin.[2]

1773	1776	1778
Д	S	И

1780	1782
П	М

1789	1790	1795	1797
&	У	Ч	Ш

From 1899 the marking of metals was standardized. The stamping with the arms of the city concerned was replaced by the so-called Kokoshnik mark (see Chapter 'Kokoshnik'). From 1899 to 1908 the Kokoshnik mark showed in addition to the *zolotnik* standard the initials of the director of the assay district, (Cyrillic) Ya.L. for Yakov Lyapunov (no. 215) and A.R. for A. Richter (no. 31) in St. Petersburg and (Cyrillic) I.L. for Ivan Lebedkin (no. 92) in Moscow. From 1908 to 1917 the assay district was given in Greek letters, alpha for St. Petersburg, delta for Moscow.

Notes

1 Foelkersam, *Opisi serebra*, vol. 1, p. 50.
2 Troinitsky, 'Farforovyya tabakerki', p. 21, no. 17, n. 31. Here there is mention of a porcelain box of Imperial manufacture in the form of a military drum, *c.* 1760, with this stamp on the gold mount.

Standard hallmarks

The *titre* of a silver or gold object, that is, the proportion of precious metal in the alloy, does not only affect the quality of a piece from the point of view of craftsmanship and technique. Its value and its estimation depend on it. This makes it necessary for objects to be stamped with a record of their *titre*.

Before the 17th century objects in precious metal were generally produced in the workshops of the Silver and Gold *Palaty* in Moscow, official state institutions which could themselves determine the standard, so that stamping was unnecessary. At most the double eagle, the State Arms, was stamped on.

With the steady increase in commercial activity, bringing with it also the circulation of foreign (precious metal) coins, some regulation of the standard of precious metal objects became necessary. The dependence of *titre*-stamping on coin circulation in 17th-century Russia is specially striking.

The first *ukaz* on the stamping of precious metal objects was issued in 1613. 'All Masters are required to produce silver articles of every sort to the standard of the *Lyubskiy Yefimok* and silver of lesser quality may on no account be used'. The '*Lyubskiy Yefimok*' denoted the *Joachimsthaler* introduced from Lübeck (Yefim = Euthenius = Joachim; thaler = dollar). The regulation meant in practice that all silver used for objects must reach at least the standard of these thalers. This standard can be given as 81-84 *zolotniki* (*c.* 850/1000).

It is true that no stamped objects from the time of this decree are known. Yet we do find, from the second half of the 17th century, pieces bearing a mark with the abbreviated word '*Yefimok*', thereby guaranteeing its standard.

In the further course of the 17th century there was a considerable rise in the price of silver, due to the constantly increasing demand for silver for minting. In 1649 and again in 1674/5 the purchase and sale of the *Yefimok* thaler were forbidden, since they were being melted down in the mints.

The consequence was that silversmiths went over to using silver of a lower standard, which however was not officially permitted until 1684. This silver was designated *levkovo* and stamped with the mark *Levok*. The *Levok titre* correspondingly amounted only to 61-2 *zolotniki* (*c.* 635/1000).

The reform of the Russian currency in 1700 by Peter the Great did away with the dependence of the silver standard indications on the *Yefimok* thaler. At the same time, on 21 October 1700, he issued an *ukaz* fixing for silver (and for gold) four different *titre* steps. These were of 96, 90, 84, and 62 *zolotniki*.

In the case of silver the use of metal of the 62-*zolotnik titre* continued to predominate (1720-32). From 1732, with the rapid improvement in the Empire's economy, the titre was raised to 72 *zolotniki*. From 1779 this was fixed as the legal standard.

This did not mean, however, that better silver was not also used at the same time. Since the middle of the 18th century silversmiths had already been accustomed to use metal with a titre of 84 *zolotniki* (875/1000). And by an *ukaz* of 1 May 1798 this became the minimum standard.

From then on until 1917 the standard mark 84 remained typical of Russia. In the 19th century, however, the more eminent firms of silversmiths frequently used silver of a titre of 88 and 91 *zolotniki* for articles of higher quality. These are mostly distinguished, too, by greater technical perfection.

With gold the fixing of the standard developed differently from that of silver. Though documents for the 17th century are hardly to be found, it can be established that gold in use at this time was generally of higher quality. This indeed is also due to the fact that gold objects were produced in smaller numbers than silver, so that more importance could be attached to its *titre*.

The regulations in Peter I's *ukaz* of 21 October 1700 governing the gold standard denote the steps as '1. higher than ducat gold (!), 2. of the same value, 3. and 4. lower'. The reference here is obviously to coins, which in the case of silver ones had just been abolished.

During the 18th century the gold standard was generally high. Gold boxes from St. Petersburg have gold *titre* stamps of 80, 84, 85, and 88 *zolotniki* (20-22 carat).

At the beginning and more especially from the middle of the 19th century the *titre* of gold sank generally to 72 *zolotniki* (18 carats) and from about 1880 to 1917 a *titre* of 56 *zolotniki* (14 carats) was usual. The more important firms of goldsmiths, however, used to make their pieces of higher artistic and technical quality of 18-carat gold (72 *zolotniki*).

Literature

Goldberg, T. and M.M. Postnikova-Loseva, 'Kleymenie serebryanykh izdeliy v 18 - nachale 18 vv.', in *Trudy Gosudarstvennago istoricheskogo muzeya*, XIII (1941), pp. 11-15.
Goldberg, T., Mishukov, F., Platonova, N. and M.M. Postnikova-Loseva, *Russkoye zolotoye i serebryanoye delo XV - XX vekov*, Moscow, 1967, pp. 141ff.
Postnikova-Loseva, M.M., *Russkoye yuvelirnoye iskusstvo*, Moscow, 1974, pp. 185ff.

Import marks

Precious metal objects imported into Russia from abroad sometimes bear Russian marks. For the 18th century and the first half of the 19th it can be taken as the rule that objects from abroad were not required to be stamped until they were sold in Russia itself. This means that any pieces which reached the customer or collector directly from abroad do not bear additional Russian marks. Only when they were resold by a goldsmith were they required to be stamped with a control mark. This then took its place, like the usual assay mark, with the master's mark of the goldsmith who offered the piece for sale.

An early example is a Hamburg standing cup by Johan Janes, a master of the first half of the 17th century, which bears the master's mark DD, the Moscow assay mark of Hans Schlatter (no. 283), and the year mark 1731.[1]

The silver service presented by Empress Catherine II to Prince Grigoriy Orlov is famous. It was ordered in Paris in 1770 from Jacques Nicolas Roettiers. When imported into Russia it was evidently delivered direct to Orlov. At any rate it bears no Russian marks stamped at this time. Not till after the death of Orlov in 1784, when the Empress bought the service back from the heirs, was it given Russian marks: those of the assay-master Nikifor Moshchalkin (1772-1800) (no. 163), the city mark of St. Petersburg with the date 1784, and the *zolotnik* mark 91.

A later example of an import mark is to be found on a Swiss enamelled gold box with Geneva marks around 1830. On the side in miniature format is the city mark of St. Petersburg, *zolotnik* mark 72, and the mark I.L.[2] This last is the initial of the goldsmith Johann Lilieberg (no. 297), who evidently resold the box in St. Petersburg.

From the middle of the 19th century onward we find marks showing the Cyrillic letters ПТ together with the city arms. These stand for *privoznye tovary*, meaning 'imported goods'.[3] Such marks have been found with the city arms of St. Petersburg and of Odessa (no. 179). From 1908-17 a modified *kokoshnik* mark in the form of a truncated oval served to indicate an import.[4]

Notes

1 Auction catalogue, Christie's, Geneva, Silver, 17th Nov. 1980, Lot 183.
2 Auction catalogue, Christie's, London, Fine Objects of Vertu, 1980, Lot 240.
3 Postnikova-Loseva, *Russkoye yuvelirnoye iskusstvo*, p. 270.
4 Postnikova-Loseva, *Russkoye yuvelirnoye iskusstvo*, p. 305.

Kokoshnik marks

The name *kokoshnik* mark is taken from the stylized design of a girl's head with a *kokoshnik* appearing in the mark. The *kokoshnik*, originally a peasant head-dress, forms part of the Russian national costume. It was made of a textile material and worn in the hair like a diadem. In the 19th century a form of ornamental jewellery evolved from it.

The introduction of the *kokoshnik* mark brought about the standardization of the precious metal stamp by replacing those with the arms of different cities. In 1896 it was the subject of an *ukaz* which however did not come into force till 1 January 1899, because the marking system was being generally reorganized and some 2400 new die stamps had to be made.[1] The new dies showed the design of a girl's head with *kokoshnik*, looking left. They were stamped in outline, with the later addition of the initials of the assay master.

In 1908 a new mark was introduced in relief, also with the girl's profile, but this time she faced right. The assay-master's initials were replaced by Greek letters giving the appropriate stamp and assay districts (cities). The corresponding *kokoshnik* marks thus indicate both the places of assay (usually that where they were made) and definite periods of time, that is 1899-1908 and 1908-17.

 1899-1908
St. Petersburg: Assay-master Yakov Lyapunov

 Assay-master A. Richter

 Moscow: Assay-master Ivan Lebedkin

 1908-17
St. Petersburg

 Import mark

 Moscow

 Stamps for objects or sections weighing less than 8.5 gr. (2 *zolotniki*)

Proofing region symbols with Greek letters

α St. Petersburg

Δ Moscow   O Caucasus region τ Kostroma

χ Odessa π Vilna υ Kazan

ν Kiev ς Riga   X Don region, Astrakhan, Terek

Note

1 Postnikova-Loseva, *Russkoye yuvelirnoye iskusstvo*, pp. 193 f.

Zolotnik

The *zolotnik* is an Old Russian denomination of weight, corresponding to 4.25 grams and one ninety-sixth of a Russian pound (1 *funt* = 408 gr.). The *zolotnik* was subdivided into 96 *doli* (singular *dolya*), giving 0.044 gr. per *dolya*.

Indications of weight in the above denominations *funt, zolotnik, dolya* are sometimes found engraved on silver objects. In the larger silver services they served to identify the individual pieces, which would all have more or less different weights.

The number of *zolotniki* of pure precious metal per pound of an alloy served to define the *titre*. Consequently the number of *zolotniki* per pound was indicated on the *titre* stamps. It starts from the value of 96 *zolotniki* for pure precious metal.

Conversion Table for *zolotniki*, 1000/1000 and Carats

1 zolotnik	— 10.4166/1000	— ¼ carat
2 zolotniki	— 20.83/1000	— ½ carat
3 zolotniki	— 31.25/1000	— ¾ carat
4 zolotniki	— 41.66/1000	— 1 carat
10 zolotniki	— 104.17/1000	— 2½ carats
20 zolotniki	— 208.33/1000	— 5 carats
30 zolotniki	— 312.50/1000	— 7½ carats
40 zolotniki	— 416.67/1000	— 10 carats
50 zolotniki	— 520.83/1000	— 12½ carats
56 zolotniki	— 583.33/1000	— 14 carats
62 zolotniki	— 645.83/1000	— 15½ carats
72 zolotniki	— 750.00/1000	— 18 carats
82 zolotniki	— 854.17/1000	— 20½ carats
84 zolotniki	— 875.00/1000	— 21 carats
88 zolotniki	— 916.67/1000	— 22 carats
90 zolotniki	— 937.50/1000	— 22½ carats
91 zolotniki	— 947.92/1000	— 22¾ carats
92 zolotniki	— 958.33/1000	— 23 carats
94 zolotniki	— 979.17/1000	— 23½ carats
96 zolotniki	— 1000/1000	— 24 carats

213 A pair of candlesticks and an oval box, master's mark M T, assay-master N. Dubrovin (158), Moscow 1821, the candlesticks 28.5 cm high, the box 18 cm long.

214 Oval silver glass-cooler, decorated in Empire style with dolphins intertwined in pairs, the handles modelled as snakes, applied with the arms of Count Potocki, master's mark of Friedrich Joseph Kolb (274, 307), St. Petersburg about 1820, 34.5 cm long.

215 Parcel-gilt travelling canteen with two crystal flacons, cover and sides set with coins of Peter Duke of Courland in an acanthus and foliage relief, signed Johan Theodor Buntzell (301), St. Petersburg 1826, 20 cm long.

216 Large silver casket on *rocaille* feet, applied with double eagle and the crowned cypher O N, signed with the initials of Karl Johan Tegelsten (262-4), St. Petersburg 1840, 23 cm long.
The cypher is that of the Grand Duchess Olga Nikolayevna, the daughter of Nicholas I and later Queen of Württemberg, to whom the casket belonged.

217 Parcel-gilt silver box, naturalistically formed as a hen sitting on the nest, Imperial Warrant mark of Gubkin (77), Moscow 1858, 15 cm long.

218 Stirrup-cup in the form of a hare with naturalistically engraved pelt, interior gilt, mark with the initials of Samuel Arnd (321), St. Petersburg 1851, 15.7 cm high.

219 Stirrup-cup in the form of an elephant's head with naturalistically engraved hide and polished ears, mark with the initials of Samuel Arnd (321), St. Petersburg 1857, 11.5 cm high. The quality of Arnd's animal sculptures is entirely comparable with that of Fabergé's, and in the context of naturalistic representation they are to be regarded as forerunners of Fabergé animals.

226

227

228

229

230

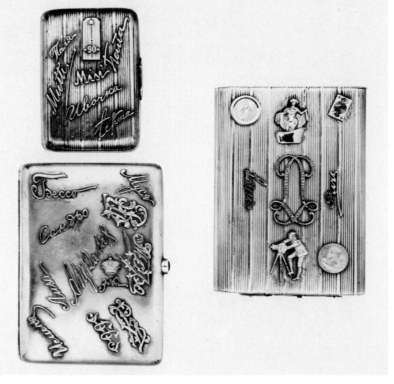

231

232

233

234

236

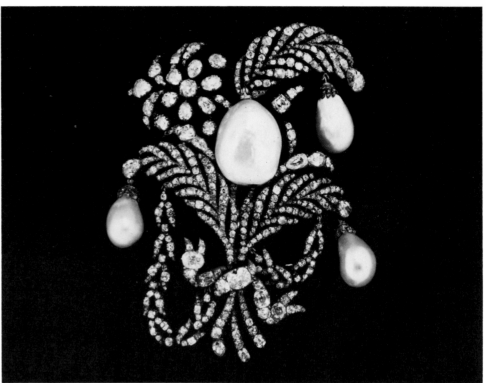

237

238

220 Vodka service with frosted glass carafe and eight *charki*, all cased in silver, shaped naturalistically as wickerwork of birchwood, the cover of the carafe simulating cloth, master's initials (Cyrillic) P D, St. Petersburg 1899-1908, the carafe 17.5 cm high.

221 Soup-tureen with engraved basketwork decoration, the feet in the form of branches, signed Grachev (43), St. Petersburg 1888, 22 cm high.

222 Pitcher, with basketwork and birch-bark decoration, the cover modelled naturalistically as a cloth stopper, late 19th century.

223 Sugar-bowl in the form of a basket covered with a cloth, late 19th century.

224 Tea service with tea-pot, tea-box and cream-jug of plain rectangular form with ivory handles and the engraved cypher V. B. under a prince's coronet, St. Petersburg about 1840. Services of this kind are typical of the firm Nicholls & Plincke, and modelled on English silver.

225 Model of the Tsar's canon in the Kremlin at Moscow, by P. Sazikov (181), Moscow 1851, 19 cm long.

226 Two illustrations of table centrepieces and goblets by Sazikov, from the catalogue of the Great Exhibition of the Works of Industry of All Nations, London 1851.

227 Silver-gilt, quarter-repeating carriage clock, movement of Earnshaw type, spring *détente* escapement, with calendar, signed Sazikov, Moscow 1859, 13.5 cm high.

228 Tea-pot in the form of a quince, the stalk and leaves as handle, master's initials of Carl A. Seipel (250/251), St. Petersburg 1866, 21 cm high.

229 (left) Silver-gilt box, naturalistically chased (in the likeness of a packet tied with string), signed with the initials of P. Sazikov, St. Petersburg about 1875, 6.8 cm long;
(middle) Rectangular silver-gilt box, the lid with a scene in relief of a girl welcomed with open arms by an angel, master's initials G K, Moscow, 1882, 10 cm long;
(right) Salt-cellar formed naturalistically as a plate with folded napkin, bread, and miniature salt-cellar in the form of a throne, silver-gilt, master's initials of Moisey Ivanov, St. Petersburg about 1875, 6.2 cm high.

230 Silver cigar box with engraved imitation of the grain of the wood, also tax bands, and the name of the firm *Fabrika Bostandzhoglo*, engraved on the side '25 cigars', master's initials (Cyrillic) P A, Moscow 1899-1908, 11.8 cm long.

231 Three silver cigarette-cases with souvenir inscriptions and signatures:
(left top) With signatures and an officer's epaulette, Moscow 1908-1917, 7.4 cm long;
(left bottom) Signed with the initials (Cyrillic) F P, Moscow 1908-1917, 10.4 cm long;
(right) Case with applied souvenirs, signed with the initials (Cyrillic) I. F., Moscow 1908-1917, 10.7 cm long.

232 (left) *Nielloed* silver-gilt spoon, unmarked, 18th century;
(middle) A *nielloed* silver-gilt spoon in the form of an arrow, decorated with a landscape scene, by A. Zhilin, Velikiy Ustyug, about 1820;
(right) *Nielloed* parcel-gilt spoon, decorated with a fountain and two swans, about 1800, 18 cm long.

233 Parts of a silver table service with chased handles by Nicholls and Plincke, workmaster Anders Long, St. Petersburg 1844-9.

234 Silver-gilt *nielloed* spoons, 17th century, without marks (from left):
(left) Spoon with flower ornaments, 19 cm long;
(middle) Spoon with fan ornaments, 17.3 cm long;
(right) Two spoons fitting into one another and thus composing a travelling service, the larger 21 cm long.

235 Portrait of Catherine II by Stefano Torelli, about 1775. The Empress is here wearing a Russian national costume richly bedecked with jewels and with the typical *kokoshnik* head ornament, evidently on the occasion of a masked ball. In the 19th century this kind of jewelled *kokoshnik* became court dress for the court ladies. In Paris the *kokoshnik* became known by the name *tiare russe*.

236 Pearl and diamond brooch in the form of a flower spray with feathery leaves, set with diamonds and with baroque pearls, mounted *en tremblant*, the mount silver-gilt, about 1760, 10.8 cm high.
This brooch belonged to the Russian crown jewels and is mentioned in the inventory of 1924-6. It was sold for 350 guineas as Lot 99 in the auction of the 'Russian State Jewels' by Christie's in London.

237 A pair of diamond brooches formed as flowers with bows, the silver mount closed at the back. These flower ornaments were sewn in numbers along the hems of dresses. St. Petersburg, about 1760, 3.5 cm long. The pieces illustrated came from the Russian crown jewels and were sold in London in 1927.

238 Portrait of the jeweller Jérémie Pauzié, pastel, about 1755.
(Musée d'Art et d'Histoire, Geneva)

Old Russian numbers and the dating system

In the convention of Slavonic writing numbers were indicated by letters and combinations of letters. This system of writing was in use during the 17th century and continued into the early 18th. With the reforms of Peter I Arabic numerals were introduced alongside it.

Apart from the system of writing there is a further problem with dates, the problem of chronology. Old Russian chronology begins with the first of September 5509 B.C., the presumed date of the Creation. The chronology of the present day must thus be calculated by deducting the Old year number 5509 (or 5508, according to the month of the year). Besides that it was usual not to indicate the thousands in the old date so that one must add the figure 7.

Example: CS =   206   plus initial number 7 for the 000s.
                       7206
            less   5509
                    ─────
                     1697   (up to 31 August; 1698 from 1 September)

This chronology was abolished by Peter I in the year 1700. On coins and silver marks (Moscow) the dates now appear *ab Anno Domini (A.D.)*, 'from the birth of Christ'. But at this period the system of writing had not yet been changed. The dates 1701 to 1724 were given in Slavonic 'numerals' (i.e. letters). By about 1730 Arabic numerals for dates had become established in Russia.

Specimen date stamps from Moscow with Old Slavonic figures

  1683-1684   1702   1724

  1693-1694   1713

Old Slavonic numerals

А	1	А̄І	11	Ѕ̄	60	Т̄	300
В	2	В̄І	12	О̄	70	Ӯ	400
Г	3	Є̄І	15	П̄	80	Ф̄	500
Д	4	etc.		Ч̄	90	Х̄	600
Є	5	К̄	20	Р̇	100	Ѱ̄	700
Ѕ	6	К̄Д	21	Р̄А	101	Ѡ̄	800
З	7	etc.		Р̄АІ	111	Ц̄	900
И(Н)	8	Л̄	30	РКД	121	҂А̄	1000
Ѳ	9	М̄	40	etc.		҂А̄Д	1001
Т	10	Н̄(N)	50	С̄	200	҂В	2000

҂А̄Ѱ	1700	҂А̄ѰІ	1710
҂А̄ѰА	1701	҂А̄ѰАІ	1711
҂А̄ѰВ	1702	҂А̄ѰВІ	1712
҂А̄ѰГ	1703	҂А̄ѰГІ	1713
҂А̄ѰД	1704	҂А̄ѰДІ	1714
҂А̄ѰЄ	1705	҂А̄ѰЄІ	1715
҂А̄ѰЅ	1706	҂А̄ѰЅІ	1716
҂А̄ѰЗ	1707	҂А̄ѰЗІ	1717
҂А̄ѰИ	1708	҂А̄ѰНІ	1718
҂А̄ѰѲ	1709	҂А̄ѰѲІ	1719

҂А̄ѰК	1720
҂А̄ѰКА	1721

Centres of Gold and Silverwork

Moscow

As a centre of the goldsmith's art Moscow was important not only during the period when it was the capital of the Russian empire, but also in the 18th and 19th centuries, when it was the centre for all that was characteristically Russian.

In gold working this had reached its peak in the 17th century. In dependence on the Tsar's Court the most distinguished craftsmen were here employed, producing masterpieces in the Silver or Gold *Palaty* and also in the Silver row.

Typical of these are chased and engraved silver objects such as the tapering octagonal beakers with figures of sibyls. *Niello* work too was executed here with unequalled mastery. This is particularly the case with objects on which the *niello* ornament is so applied and finished that it looks 'painted'. The backgrounds of engraved flowers and figurative subjects were decorated with floral and scrolling ornaments in meticulous stippling and hatching.

Besides that, polychrome enamel technique was used with mastery in all its variants. *Cloisonné*, its compartments filled with colour and set with silver beads, and *paillettes* came splendidly into their own here. Painted enamel too, on embossed surfaces (*ronde bosse*), and exclusively gold-based, had many uses. Since in the 17th century Moscow, as the capital, dominated the state not only politically but also artistically, there is almost no problem at this period about the attribution of any particular work of art.

With the beginning of the 18th century and the transfer of the Court to St. Petersburg things changed. The workshops of the *Oruzheynaya Palata* were dissolved and some of the craftsmen moved to the new capital.

And yet it was the use of the old forms and techniques which remained typical of the work of goldsmiths in Moscow, all except for enamel, a craft which came to an abrupt end while still on traditional lines. *Niello* too ceased to be executed at its earlier level of quality.

By contrast the embossing of silver became more and more popular. Cups and goblets soon began to appear with baroque ornaments which often had immediate models in the work of German goldsmiths.[1] Pineapple and *aquilegia* cups from Augsburg were copied and Russified by crowning them with the double eagle. An additional point, however, was that these 17th-century cup models from 1740 onwards were adorned with the *rocaille* ornaments which were just then coming into fashion. The result was a typically Muscovite mixture of styles.

Later—say from 1750 to 1790—beakers with embossed birds such as eagles in *rocaille* cartouches became characteristic of Moscow. The great majority of these are more likely to be from the stylistically backward period between 1775 and 1785, when, in St. Petersburg for example, classicism was becoming more important. The traditional Imperial presentation *kovshi* continued to be made in Moscow as a matter of principle.

It is important to bear in mind that even in the 18th century and later Moscow continued to be a significant centre of trade with the provincial cities and likewise foreign countries, especially Persia and Turkey. This was a role which St. Petersburg never took over. There the main customer and business focus was the immediate circle of the Court. In Moscow, on the other hand, the importance of its trade produced a different social class characterized by its tenacity in maintaining the Old Russian traditions of the pre-Petrine era. What in St. Petersburg was disparaged as 'tradesman's taste' was often more original than the westward-looking St. Petersburg style.

The 19th century's increasing mechanization had particularly noticeable consequences in the work of Moscow's goldsmiths. The punching of patterns (flowers, garlands, acanthus leaves) was usual there from 1830 onwards. Table services and individual objects in the so-called Biedermeier style often give evidence of this kind of treatment.

In view of Moscow's insistence on tradition previously mentioned, it is easy to understand that with the advent of historicism the style found more support there than it did in St. Petersburg. From about 1860 on the production of cloisonné enamel in 17th-century style was resumed. Pieces of this kind were subsequently shown at all the world fairs. The big firms such as those of Ovchinnikov, Khlebnikov, and Sazikov regularly participated and exhibited on an ever increasing scale pieces in this typically Russian style, with its ponderous tendencies and rather 'Oriental' extravagance of colour.

St. Petersburg

With his foundation in the year 1703 of a new capital city which soon came to be called St. Petersburg, Peter the Great had it in mind to detach the Russian empire, politically and socially, from the traditionalism of Moscow. By transferring the goldsmiths' workshops from Moscow, by recruiting foreign craftsmen, and last but not least by passing new laws on the guilds it became possible for a new style to develop in St. Petersburg, with a thoroughly western orientation and yet at the same time Russian characteristics. It cannot be said that the foreign craftsmen in

St. Petersburg worked in exactly the same styles as those in Western Europe did. Individual stylistic elements and qualitative characteristics now found their way into Russian art, yet in essence it remained the same. At the beginning of the 18th century Dutch, English, and German characteristics prevailed. After Catherine II came to the throne in 1762 they were increasingly displaced by French stylistic influences.

While at an earlier period of the goldsmith's art influences from Germany (especially Dinglinger of Dresden) and Holland were noticeable, in the second half of the 18th century St. Petersburg's taste was moulded by the Empress's artistic purchases in France. The 'Orlov service' ordered from Roettiers in Paris was copied, for example. Classicism asserted itself here more quickly than in Moscow. Likewise typical of St. Petersburg was the production of snuff-boxes, which did indeed follow the Paris models but in their size and the lavish use of precious stones were recognizably Russian. Painted and *guilloché* enamel were especially popular with St. Petersburg craftsmen.

At the beginning of the 19th century the direct contact of Court circles with France was of particular importance in connection with the Napoleonic wars. In the arts and crafts *Empire* style became all the rage. And this style remained popular for another hundred years in memory of the glorious epoch of Russian history when Tsar Alexander I was celebrated as the 'liberator of Europe'.

From about 1830 onwards a fashionable liking for English things took hold of aristocratic circles in St. Petersburg. A typical example was the *Magasin anglais* of Nicholls and Plincke, which at first imported English silverware, then supplemented or copied it, and later produced Russian ware of nearly the same quality. From 1829 to about 1880 the shop enjoyed a sort of monopoly position in St. Petersburg. Around the middle of the 19th century, in contrast to Moscow, there seems to have been less mass production in St. Petersburg. The main emphasis was on individually designed articles of outstanding quality. At the same time Russian nationalist historicism had very few adherents there.

For this reason it is easily understood how a firm like Fabergé could have such success. The idea of manufacturing *objets de fantaisie*, combining stylistically all the characteristics of Western European art with work of unsurpassed technical quality, appealed to the aesthetic fancies of St. Petersburg Court society. It was for much the same reasons that the firm gained such recognition in Western Europe, especially in England.

Velikiy Ustyug

This town may be regarded as the centre for Russian *niello* ware in the 18th century. Its origins there are not yet fully understood, but it is known that in the 15th and 16th centuries the city had close trading connections with Novgorod, then an important city also in the jewellery trade. Masters of *niello* have not yet been identified here at that early date. The silversmith's craft was specially widespread in Velikiy Ustyug from the second half of the 17th century onwards and reached its peak in the 18th.

Characteristic of pieces from this city is a specially black *niello* worked over a very fine engraving and thus achieving an outstanding decorative effect. This *niello* is often found on snuff-boxes of large size which often show an imitation of the *monture à cage*. In this the edges of the box, in contrast to the *nielloed* silver sides, are emphasized with heavy gilding and a strongly engraved *rocaille* ornament. This makes it look as if the sides are mounted in frames, though the box actually is made all in one piece.

Around 1760 the designs consist particularly of genre scenes of shepherds and the chase; from 1780 onwards city views, of Velikiy Ustyug, Vologda, and Archangel, and also maps of the province (*guberniya*) embellished with statistical tables, were used as decoration.

Of the masters working in Velikiy Ustyug Mikhail Klimshin (1711-64) was already celebrated by his contemporaries as the most distinguished (no. 138). In 1745 Klimshin was summoned to Moscow as a teacher of *niello* work. Similar in quality of execution as in style of decoration were the pieces from the 'Factory of the Brothers Afanasiy and Stepan Popov', who were working from 1761 to 1776. Their signature (nos 194, 195) is found on a series of fine pieces, particularly snuff-boxes.

Velikiy Ustyug continued to be a centre of *niello* work in the first half of the 19th century. One frequent master signature (nos 9-12) is that of Aleksandr Ivanovich Zhilin, who was working between 1824 and 1841. Later, Velikiy Ustyug began a steady decline both in its production and in the quality of its pieces.

Tobolsk

The capital city of the *guberniya* of Siberia, important for the fur trade, became known for *niello* objects of extremely high quality, produced especially in the 1770s. Under the influence of Velikiy Ustyug there were a number of outstanding masters working here, and they created a style specific to Tobolsk. Typical instances are the objects with panoramic views of cities, maps of Siberia, and hunting scenes. The influence of China, to the east, produced an unusual form of *charka*, found only in Tobolsk. The *charka* here was made in the form of a fruit, rather like a round peach, with a leafy stalk for a handle. Such *charki* were worked all over in *niello*. Many of them bear a coat of arms, that of the governor of Siberia, Denis Ivanovich Chicherin.

Chicherin, governor from 1763 to 1781, had a reputation on the one hand for carrying out successful reforms and administrative innovations but on the other for being extremely fond of display. He set up in Tobolsk a School of Geodetics, a hospital, a pharmacy, and a school of arts and crafts. He lived in very lavish style, surrounded by numerous servants, and on Sundays used to go to divine service in the Cathedral dressed in the ceremonial robes of the St. Alexander Nevsky Order. The silver service adorned with his coat of arms and monogram contained pieces of every possible kind and for every conceivable use. One of his contemporaries, the Frenchman Thesby de Belcour, retailed a characteristic remark that Chicherin was said to have made: 'Dieu est là-haut, l'Impératrice est fort loin, c'est moi qui fait la loi.'[2]

However, he regularly sent the Empress splendid presents of silver and furs in order to retain her favour.

In 1765 he sent the Empress a *Relation* about the discovery of the Aleutian Islands between 1741 and 1764. To accompany it he had three silver snuff-boxes made with the map of Siberia; the north-eastern ocean areas were laid out on them in *niello*. The islands were later sold to the USA, along with Alaska, by Alexander II.

Also in the year 1765, Chicherin had a report drawn up for the Empress on the population and handicrafts of the city of Tobolsk. In this he gave it as his opinion that of the 446 craftsmen living in the city a proportion were superfluous. He proposed to send 13 of the silversmiths working in Tobolsk 'to the front' on military service.

In 1780 Chicherin fell into disfavour. The Empress became displeased with the independent leanings of her Siberian governor. He was relieved of office and died five years later, in 1785. So ended also the heyday of silver production in Tobolsk.

Notes

1 Filimonov, *Opis'*, nos 887, 888; cf. Markowa, G.A., *Deutsche Silberkunst des 16.-18. Jahrhunderts in der Sammlung der Rüstkammer des Moskauer Kremls*, Moscow, 1975.
2 Thesby de Belcour, *Relations ou journal d'un officier français aux services de la confédération de Pologne pris par les Russes et relégué en Sibérie*, Amsterdam, 1776, p. 230.

Literature

Postnikova-Loseva, M.M., *Russkoye yuvelirnoye iskusstvo*, Moscow, 1974, p. 112.
Postnikova-Loseva, M.M., Platonova, N.G. and B. L. Ulyanova, *Russkoye chernevoye iskusstvo*, Moscow, 1972, p. 18.

Baltic provinces and Finland

Baltic silver of the 16th and 17th centuries is generally of excellent quality. The forms and ornaments are influenced by the northern European states and particularly by Sweden, to which the Baltic provinces had belonged since 1561. In the course of the 17th century especially, a large number of silver articles from the Baltic provinces reached Russia. Some of them were overdecorated or provided with Russian inscriptions.

During the Great Northern War (1700-21) Peter I conquered first Narva and Dorpat (1704) and later Riga and Reval from Sweden. By capitulations with the German knightly orders and municipalities he acquired Livonia and Estonia, with their thriving cities, for his kingdom. Peter not only confirmed their ancient privileges but as an enthusiastic promoter of Western European culture was also concerned to give continued support to handicrafts. The annexation of the Baltic by Russia made them of course politically dependent on Russia, but in cultural matters the area continued its close association with the Germans.

During the Great Northern War silver production in the Baltic seems to have declined sharply, and afterwards it recovered only slowly from its effects. The pieces produced at this time kept the traditional Swedish-influenced forms: sometimes we find double eagle themes engraved or chased.

During the 18th century the punches with the coats of arms of different cities continued in use. In 1763 an *ukaz* was issued on behalf of the Goldsmiths' Office in Narva permitting apprentices to work for masters in Moscow, St. Petersburg, or Riga.[1] From the middle of the 18th century onward marks appear in Narva, Reval, and Riga which according to Russian law bear the initials of the assay-master and the corresponding dates. This is particularly the case with Narva and Riga.

While silver production obviously suffered a sharp decline in the Baltic since the 18th century, it can be established also that a great part of the Baltic goldsmiths emigrated to Russia, especially to St. Petersburg. Between 1714 and 1870 141 goldsmiths of Baltic origin were working in St. Petersburg. Most of them reached Russia during the last quarter of the 18th century, up to about 1850. One of these was Gustav Fabergé, the founder of the Fabergé firm.

Developments in Finland were comparable to those in the Baltic. During the latter half of the 19th century Finnish goldsmiths emigrated in great numbers, to St. Petersburg in particular.[2]

Notes

1 Bäcksbacka, L., *Narvas och Nyens Guldsmeder*, Helsingfors, 1946, p. 10.
2 Engmann, M., 'Finnish Goldsmiths in St. Petersburg during Two Centuries', in: *Carl Fabergé and his Contemporaries*, exhibition catalogue, Helsinki, 1980.

Important Masters, Workshops and Firms

Ador, Jean-Pierre (1724-84)

Court jeweller and goldsmith for snuff-boxes in the time of Catherine II. Ador was born in Vuittebœuf near Orbes (Vaud) in the Canton of Berne and baptized on 25 July 1724 in Peney. He worked as jeweller, *guillocheur*, and enameller in Carouge near Geneva, and in 1753 became an *habitant* (licensed resident) of Geneva. In 1757, in partnership with several other goldsmiths, he formed the firm Flournois, Ador, Bonard & Cie., which was dissolved, however, in 1759. After this date Ador is no longer registered in Geneva, which suggests that he began his journey to Russia about 1760. At the beginning of the 1760s he settled in St. Petersburg and there became one of the most famous goldsmiths in Russia.[1]

Among his earliest dated works is the Orlov Vase (now in the Walters Art Gallery, Baltimore), dated 1768, but probably of earlier manufacture was the snuff-box with Kaestner's enamel miniatures of Catherine II's accession to the throne (Smithsonian Institute, Washington). The most important collection of his works—formerly in the Empress's possession—has been preserved in the Hermitage.

During his travels (after 1759) he married Catherine Gardine, an Englishwoman. In 1782 he married again, in St. Petersburg, Andrienne Dumont. The marriage contract drawn up by the Imperial notary Jean Daniel Spies and sealed by Ador and witnesses has been preserved. Cf. facsimile on pages 189-90.

Ador worked predominantly for the Court. This is evident also from a testamentary register drawn up in connection with a dispute about the inheritance between his son Jean and his son-in-law. (Ador had died on 7 July 1784.) Here we read: '*Assets:* According to the true inventory made by M. Patot d'Orflans, in charge of the Consulate of France in Russia, at the request of Dame Veuve Ador née Dumont, it transpires that there were 1° in the Cabinet of Her Imperial Majesty the jewels and *objets d'art* detailed in the inventory nos. 3 & 7, valued at 66,674 roubles, on which it is said that the Cabinet has paid on account 12,000, net remainder 54,674 roubles.'

The total amount of the assets with other *effets & bijoux* as well as *en débiteurs bons et mauvais* comes to 170,246.16 roubles.

Facsimile of the marriage contract between Jean-Pierre Ador and Andrienne Dumont made out by the Imperial notary Jean Daniel Spies, St. Petersburg 1782.

place de la quatrieme partie qu' Elle devroit avoir de
son Bien mobil selon la teneur des Ukases du quinzième
Avril mille sept cent & seize & du dixseptième Mars
mille sept cent & trent & un pour eviter touts les
Jnconvenients qui pourroient se passer par rapport
à l'heritage entre Elle et les Enfants du premier
Lit du dit Sieur Ador. La Demoiselle Andrienne Dumont seconde Comparante acceptoit
l'Offerte du Sieur Ador son futur Epoux avec
Reconnoissance, la dessus le dit Sieur Jean Pierre
Ador signoit cet acte de sa main & apposoit
le Sceau en Chifres. J.P. Ador

En foi de quoi Nous avons fait & signé cette
Minute, signé & cacheté par le Sieur Jean
Pierre Ador Fabriquant en Bijouterie dans
cette Ville de St. Petersbourg en notre presence
& des Temoins sousscrits, Solennellement requis,
pour Solenhiser ce Contrat de Mariage.

Fait & passé à St. Petersbourg comme cy
dessus.
                        Jean Daniel Spies,
                        Notaire Jmperial public &
                                juré approve

Louis desaugy Conseiller   Cristofaro Arnaboldi dasso il
honoraire au Cabinet de   Comaschino al servizio di
S. M. J. de toutes les Russie   S. M. J. de toutes les Russies

Further particulars of the family history had not been known previously and were discovered in the possession of his descendants. Ador, who did not belong to the Guild, usually signed his boxes on the rim with the inscription 'Ador à St. Petersbourg' or with the initials IA, crowned or inside a crown.

Index of marks nos 286, 287.

Note

1 The exact date of Ador's arrival in St. Petersburg in still not known. M. V. Martynova, *Precious Stones*, p. 41, mentions that Ador came to Russia at the end of Empress Elizabeth's reign.

Bolin

Firm of jewellers founded in St. Petersburg at the beginning of the 1830s by Carl Edvard Bolin. In 1834 he married Ernestine Römpler, a jeweller's daughter, and died in 1864.

His younger brother Henrik Conrad at first worked with him, then in about 1850 moved to Moscow and with an associate founded the firm 'Bolin & Jahn'. The firm was highly successful under Henrik Conrad Bolin's management and he became a Court Jeweller. The parure of which part is illustrated in Pl. 244 was by him. After his death in 1888 his son Vasiliy Andreyevich carried on the business, which after Jahn's retirement subsequently merged with the continuing firm of Bolin in St. Petersburg.

By 1900 Bolin was the most important firm of jewellers in Russia after Hahn. It continued there till the Revolution and had a branch in Stockholm. Apart from jewellery Bolin also produced utensils and ornaments in silver, gold, and enamel in the manner of Fabergé.

R. Schven is known for his work in the firm as workmaster-jeweller.[1] Index of marks nos 246, 253, 327.

Note

1 Fersman, *Les Joyaux du Trésor de Russie*, vol. I, no. 139.

Fabergé (1842-1918)

Firm of goldsmiths and jewellers founded by Gustav Fabergé in 1842 in St. Petersburg. The Fabergé family was descended from French Huguenots who emigrated by way of Germany into the Baltic region, where Gustav Fabergé was born in 1814 in Pernau. His son Karl Gustavovich, born 1846, took over his father's business in 1870. Karl Fabergé was not himself an active craftsman goldsmith. His genius was for organization. Under his direction his father's firm expanded to a point where at times it was employing 500 artists and craftsmen. The technical management was entrusted by Fabergé to head workmasters, successively Erik Kollin (1870-86), Mikhail Perchin (1886-1903), and Henrik Wigström (1903-18). He concerned himself with the artistic and technical supervision. Every piece leaving the firm's premises on the Bolshaya Morskaya had to undergo a severe quality control. Artistically he combined mainly the French Louis XV, Louis XVI, and Empire styles with Russian national elements and also the Art nouveau style. In his revival of historical styles and their mixture with contemporary 19th- and 20th-century styles Fabergé was a follower of the ideas of the *Mir iskusstva* ('World of Art') movement. The firm's achievements, particularly in enamel technique (especially *guilloché*) and stone carving, were of outstanding virtuosity.

The firm received the Imperial Warrant in 1884-85. This was connected with the first production of an Easter present in the form of an egg for the Emperor Alexander III. Altogether Fabergé made a series of 56 of these Imperial Easter eggs from 1894 onwards for Nicholas II as presents for the Empress Alexandra Fedorovna and the Dowager-Empress Mariya Fedorovna.

Fabergé had branches in Moscow (from 1887), Odessa (1890-1918), Kiev (1905-10), and London (1903-15). This last branch supplied the British royal family and the Western European aristocracy.

Fabergé's signatures (see Index of marks)
no. 197   St. Petersburg only
nos 125, 126 Moscow only
no. 124   St. Petersburg: silver objects by Nevalainen, Rappoport, Wäkewä, ICA
nos 122, 123 St. Petersburg or Moscow for small objects and jewellery
nos 254, 272 Objects for export to England

The workmasters' signatures were as follows:
Johann Victor Aarne
Fedor Afanasev
Karl Gustav Hjalmar Armfeldt
Andrey Goryanov
August Frederik Hollming
August Wilhelm Holmström
Erik August Kollin
G. Lundell
Anders Johan Nevalainen
Gabriel Ninkkanen
Mikhail Yevlampievich Perchin

Aleksandr Petrov
Oskar Pihl
Julius Rappoport
Wilhelm Reimer
Philip Theodor Ringe
Fedor Rückert
Eduard Wilhelm Schramm
Vladimir Soloviev
Alfred Thielemann
Stephan Wäkewä
Alexander Wäkewä
Henrik Wigström
ICA (First Silver Artel) (no. 289)
A R (no. 234)
J. W. (no. 304)
(Russian) I. P. (no. 96)

Literature

Bainbridge, H. C., *Peter Carl Fabergé*, London, 1949, 1966.
Habsburg-Lothringen, G. von and A. von Solodkoff, *Fabergé, Court Jeweller to the Tsars*, Fribourg-London, 1979.
Snowman, A. K., *Carl Fabergé, Goldsmith to the Imperial Court of Russia*, London, 1979.

Grachev

Firm of goldsmiths founded in St. Petersburg in 1866 by Gavriil Petrovich Grachev, taken over after his death in 1873 by his sons Mikhail and Semen. The business became well known under the name 'Grachev Brothers', received the Imperial Warrant in 1896, and survived until 1917. The firm worked in gold, silver and enamel and also produced sculptural objects in electroplate. Workmasters with the initials A P and K R (Russian) are known.
Index of marks nos 43, 69.

Hahn

Firm of jewellers founded by Karl Karlovich Hahn during the later half of the 19th century. It received the Imperial Warrant. In 1911 the firm was located in St. Petersburg (Nevsky Prospekt 26) and was then apparently managed by the founder's son, Dmitriy Karlovich Hahn.[1] In 1896, before the coronation of Nicholas II, Hahn received an Imperial commission to make a copy of Duval's 'small crown of the Empress'. The original was worn by the Dowager-Empress, whereas Empress Alexandra Fedorovna wore the replica from Hahn.[2]

Alongside mainly unsigned pieces of jewellery, Hahn produced gold and enamel objects of highest quality including Imperial gifts. He was one of Fabergé's greatest rivals.[3] Hahn frequently used large precious stones, also for *objets de fantaisie*.

Among workmasters were Alexander Tillander (nos 237, 238) and a master known by the initials C B (no. 183). Cartier is said to have produced objects for the Hahn firm.[4]

Index of marks no. 120.

Notes

1 See *Ves' Peterburg*, 1908, *s.v.* 'Jewellers'.
2 Fersman, *Les Joyaux du Trésor de Russie*, vol. III, no. 82.
3 See Pl. 211 and the so-called Tercentenary Triptych in the Forbes Collection, New York; Waterfield/Forbes, *Fabergé*, p. 106.
4 Ross, *The Art of Carl Fabergé*, p. 90.

Keibel

Firm with its own workshop in St. Petersburg, founded in 1797 by Otto Samuel Keibel. It survived until 1917. Keibel, born in Pasewalck, Prussia, in 1768, a jeweller, was chief warden of the guild and in 1807-1808 an alderman. He produced a series of outstanding gold snuff-boxes for the court. He died in 1809, leaving his business to his son Johann Wilhelm, who continued to use his signature and received the Imperial Warrant.

Johann Wilhelm Keibel was also a goldsmith and jeweller. In 1826 he reworked the Imperial Crown for the coronation of Nicholas I. From 1828 on he was president of the foreigners' guild. From 1836 to 1841 his firm was charged with the production of insignia for orders. After his death in 1862 the firm carried on until 1917 and specialized mainly in insignia production.

Index of marks nos 20, 305.

Khlebnikov

This firm was founded in 1867 by Ivan Petrovich Khlebnikov in St. Petersburg. In 1871 the whole business was transferred to Moscow, where it survived till 1917. It was one of the more distinguished in Russia and a warranted Court purveyor. In 1882 some 200 craftsmen were employed by Khlebnikov.

239 Square-cut emerald of 19.4 carats engraved with the portrait of the Empress Catherine II in profile looking left, signed on the shoulder *Eger (Jaeger)*. The stone is in a later mount as a pendant. Eger was the medal-maker by whom a series of medals of this Empress are known.

The emerald was a gift of the Empress to Prince Grigoriy Orlov. A similarly engraved stone was among the Russian crown jewels (today in the Diamond Fond of the USSR). The photograph is enlarged 1.83 times.

240 Badge of the Order of St. Andrew set with diamonds, the St. Andrew's cross with the saint in painted enamel, the closed gold mount engraved on the reverse with the eagle's plumage. A later inscription says that the Order was worn on 26 November 1890 by the Empress Mariya Fedorovna. The Badge belonged to a member of the Imperial family and it may be presumed that it was made for an imperial coronation. There were similar Orders among the crown jewels and these were dated in the 1925-7 Catalogue to the closing years of the 18th century. Consequently the coronation in question was probably either that of Paul I (1797) or that of Alexander I (1801). No marks, 13.3 cm long.

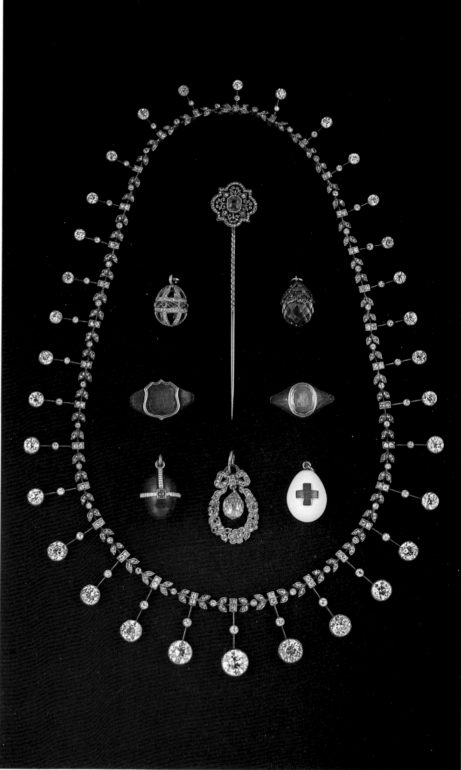

Khlebnikov's pieces were executed in the Russian national style and consisted principally of silver and enamel (*cloisonné* and more especially *plique-à-jour*).

The firm often exhibited at world fairs and received a distinguished mention at that of 1873 in Vienna.

Index of marks nos 99, 208, 209.

Morozov

The firm was founded in the Gostinniy Dvor in St. Petersburg in 1849, by Ivan Yevdokimovich Morozov. The business was principally mercantile, a house for the sale of goods made by other goldsmiths. Morozov himself also had his own workshop as a master goldsmith. The firm continued in existence until 1917 and was a purveyor to the Court: silverware and enamels by Morozov are known. Master foremen working for the firm were: Anders Johann Seppänen, Fredrik Tiander, and a master with the (Cyrillic) initials I. P. and B. K.

Index of marks no. 144.

241 Part of a diamond and spinel *parure* consisting of diadem, a smaller diadem-like hair ornament, a necklace, and a pair of ear-rings. The stones are mounted in silver on gold. The *parure* belonged to the Princess Yekaterina Pavlovna Bagration (1783-1857), who was a celebrated beauty at the time of the Congress of Vienna, and it no doubt dates from that period. Spinels were not distinguished from rubies until well into the 19th century and at that time had the same high value.

242 (top) A lozenge-shaped diamond pendant with the portrait of Alexander II in miniature under a table diamond in a silver and gold mount. The ornament was a kind of family decoration inside the Imperial house and was worn on the light blue ribbon of the Order of St. Andrew, unmarked, about 1865.

(bottom) Diamond-set Star of the Order of St. Alexander Nevsky with enamelled central medallion, the mount silver-gilt. Unmarked, about 1870.

243 Diamond necklace in a gold mount by Fabergé, unmarked, about 1910, 40 cm long; gold tie-pin with ruby and rose-diamonds, signed with the initials of Fabergé (122), St. Petersburg 1899-1908; miniature Easter egg with rose-diamonds and rubies, unmarked, probably by Fabergé; miniature Easter egg with a faceted aquamarine in an open mount with diamonds, master's initials of August Holmström, Fabergé; two rings by Fabergé, workmaster for jewellery Alfred Thielemann (236), left cornelian, right sapphire; miniature Easter eggs, left nephrite with white-enamelled gold mount and cabochon ruby, right with enamelled red cross; bottom middle, brooch pendant designed as a wreath of flowers set with diamonds and rubies, with bow and pendant of briolette-cut diamond, workmaster August Holmström (229), Fabergé, 2.5 cm high.

244 Diamond and ruby tiara with stylized flower motifs in gold and silver mounts. The tiara has its own case with the stamp of the Bolin firm, Moscow. It is part of a large ruby *parure* which the Emperor Alexander II presented to his daughter the Grand Duchess Mariya Alexandrovna on the occasion of her marriage to Alfred, Duke of Edinburgh in 1874.

245 Diamond necklace, about 1870. Typical of Russian work is the enclosure of the large diamonds within pavé-set rose diamonds so as to even out the inequalities of cut and carry over to the surround. Coloured gems too were treated in this way.

Nicholls & Plincke

Firm of silversmiths in St. Petersburg from 1829 to 1898. Plincke had a workshop already in 1815, and in 1829 it became part of a combined business with the Englishman Charles Nicholls as partner.

Until about 1880 the shop was the most important of its kind in St. Petersburg and early on received the Imperial Warrant. The basis of its remarkable success was the idea of importing silver from England to St. Petersburg and there selling copies of the pieces. For that reason the shop was also called the *'Magasin anglais'*, or MAG. ANG for short as it appeared in the signature (index of marks no. 312).

Apart from the Imperial Court, which in 1852 for example ordered 40 services each with coffee-jug, sugar-bowl, and milk-jug, and also had the great court services enlarged, all of St. Petersburg society shopped at Nicholls & Plincke.[1] It was Fabergé who from 1880 onward began to win away its custom, so that by 1898 it had become relatively unimportant. It is probable, however, that even before this Waldemar Nicholls had joined the jewellers' firm of Nicholls & Ewing as a partner; this firm survived until 1917.

Apart from silverware enamel pieces also are known from this firm. Workmasters were: Samuel Arnd (no. 321), J. Henrikson (nos 295, 296), A. Tobinkov, and a workmaster with the initials P K (Plincke?) for silver (314) and KA for enamel.

Index of marks nos 310, 311, 312.

Note

1 Lady Londonderry mentions Mr. Nicholls in her *Russian Journal* of 1836-1837 (ed. W. Seaman/ J. Sewell, London 1973, p. 97): 'We dined at Lord Durham's (the British ambassador in St. Petersburg) and met a large number of English bankers and merchants. I was much surprised to meet Mr. Nicholl [sic], one of the proprietors of the English *magazine* and who literally stands behind the counter.'

Ovchinnikov

Firm of goldsmiths founded in 1853 by Pavel Akimovich Ovchinnikov, alongside Fabergé the most important in Russia. The business was carried on after the founder's death by his sons Mikhail, Aleksandr, Pavel, and Nikolay, and survived until the Revolution.

In 1873 the business had 173 workmen and in 1881 300, making it larger than any of its competitors at that period. Its production was correspondingly large. For the training of young craftsmen the firm had set up a school in Moscow, which at times had over 130 pupils. In 1873 a branch with its own workshop was set up in

St. Petersburg. It was located at Bolshaya Morskaya no. 35. The firm received the Imperial Warrant in 1883.

Ovchinnikov was the first business to devote itself entirely to the manufacture of articles in Russian national style. Its *cloisonné*, *champlevé* and *plique-à-jour* enamelware is outstanding, and won the firm first prizes at every important Russian exhibition, for instance at the Manufacturing Exhibition of 1865 and the All-Russian Exhibition of 1882 in Moscow. It also exhibited at every world fair and in particular earned honourable mention at those in Chicago in 1893 and Paris in 1900. The Cartier archives in Paris show that from 1904 to 1906 Ovchinnikov supplied this firm with articles of semi-precious stone.

Index of marks nos 13, 174.

Pauzié, Jérémie (1716-79)

Goldsmith and jeweller, born in Geneva. In 1729 he accompanied his father when he emigrated to Russia and served his apprenticeship as a goldsmith with Gravero. From 1740 onwards he worked as an independent master, particularly for the Court. He was Court Jeweller for the Empress Elizabeth, for whom he made a series of gold snuff-boxes, some richly adorned with gemstones. In 1750 he paid a short visit to his home city of Geneva. During this journey he made some important business contacts, and also stopped at Dresden where he visited the art collection called the 'Green Vault'.

In 1762 Peter III appointed him as his Court Jeweller with the rank of brigadier, which gave him immediate access to the Court. After the *coup d'état* by the Grand Duchess Catherine in 1762 he received the commission to make a new crown, which was subsequently used at all coronations as part of the Imperial insignia and is today preserved in the Kremlin in Moscow. In 1764 he left Russia with his family and settled in Geneva. He no longer worked as a jeweller and led a retired life until his death on 2 December 1779.

Pauzié did not belong to any guild and always worked directly for the Court. This is the reason why none of his pieces were signed or marked. He was the best jeweller of his day, at any rate in Russia. His work may be defined artistically as typically Russian for he passed his youth and served his apprenticeship in St. Petersburg. His style was no doubt influenced by imported pieces from Western Europe, as also by his experiences during his travels of 1750 and 1751. He always knew, however, how to appeal exactly to his customers' Russian taste, which showed itself particularly in his heavy gem-set snuff-boxes and the Empresses' splendid jewellery.

Pauzié's interest as a person in the framework of social and craft conditions is immeasurably increased by the fact that after his return to Switzerland he wrote his memoirs. The insights thus given into the life of a court craftsman in the first half of the 18th century are hardly to be equalled.

The memoirs, written in French, were published in a Russian translation in 1870.[1] An 18th-century manuscript copy of the original came to light in the Public and University Library of Geneva. It corresponds in its contents to the translation but for a description of the Geneva journey of 1750 which that omitted. The memoirs contain descriptions of Pauzié's personal and family affairs, general historical records and business commissions by the Empresses, together with technical questions of workshop practice.[2]

The memoirs are an interesting document on the activities of a goldsmith and jeweller as craftsman and businessman in the 18th century. Particularly informative about these are the hitherto unpublished descriptions of his journey from St. Petersburg to Geneva at the end of November 1750. It took him through the Baltic provinces to Berlin, Leipzig, Strasbourg, Mühlhausen, Basle and Geneva, then back through Frankfurt, Leipzig, Dresden, Berlin and Danzig to St. Petersburg.

In all the larger cities he made contact with jewellers and bought objects of art and jewellery. In Leipzig he made the acquaintance of Monsieur Benelle, 'with whom I established business connections. I bought from him *galanterie* to the value of 5,000 crowns, almost half the capital I had brought with me, and I have done a lot of business with this house since my return to Russia, as also with that of Herr Jordan in Berlin'.[3] In Geneva again he established business contacts with Monsieur Pallard 'the famous jeweller who had retired with a great fortune from the Court of Vienna'.[4]

Pauzié's stay in Dresden is interesting for his visit to the Grünes Gewölbe ('Green Vault'), one of the most important art collections in Europe. His description also gives a glimpse of 18th-century 'tourism'.

'We set out next morning for Dresden. I had a letter of recommendation from Chancellor Vorontsov for Count Brühl, prime minister of this Court, also two further letters from Herr Benelle and Monsieur Pallard for good dealers, which were just as useful to me as the Minister's. On arriving in this city we took quarters in the finest inn, belonging to a certain Dagobert, who received us very warmly although it was already midnight. He gave us a very good supper and excellent beds, of which we had special need, tired as we were.

'On the next day I asked the landlord to drive me to the Minister von Brühl. I found him on the point of leaving for the Court. I handed him Chancellor Vorontsov's letter. After reading it, he seemed to me to be very pleased with it. After congratulating me on my arrival he asked me if I planned to stay a while and begged me to take the evening meal with him on Wednesday, the day on which he dined at home. I thanked him for the honour, but begged him to excuse me in view of the fact that I could only stay two days. "But you won't have time to see all the sights if you leave again so soon." I only begged him to make it possible for me and my companions to view the jewellery of His Majesty and the Cabinet of Curiosities. "But certainly" he replied "when would suit you, so that I may send you my secretary to show them to you?" I thanked him and said, "if it pleased him, then that same afternoon." In the meanwhile I handed over my other letters to the dealers, who showed me every friendship and with whom I established business relations. I also saw there Mons. Poncet, the King's Clockmaker, who also received me with every friendship.

'Herr von Brühl's Secretary fetched us from the inn and conducted us to the "Green Vault", where we viewed all the curiosities, the pictures and fine china there were to see there. After that we were in the King's and Queen's apartments and in the room where the jewels were kept, and these I found very fine and well arranged. From there we were taken to see the splendid gardens of Herr von Brühl, where we were given refreshment. After that the Secretary showed us the most interesting of the city quarters for sightseers.'[5]

Pauzié's most important commission for the Russian Court was the making of the crown for Catherine II in the year 1762. He gives the following account:

'After the Emperor [Peter III] had been arrested and the Empress had returned to the city, all the troops who had been posted in the streets were removed and everyone was freed from the fears which beset us. Three days later we learned of the death of this unfortunate prince, of which however I shall give no account...'

'A few days later the Empress sent for me to say that she had ordered Chancellor Betzky [Betskoy] to go through the crown jewels and take out all the pieces which were not modern to be broken up and used for a new crown which she wanted made for her coronation. I was to work together with him. I was glad of that because it meant that I could leave to him all the problems and difficulties which would arise as a consequence and which all those entrusted with the supervision would be able to deal with. I agreed to everything that Chancellor Betzky wanted, since all he cared about was fame, and confined myself to helping him in matters which were my concern. I procured for him a French craftsman who was extremely able, Auroté by name, and in fact turned out very well.

'From among all the jewels I selected those which would best suit, and since the Empress told me she wanted the crown to be preserved after the coronation, I selected all the large stones, which were less suitable for modern jewellery. The result was a set of diamonds and coloured gems making the whole piece one of the richest in all Europe. Despite all the measures we took to keep the crown light and using only as much metal as was necessary to hold the stones, it still weighed five pounds. I tried it on the Empress's head, much fearing that she would be unable to bear the weight. She told me she was very satisfied and that she could very well wear the crown for the four or five hours the ceremony would last. She asked me if I should be staying in Moscow for the coronation. I answered that it would give me the greatest pleasure to have the honour of following her wherever she wanted but begged her to give me leave to ease my mind about the Emperor's debts, which amounted for one in my position to a very considerable sum, and said that my friends who had given me credits were pressing me for payment.'[6]

The costs of making the crown, even though the jewels had been supplied from the Imperial treasure, amounted to almost the whole sum provided for the coronation ceremonies, 50,000 roubles. This did however include *'le supplément d'une livre d'or fin et de plusieurs livres d'argent'*.[7] It should be observed that Pauzié did not do all the work himself but—as for instance later in Moscow—employed up to ten master goldsmiths as assistants.

Though Pauzié worked also with gemstones of great value, and evidently demanded big sums in wages for the work, his financial position was generally difficult. The reason was that he had not founded his business with his own capital but had to work with loans which he could often hardly repay because of his customers' unscrupulousness about prompt settlement of bills. This was a typical feature of the craftsman's situation in the 18th century, especially that of the master who was not attached to a guild. Complaints about payment difficulties take up a lot of space in the second half of Pauzié's *Memoirs*. In the end he thought to solve his credit problem by founding a company with the Geneva jeweller Louis David Duval, shortly before 1762. Duval brought into the company, as capital valued at 5,000 roubles, *'tabatières de pierre aventurine, des montres de Dames et d'Hommes et des étuis à instruments montés sur or et Pingebec'*.[8] According to Pauzié, aventurine and pinchbeck had not previously been known in Russia. Duval had objects of this kind sent by his brothers from London, where they were Court jewellers. But the company was dissolved after three years because, it is said, Duval had lost his reason.

The payment difficulties remained despite Pauzié's further successes. They are thus illustrated in his memoirs: 'I recall an event that happened after the funeral of the Empress Elizabeth, and the circumstances I had to endure. I should have to go into too much detail if I were to recount all the mishaps that occurred. The burglaries committed on my premises, the fires from which I so many times suffered great losses, and the continual problems of the critical business dealings with the nobility, whose only concern was to buy on credit without sparing a thought for how they were ever going to pay. Often I was compelled, when I saw five- or six-horse carriages driving up, to shut the house doors and send down to say that I was not at home, to avoid jeopardizing my fortune and those of my friends who had entrusted theirs to me. In truth I have not words to express all the anxieties and tortures I had to endure, and I had nobody outside the house to help me with business deals.'[9]

The Empress clearly was an exception: 'She bought many things from me which she needed as presents, and since she had me paid with great punctuality, I was even in a position to send remittances to my correspondents in Holland, to whom I owed over 300,000 guilders besides that which I owed to correspondents in Germany. From the gentry, it is true, I could not get a penny. I had to make great efforts to resist giving them as much credit as they wanted. I dared not complain to Her Majesty, since she was very attached to them.'[10]

Even on his last commissioned work, a star of the Order of St. Andrew for Count Stanislaus August Poniatowski which he delivered to the Empress, Pauzié writes, *'je luy baisai la main et la priai de vouloir bien ne pas m'oublier pour la somme de cet ordre étant obligé de payer les brillants à ceux de qui je les avois pris.'*[11]

To escape all further money problems and to 'save'[12] his fortune, which amounted to 28,000 roubles in goods, Pauzié sold his St. Petersburg workshop. On 4 January 1764 he received his passport and thereupon left Russia with his family to settle in his native Geneva. Here he was able to live on the capital he had laboured to accumulate. In his will he left extensive property to the members of his family.[13]

Notes

1 *Russkaya starina*, I, 1870, pp. 16-27, 77-103, 197-244.
2 In the corresponding chapters I have quoted from the memoirs on Orders, Easter eggs, jewellery and snuff-boxes.
3 Pauzié, manuscript, p. 14 recto.
4 Pauzié, manuscript, p. 16 verso. Jean-Jacques Pallard, born 1701 (?) in Geneva, jeweller in Vienna and Dresden.
5 Pauzié, manuscript, pp. 18 verso, 19 recto.
6 Pauzié, manuscript, p. 31 verso.
7 Fersman, *Les Joyaux du Trésor de Russie*, vol. II, p. 13.
8 Pauzié, manuscript, p. 25 recto.
9 Pauzié, manuscript, p. 24 verso.
10 Pauzié, manuscript, p. 32 verso.
11 Pauzié, manuscript, p. 34 verso.
12 Pauzié, manuscript, p. 33 recto.
13 Fontaine-Borgel, C., *Notes sur Jérémie Pauzié*, Geneva, 1899, pp. 24-27.

Sazikov

Important silversmiths' business founded as a workshop in Moscow in 1793 by Pavel Fedorovich Sazikov. From 1810 onwards the workshop is described as a 'factory', which indicates that the firm had grown substantially. In 1842 a branch was opened in St. Petersburg, and from 1846 the firm had the Imperial Warrant.

Pavel Sazikov's son Ignatiy Pavlovich carried on the firm and was followed in his turn by his own sons. Of these Pavel and Sergey were responsible for Moscow and Valentin Ignatevich for St. Petersburg. The business survived until 1917.

It was known for high quality silverware and later too for silver sculptures and *cloisonné* enamels. Sazikov exhibited a large number of cups and centre-pieces at the Great Exhibition of 1851 in London.

Index of marks nos 181, 182.

Lists of Masters

Cloisonné enamel

The most important master workshops for *cloisonné* enamel functioning towards the end of the 19th and at the beginning of the 20th century are set out below, with details of styles used. (Workshops given without a place-name were situated in Moscow.) The figures refer to the marks as given in the index.

ADLER, Maria   Dealer in silver with her own workshop at the beginning of the 1880s. Very stylized foliage, not enamelled throughout, matted gold ground (228)

AGAFONOV, Vasiliy Semenov   Around 1900. Traditional with painted shaded enamel coating; colours: pink, (bright) green, cream (48)

AKIMOV, V.   Active in the second half of the 19th century, traditional style, large flowers; colour: royal blue (47)

ALEXEYEV, Nikolay Vasilevich   Exhibited in 1896 at the Exhibition in Nizhniy Novgorod. Shaded flowers, predominantly turquoise-blue (156, 157)

ARTELS   Of the artels founded in the 1890's the following worked in *cloisonné*:
 1st Artel: traditional style
 3rd Artel: traditional style (330)
 6th Artel: the objects are completely covered with enamel, the cells painted in
  shades, colours traditional: olive-green, blue, cream (331)
 7th Artel: traditional style
 8th Artel: Art nouveau influences
11th Artel: complete enamel covering, Art nouveau influence with triangular and
  rectangular enamel cells, volutes, spirals, silver beads, green, ochre, violet-
  and-cream tints in a hazy 'water-colour' style (332)
20th Artel: similar to the 11th Artel in its Art nouveau style, often too with quite
  traditional flowers alongside the Art nouveau bands. Shaded blues (333)

DUBROVIN

FABERGÉ   The only workmaster for *cloisonné* in this firm was Fedor Rückert (q.v.). Fabergé bought his objects and overstamped Rückert's signature with his own mark (125)

GRACHEV Firm of the brothers Mikhail and Semen Grachev, founded by their father Gavriil in 1866 in St. Petersburg. The firm had the Imperial Warrant until 1917 and won a gold medal at the Paris World Exhibition of 1889. Style: traditional; colours: bright green, dark blue, also *champlevé* enamel. Workmasters with the initials (Cyrillic): AP, KR. (43, 69)

GUBKIN, Ivan Semenovich Manufacturer, founded his firm in 1841. It was carried on after him by his sons Sergey and Dmitriy. Imperial Warrant. (76, 77)
Marks: frequently his name written out in full.

IVANOV, Moisey Master from 1849, died 1893, worked in St. Petersburg. Highly stylized foliage with narrow enamel bands

KHLEBNIKOV One of the more important firms of silversmiths (q.v.) in Russia, active in Moscow from 1871 on. Exhibited at the World Exhibition in Vienna in 1873. Enamel objects of very high quality in all techniques, often *cloisonné*, *champlevé* and *plique-à-jour* side by side in the same piece. Colours: pastel tones, also violet, green, yellow. Workmasters: initials (Cyrillic) D S (208, 209)

KLINGERT, Gustav Gustavovich Firm with 55 employees, founded 1865, active till 1917. At the Chicago World Fair of 1893 the firm 'G. Klingert J. Levitt' was named as among the most important. Klingert had a representative in Paris (Krantz, *Exposition Internationale de Chicago*, p. 40). Until about 1899 his mark was in Latin characters, thereafter in Cyrillic. Traditional style, without shaded painting. Typical is the use of turquoise-coloured enamel over large surfaces relieved only by a filigree tracery (63, 278, 306)

KRUTIKOV, Ivan and Petr Kirilovich Silversmiths whose workshop is known from 1894 onwards and was functioning until 1913. Traditional enamel style; colour: bright green grounds (90)

KURLYUKOV, Orest Fedorovich Dealer and silversmith, active 1884-1916. Painted *cloisonné* enamel, colours: especially bright blue on a cream ground. In 1895 he won the Finance Ministry's Medal of Honour and made objects for Tiffany, New York (165, 166)

KUZMICHEV, Antip Ivanovich Manufacturer, functioning from 1856. Mark, initials or name written out in full. This firm did *plique-à-jour* enamel (17, 18)

LYUBAVIN, Alexander Benediktovich Manufacturer, functioning in St. Petersburg from 1893 onwards. Traditional style, unshaded flowers (130)

MAKHALOV, V.S. Master, in 1823 founded a firm which was carried on by his sons Nikolay and Vladimir. Exhibitors at the Paris World Exposition, 1867. Traditional enamel, not shaded. Colours: bright blue and turquoise (51)

MILYUKOV, Petr Pavlovich In 1877 opened a workshop in which in 1894 he was employing 33 workmen. The firm survived until 1912 (173)

MISHUKOV, Yakov Fedorovich Founder in 1880 of a firm which was carried on by Pavla Alexandrovna (172) and Fedor Yakovlevich Mishukov. It was known especially for icon *oklady* (222)

MOROZOV, Ivan Yevdokimovich Silversmith and dealer in St. Petersburg, died

1885. The firm had the Imperial Warrant and was still in business at the beginning of 1900. Among the workmasters were F. Tiander and A.I. Seppänen (144)

NEMIROV-KOLODKIN, Nikolay Vasilevich   Manufacturer from 1875 until the Revolution, with 39 fellow workers. Art nouveau influences, colour: dark blue. He manufactured articles which were sold at Tiffany's, New York. Workmasters with the initials AK, and CK (Semen Kazakov) (983, 23, 159)

NICHOLLS & PLINCKE   Famous silverware shop (cf. Important Masters, Workshops and Firms) called *Magasin anglais* in St. Petersburg, 1829 to 1898. Objects in *champlevé* enamel are known from this firm. Workmaster KA

NIKOLAYEV, Dmitriy Nikolayevich   Active in the second half of the 19th century. His style of ornament shows slight Art nouveau influences. Colours: pink, bright blue, green, cream (80)

OLOVYANISHNIKOV, Ilya   Had a workshop in Yaroslavl, but later came to Moscow, where the firm was carried on by his sons. Here around 1900 they produced almost exclusively church utensils (167)

OVCHINNIKOV   One of the most important silversmith businesses in Russia, functioning from 1853 till the Revolution. This firm produced the best enamel in Russia, perhaps rivalled only by Rückert. Its pieces use all the enamel techniques and colours. The colours often occur in all possible shades, the greens and blues for instance, and with them—technically difficult—a transparent red. Ovchinnikov likewise used the traditional lacquer technique. The style embraces everything from folkloristic to Art nouveau, the former being particularly in evidence with vessels for the bread and salt ceremony. The *plique-à-jour* enamel pieces are always of outstanding quality (174, 13)

OZERITSKY, I.   Active around 1900. Traditional enamel, not painted throughout. Also did *plique-à-jour*. Colour: turquoise-blue (95)

POSTNIKOV, Andrey Mikhaylovich   Active 1868 until 1898 (27, 28, 30)

RÜCKERT, Fedor I.   Active from about 1890 until the Revolution, highly original enameller of exceptional quality who sold the greater part of his production at Fabergé's, other pieces also direct to the customer, or through other dealers, as for instance Kurlyukov. His style is highly individual and often influenced by Art nouveau. *Cloisonné* and enamel painted *en plein* are often found combined in his work. The pieces are as a matter of course completely clothed in enamel, the wire ridges often assuming a purely decorative character, especially in the case of spirals and individual lines and points. The colours are kept to pastel tones. A typical feature of Rückert pieces was that after enamelling he very often heavily gilded or silvered again the exposed metal of the *cloisons* (207)

SALTYKOV, Ivan Dmitriyevich   Master workshop from 1884 onwards, produced objects of extremely high quality in all styles and techniques. He combined *cloisonné* and enamel painted *en plein* on boxes and cases. The colours are specially brilliant. The workshop kept going only until 1897 (98)

SAZIKOV   Important firm of silversmiths, from 1793 until the Revolution in the hands of a single family. Enamel objects in all techniques, mostly traditional in style (181, 182). Cf. Important Masters, Workshops and Firms

SBITNEV, Grigoriy Mikhailovich   Master workshop from 1893 until the Revolution. Enamel with shading, Art nouveau influence. Colours: grey, olive-green, dark blue, yellow (74)

SEMENOV, Vasiliy   Master workshop from 1852 (57, 58, 59, 60). The business was carried on until the Revolution by his daughter

SEMENOVA, Mariya Vasiliyevna   Working from about 1890 (?). Her pieces are of outstanding quality, especially in the painting of the *cloisons*. Her style tends more to the traditional, less often Art nouveau. The magnificent *cloisons* of her flowers (on a matted gold ground) are shaded with violet tones. Other typical colours are white and green, with frequent frames of round turquoise pearls. Also from her hand are enamel paintings *en plein* combined with *cloisonné* frames, mark MC (150)

VERKHOVTSEV, Fedor Andreyevich   Founded in 1819 in St. Petersburg, a firm of goldsmiths, which became well known for church utensils. His son Sergey took over the business in about 1865 and produced objects with *champlevé* enamel (184, 203)

Presentation *kovshi*

ARTEMIEV, Ilarion   Moscow 1732-42. The *kovshi* often bear the engraved signature 'made by Larion Artemiev'. (127)

BUD, Yakov   Moscow 1681-1720 (102)

GERASIMOV, Andrey   Moscow 1739-63 (5)

GOMULIN, Andrey   Moscow 1641-68

GRIGORIEV, Ivan   Moscow 1678-81

DANILOV, Ivan   Moscow, at work about 1630

IVANOV, Vlas   Moscow 1668-74

IVANOV, Petr   Moscow 1686-1708 as master for *niello*

IPATIEV, Frol   Moscow, mentioned 1635

KONONOV, Vasiliy   Moscow 1680-1708, master for *niello*

KUZMIN, Kyrill   Moscow, mentioned 1624 and again in 1635

MASLENNIKOV, Yakov   Moscow 1756-90 (216, 217)

MALOSOLETS, Vasiliy   Moscow, master 1621, mentioned 1634

NASSYKA, Vasiliy   Moscow 1619-35

NEKRASOV, Boris   1622-4

OVDOKIMOV, Gavrila   Moscow, at work 1635

PESTRIKOV, Dmitriy Kirillov   Moscow, mentioned 1664-73

PESTRIKOV, Kyrill   Moscow, mentioned 1622-73

POPOV, Ivan   Moscow, at work 1619-35

POPOV, Vasiliy Ivanovich   Moscow 1816-40 (52, 53, 54)

SILUYANOV, Timofey Filipovich   Moscow 1760-1802 (192, 193)
TIMOFEYEV, Arkhip   Moscow, mentioned 1622-35
TIMOFEYEV, Ivan   Moscow, mentioned 1622
WEGENER, Christoph Friedrich   St. Petersburg 1765-85 (255)
ZONTAG (Sonntag), Gabriel   Moscow 1747-80 (62, 281)
E. K. (84)
I G K (292)
B M (50)
M. Ts. S. (151)

Objets de fantaisie. Fabergé's competitors

Workshops of which the location is not stated were in St. Petersburg.

ARND, Samuel   Master 1845-90, used *guilloché* enamel for smaller articles of jewellery (321)
ARTEL, 3rd   St. Petersburg 1908-17. Chased objects of gold *en quatre couleurs*. Enamel in pastel shades: green, blue, raspberry, opalescent white (330)
ASTREYDEN, A.   About 1900-17. Enamelled cigarette-cases in shades of light blue, violet-mauve, salmon pink and white (1)
BOK, Karl   Moscow, produced gold cigarette-cases (41, 119)
BOLIN   Between 1890 and 1917 he also produced gold and silver articles with *guilloché* enamel. Art nouveau influence. Cf. Important Masters, Workshops and Firms (246, 327)
BOITSOV, Vasiliy Vasilevich   Enameller
BRAGIN, Andrey Stepanovich   Master 1852, produced gold cigarette-cases (42)
BRITZIN, Ivan Savelevich   Firm founded in 1860, one of Fabergé's most important competitors in enamel. The firm had its offices at 12 Malaya Konyushenaya and advertised in address books especially 'Russian Enamel', although it was in fact *guilloché* enamel. Britzin used mostly pastel colours—green, light blue, violet, turquoise, pearl-grey, and also white. From about 1900 until 1917 he also exported to Britain and America. It has been suggested but not proved that Britzin was apprenticed to Fabergé (44, 86a).
BURKHARD, E.   About 1900, gold cigarette-cases
CHERYATOV, Yegor Kuzmich   Moscow 1912-16, had started work in the firm of Lorié, gold cigarette-cases (78, 79, 85)
DENISOV-URALSKY   About 1908-17, semi-precious stone articles with chased and enamelled mounts. The Cartier archives show that Denisov supplied articles of semi-precious stone to this firm from 1911 to 1917. Workmaster with the initials A P
FABERGÉ   1842-1918, used 144 shades of enamel, which have been preserved on a specimen table. Cf. Important Masters, Workshops and Firms

GRACHEV   A firm which for example produced, around 1900 *samorodok* cigarette-cases. Cf. Important Masters, Workshops and Firms

HAHN   Between 1890 and 1917 he produced *objets de fantaisie* of high quality in gold, silver, and *guilloché* enamel (120). Cf. Important Masters, Workshops and Firms (183) Hahn had workmasters with the initials C B (183) and A T (237, 238)

KÖCHLI (Kekhli)   Firm of goldsmiths and jewellers founded in the latter half of the 19th century by Friedrich Köchli and headed in 1908 by Friedrich-Theodor Köchli. The address of the firm with its masters' workshop was 17 Gorokhovaya. Köchli towards the end of the 19th century produced a series of gold cigarette-cases which, provided with a double-eagle set with diamonds, served as Imperial gifts. He also used enamel and precious stones. The firm's stamp was *Frid. Kekhli* (275)

KUZMICHEV, Antip Ivanovich   Moscow, 1856-1917, *samorodok* cigarette-cases (17, 21)

LORIÉ, Fedor Anatolevich   Moscow, 1871-1917, gold cigarette-cases. The workmaster with the initials (Cyrillic) E. Ch. was Yegor Cheryatov, who later made himself independent (198, 129, 204, 205)

MARSHAK, Iosif Abramovich   Kiev 1878-1917, goldsmith and jeweller (131)

MOROZOV   Produced gold cigarette-cases around 1900. Cf. Important Masters, Workshops and Firms (144)

ROSEN, Yakov Mikhailovich 1909-17   Gold cigarette-cases (221)

SUMIN, Avenir Ivanovich   Owner of a workshop at 60 Nevsky Prospekt. This firm produced articles in *guilloché* enamel comparable in quality with Britzin's and like his following Fabergé in style. In address books of 1908 and 1914 Sumin advertised 'Stones from Siberia and the Urals' (189)

TILLANDER, Alexander Eduard (1860-1917) and his son Alexander Theodor   Predominantly makers of enamelled gold badges and *jetons* (237, 238)

VERKHOVTSEV, Fedor Andreyevich   In 1819 founded a firm of goldsmiths which was carried on right up to 1917 by his son Sergey. Gold cigarette-cases (201, 202, 203)

Jewellery

St. Petersburg

ANTOIN, Peter   Jeweller about 1880

ARND, Samuel   Goldsmith and jeweller, master 1845-90 (321)

BOCK, K.   Jewellery firm about 1900-17

BOIANOWSKI, Carl   Silversmith and jeweller, 1825-60, Imperial Warrant (244, 245)

BOLIN   Important firm of jewellers, 1850-1917. Cf. Important Masters, Workshops and Firms

BUTZ, Alexander Franz   Goldsmith and jeweller 1849-57. At first in business under the name Butz & Bollien. The business was carried on by his son Julius Agaton Butz until 1893

FABERGÉ   Workmasters in chief for jewellery were Alfred Thielemann and Albert and August Holmström. The founder of the firm, Gustav Fabergé, had mostly produced traditional gold jewellery (1840-70) (236, 229). Cf. Important Masters, Workshops and Firms

HAHN, Karl Karlovich   About 1890-1910. Cf. Important Masters, Workshops and Firms

JAHN, Gottlieb Ernst   Master 1812, founded the firm Jahn & Bolin (Moscow), which remained in business until the end of the 19th century

JOHANSSON, N.   Jeweller in the late 19th century, produced diamond-set *chiffres*

KAEMMERER & ZAEFTIGEN   Exhibited in 1851 at the Exhibition of Works of Industry of all Nations in London (Catalogue no. 376)

KEIBEL   Also produced jewellery at the beginning of the 19th century. Cf. Important Masters, Workshops and Firms

KURKI, Andreas, master 1857-86.   The firm was still in business around 1900 (19)

LINDEN, Nikolay   Firm of jewellers, end of 19th century

MADSEN, Peter   Goldsmith and jeweller 1850-61 (316)

MOROZOV, 1849-98. Cf. Important Masters, Workshops and Firms

NICHOLLS & PLINCKE   Though specialized on the whole in silverware this firm around 1840 was also producing jewellery. One of the firm's workmasters: Samuel Arnd (see above)

NICHOLLS & EWING   Jewellers in the second half of the 19th century. Workmaster with the initials A H (231)

PENDIN, Hiskias   Working around 1840 in association with Gustav Fabergé

SCHUBERT, Carl Reinhold   Goldsmith and jeweller 1844-80

SPIEGEL, Andreas Ferdinand   Goldsmith and jeweller, about 1830-62 (235)

STENBERG

TEMNIKOV, Paul   Jeweller about 1830

TENNER, Paul Magnus   Master 1803-19 (318, 325)

TILLANDER   Firm of goldsmiths and jewellers, 1860-1917 (237, 238)

TREIDEN, A. A.   Jeweller, end of 19th century

Master with the initials R S. Probably R. Schven, a workmaster of the Bolin firm (319)

Moscow and Kiev

BOLIN and Bolin & Jahn 1850-1917. Cf. Important Masters, Workshops and Firms

MARSHAK   A large jewellers' firm in Kiev (131)

Niello work

17th Century

AGEYEV, Matvey   Moscow 1681-1700
BESEKIRSKY, Filipp   Moscow *c.* 1681
BULGAKOV, Ivan   Active in the silver *palata* in Moscow 1622-4
VARFOLOMEYEV, Semen   Moscow 1680-7
VLASOV, Pavel   Moscow *c.* 1622
GANKA   Moscow *c.* 1622
GRIGOREV, Semen   Moscow *c.* 1623
IVANOV, Zakhar   Moscow *c.* 1622
IVANOV, Petr   Active 1686-1709 in the silver *palata* of the Moscow Kremlin. Most of his work was for the Tsar's Court and he received an annual pension of 10 roubles. Cf. Pls. 95-6 (171)
KONONOV, Vasiliy   Moscow 1678-1700, pupil of Osip Astrakhanets. For some time he worked with Petr Ivanov
KOSTRIKIN, Timofey   Moscow 1683-1700
KUTNEV, Maksim Semenov   Moscow 1676-1700
MALOSOLETS, Vasiliy   Moscow 1622-4
MIKULAYEV, Fedor   Moscow 1663-80
MIKHAILOV, Mikhail   Moscow 1664-85
NEKRASOV, Boris   Moscow 1622-4
PAVLOV, Andrey   Moscow 1663-85
PESTRIKOV, Tretyak   Moscow 1617-24
POPOV, Dimitriy   Moscow 1624-45
POPOV, Ivan   Moscow 1619-37
SEMENOV, Afanasiy Ivanov   Moscow 1662-4
SEMENOV, Stepan   Moscow *c.* 1666
TIMOFEYEV, Ivan   Moscow 1623-4
TIMOFEYEV, Trofim   Moscow 1680-1700
FEDOROV, Anton   Moscow *c.* 1659
FEDOSEYEV, Ivan   Moscow 1684-91
CHEKALO, Varfolomey Kuzmin   Moscow 1669-87
YAKOVLEV, Vasiliy   Moscow 1663-87
YAKOVLEV, Ivan   Moscow 1679-87, pupil of Mikulayev; on 30th March 1682 he received 'a pound of Yefimok silver to make two silver cups with Turkish *niello*'

18th Century

ANDREYEV, Petr Grigorev   Velikiy Ustyug *c.* 1760

AREFEV, Andrey   Vologda *c.* 1798

AREFEV, Ivan   Vologda 1782-94 (86)

BELKOV, Alexey Prokopev   Velikiy Ustyug, born 1783

BELKOV, Vasiliy Prokopev   Velikiy Ustyug, born 1755, died 1810

BELKOV, Prokopiy Timofeyev   Velikiy Ustyug, died 1805

BURAVKIN, Nikita Ivanov   Velikiy Ustyug *c.* 1750, 1774 lived in Solvychegodsk

BUSHKOVSKY, Fedor Klimov   Velikiy Ustyug 1795-1834, was head of the guild from 1823 to 1825. One of the best masters of his time (199 [1813-15], 200 [1817-34])

GRIGOREV, Ivan   Born 1721, Moscow 1748-85 (104, 105, 106)

GRIGOREV, Yakov   Moscow *c.* 1703-40 (212, 213, 214)

GUSHCHIN, Semen Andreyev   Velikiy Ustyug *c.* 1760

ZHILIN, Ivan Petrov   Velikiy Ustyug, born 1750, died *c.* 1810, was head of the artisans in 1804-5 (107 [1782-96], 108 [1796-1812])

ZHILIN, Mikhail Petrov   Velikiy Ustyug, born 1749, still active in 1805. From 1790 to 1796 Petr Rusanov was his pupil (136)

ZHILIN, Petr Petrov   Born 1755, active at Velikiy Ustyug, 1787-1821 (170)

ZHILIN, Petr Yakovlev   Velikiy Ustyug, born 1713, father of the three masters mentioned above

ILIN, Timofey   Moscow 1704-21 (190, 191)

KAYAVKIN, Vasiliy Maksimov   Solvychegodsk *c.* 1722

KLIMSHIN, Andrey Matveyev   Velikiy Ustyug *c.* 1744

KLIMSHIN, Ivan Mikhailov   Velikiy Ustyug 1792-1805

KLIMSHIN, Mikhail Matveyev   Merchant and leading *niello* master in Velikiy Ustyug, born 1711, died 1764. In 1745 he was summoned to Moscow to teach *niello* work. He returned on 30th December of the same year (138)

KOZOMANOV, Semen Ivanov   Velikiy Ustyug from 1796 onwards

KONSTANTIN   Solvychegodsk *c.* 1722

KUZOV, Semen Petrov   Moscow 1780-99 (186)

KUNKIN, Vasiliy Matveyev   Master in Moscow for silver, *niello* and enamelwork, born 1726, died 1762. From 1751 he described his workshop as a *fabrika* in which he employed several masters and apprentices. He was a merchant of the first guild and had learned *niello* work in 1745 from M. M. Klimshin (168). An *ukaz* of 21 May 1752 ordered Kunkin to give his objects a new mark to show that they were made in the factory

MASLENNIKOV, Yakov Semenov   Moscow 1756-96

MIKHAILOV, Ivan   Moscow, born 1705, still active 1774 (94)

MOISEYEV, Yakov Gerasimov   Velikiy Ustyug, born 1773, still mentioned in 1811. He had several pupils (218 [1789-1804], 219 [1804-11])

MOLOKOV, Osip Vasilev   Velikiy Ustyug, in 1744 lived in Arkhangelsk

MOLOKOV, Prokopiy Osipov   Velikiy Ustyug *c.* 1787, died 1805

MOLOKOV, Stepan Stepanov   Velikiy Ustyug 1786-1821

MOSHNIN, Alexey Ignatiev   Velikiy Ustyug, born 1721, active *c.* 1750. One of the best *niello* masters in Ustyug (22)

OSTROVSKY, Ivan Alexandrov   Velikiy Ustyug, born 1759, died 1828 (110 [1796-1804], 111 [1791?-1821])

PESTOVSKY, Ivan Fedorov   Velikiy Ustyug 1787-1821 (112)

PESTORZHEVSKY, Ivan Fedorov   Velikiy Ustyug, born 1746, still mentioned 1806

PETROV, Efim   Yakutsk *c.* 1798

PETROV, Fedor   Moscow 1760-89 (155)

PLOTOV, Grigoriy Andreyev   Moscow 1753-75 (65, 280)

POPOV, Ivan Fedorov   Velikiy Ustyug 1792-1805

RATKOV, Alexey Ivanov   Moscow 1777-1821

RATKOV, Grigoriy Stepanov   Kostroma 1783-8 (66)

RUSANOV, Petr Prokopev   Born 1777, Velikiy Ustyug 1798-1840

SEREBRENIKOV, Petr Fedorov   Kostroma 1781, died 1817 (175)

STUDENTSOV, Fedor Petrov   Moscow 1776-80

SHEVYAKOV, Vasiliy Ekimov   Kostroma 1794-1817

SHEVYAKOV, Ivan Kuzmin   Kostroma 1785-1806, active in 1794 with his son Andrey   (100)

19th and beginning of 20th century

AGAFONOV, Vasiliy Semenovich   Moscow 1893-1917 (48)

BAKH   St. Petersburg, exhibited *niello* work at the 1876 World Exhibition in Philadelphia

BURAVKIN, Grigoriy Petrov   Velikiy Ustyug, born 1775, died 1837

BUSHKOVSKY, Mikhail Fedorov   Velikiy Ustyug 1828-68

VASILIEV, A.   Moscow *c.* 1860

WÄKEWÄ, Stephan   St. Petersburg from 1856 onwards, worked for Fabergé later (323)

GOROKHOVSKY   Velikiy Ustyug until 1828, later in St. Petersburg

GRECHUSHNIKOV, Matvey   Moscow 1818-40 (134)

GRIKUROV   Workshop in St. Petersburg during latter half of 19th century, exhibited at the 1876 World Exhibition in Philadelphia

GUBKIN   Firm in Moscow, made *niello* work *c.* 1850 (76, 77)

DALMAN, Alexander Karlovich   Owner of factory in St. Petersburg from 1880 onwards, exhibited at the 1897 World Exhibition in Stockholm

DMITRIYEV, M.   Moscow *c.* 1860 (135)

EGOROV, Fedor   Velikiy Ustyug from 1803 onwards

ZHILIN, Alexander Ivanov   Velikiy Ustyug from 1817 onwards, born 1800, died *c.* 1842. Made objects of high quality with original decoration and heavy gilding (9 [1824-27], 10 [1828-30], 11 [1831-32], 12 [1832-40])

ZHILIN, Andrey Alexandrov   Born 1824, Velikiy Ustyug, 1846-68

ZHILIN, Ivan Alexandrov   Born 1832, Velikiy Ustyug

ZALESOV, Vasiliy Fedorovich   Velikiy Ustyug 1832-40

ZUYEV, Alexander Ivanov   Vologda 1854-65. Marks with initials (Russian) A Z

ZUYEV, Ivan Matveyev   Born 1786, Vologda, died 1860. Exhibited *niello* work at the fair in Vologda province in 1837 (87 [1810-15], 300 [1816], 88 [1827-28], 109 [1840-44])

IGUMNOV, Ivan Matveyev   Velikiy Ustyug 1846-80

KALTYKOV, Ivan   Moscow 1820-34 (89)

KLADOVNIKOV, Andrey Vasilev, Vasiliy Lvov, and Prokopy were masters in Velikiy Ustyug during the first half of the 19th century

KOSHKOV, Ivan Alexeyev   Born 1782 in Velikiy Ustyug, 1812-15 was apprenticed to F. Bushkovsky, died 1821

KOSHKOV, Mikhail Ivanov   Velikiy Ustyug 1838-96, received a prize at the All-Russian Exhibition in Moscow in 1882 (137)

LAVROV, Martyn Nikitin   Moscow 1821-45 (141)

MINEYEV, Ilya Stepanov   Velikiy Ustyug 1835-68, pupil of F. Bushkovsky and apprenticed to A. Zhilin (93)

MINEYEV   Nikolay Ilin, Velikiy Ustyug *c.* 1877

MINEYEV, Stepan Sergeyev   Velikiy Ustyug, died 1836

MOTOKHOV, Nikolay Grigorev   Velikiy Ustyug 1835-53 (162)

OVCHINNIKOV   Firm in Moscow and St. Petersburg 1853-1917. Exhibited *niello* work at the 1876 World Exhibition in Philadelphia (174). Cf. Important Masters, Workshops and Firms

PODYAKOV, Alexey Ivanov   Velikiy Ustyug *c.* 1830

POTAPOV, Vasiliy Petrov   Velikiy Ustyug from 1821 onwards

POPOV, Vasiliy Ivanov   Moscow 1816-40

POSTNIKOV, Andrey Mikhailovich   Firm 1868-1908 (30)

ROMANOV, Vasiliy Ivanov   Born 1772, Velikiy Ustyug until 1831 (55)

RUDAKOV, Andrey Grigorev   Born 1788, Velikiy Ustyug until 1868

SAZIKOV   Firm in Moscow 1793-1918, exhibited at the 1862 World Fair (181, 182)

SAZONOV, Alexey   Yakutsk *c.* 1829

SEMENOV, Vasiliy Semenovich   Owner of factory in Moscow 1852-1918, exhibited at the All-Russian Exhibitions in 1867 and 1882 (57, 58, 59, 60)

SKRIPITSYN, Sakerdon Ivanov   Vologda 1837-44 (187, 188)

SOKOLOV, Alexey Isayev   Moscow 1821-31. Exhibited *niello* snuff-boxes at the 1831 Moscow fair (32)

SOKOLOV, M. F.   Moscow 1860-90 (149)

SOKORIN, Vasiliy Petrov   Velikiy Ustyug 1835-46

STUDENTSOV, Prokopiy Petrov   Velikiy Ustyug 1831-62
TOTMAKOV, Matvey Grigorev   Velikiy Ustyug 1805-34
USTINOV, Gavriil   Moscow 1806-51 (75)
FULD, Alexander Iosifovich   Owner of factory in Moscow 1862-1918 (34, 35)
KHLEBNIKOV   Factory in Moscow 1871-1918, exhibited *niello* work at the All-Russian Exhibition in 1882 (99, 208, 209). Cf. Important Masters, Workshops and Firms
KHODZHOYAN, Karapet Stepanovich   St. Petersburg 1876-97
CHIRKOV, Mikhail Pavlovich   Velikiy Ustyug *c.* 1900 (152)
CHICHELEV, Ivan Dmitriyevich   Moscow 1815-76 (117)
CHULKOV, Mikhail Ivanov   Vologda, died 1864 (153)
YAKOVLEV, Mikhail   Moscow 1821-23 (154)

List after M. M. Postnikova-Loseva, N. G. Platonova, B. L. Ulyanova, *Russkoye chernevoye iskusstvo* (Russian *niello* art) Moscow, 1972, pp. 133-41

Snuff-boxes

St. Petersburg

ADOR, Jean-Pierre   *c.* 1763-84 (cf. section on Ador)   Swiss by birth from Canton of Berne, in St. Petersburg from about 1763, Court Jeweller without being a member of the Guild, died 1784. One of the best masters in Russia for gold boxes with enamel. Engraved signatures *Ador à St. Petersbourg* or marks (286, 287)
BARBÉ, Carl Helfried   1806-11   born 1777 in Frankenthal, apprenticed from 1796 to A. W. Reinhardt, master 1806, member of the Russian Guild 1811 (240)
BECKER, Johann Andreas   1806-24   born in Hamburg, from 1798 in St. Petersburg, master 1806
BERNARDI   *c.* 1750-60   jeweller and dealer in *galanterie*, mentioned in Catherine II's *Memoirs* in the year 1759
BLERZY, Jean Charles   1794-1811   Frenchman, from 1793 in St. Petersburg, from 13 August 1794 master of *galanterie* in the Foreigners' Guild, from 1811 in the Russian Guild. This master is not to be confused with Joseph Etienne Blerzy, who was *maître orfèvre* in Paris
BOCK, Matthias Michelson   1726-72   Swede, 1717-24 pupil with Abraham Dey, master 1726, 1750 alderman (308)
BOUDDÉ, Jean-François (Xavier)   1769-89   born in Hamburg, master on 10 January 1769, alderman of Foreigners' Guild 1779-85, made gold boxes in French style with *émail en plein*. Engraved signatures *Bouddé à St. Petersbourg* and mark (277)

BUCH, Ivar Wenfeldt   1776-1811   born 1749 in Norway, 1776 master, his son Jørgen Buch became a master in 1802. Boxes around 1800 bear the engraved signature *Fabrique De Buch à St. Petersbourg* (249)

DAHLBERG, Andreas   1786-1818   Swede from Nyköpping, *galanterie* master and engraver from 1786, died 1818

DUC, Jean   1770-85   Frenchman, born in Frankfurt on Main, jewellery master from 1 March 1770, alderman 1778-85, engraved signature *Duc à St. Petersbourg*

DUVAL, Louis David   1753-7   born in Geneva, came to St. Petersburg in 1753 and worked together with Pauzié. Through his brothers he imported from London boxes and cases of gold and pinchbeck. He is said to have lost his reason, and emigrated to England

EILER (Eylerdt), Carl   1830-49   master goldsmith from 1830 (252, 268)

ERNST, Carl   1800-50   master of *galanterie*, in 1849 had his shop on the Nevsky Prospekt. Mark: C E

GASS, Johann Balthasar   1760-93   master from 31 December 1760, in 1773 received the title of an 'Imperial medallist'. Engraved signature *Gass à St. Petersbourg* (Cf. chapter on Medals)

GEDDE (Gaudé), Christian   1786-98   born in St. Petersburg, apprenticed to Bouddé, master 1786 for *galanterie* in the Foreigners' Guild, died 1798

GENOU (Genu), Jean   1785-?   born in Paris, master goldsmith from 8 September 1785

GODEFROY, Carl Dietrich   1782-1816   from Mitau, master 1782, elder of the Foreigners' Guild 1793-4. His sons too were goldsmiths: Carl Robert, 1805-26, apprenticed to Otto Keibel; Christoph Friedrich, 1810-25

GOEBEL (Göbelt), Christian Gottlieb   1760-80   master from 31 December 1760, 1780 still a guild member, occasionally worked in collaboration with J. G. Scharff. Engraved signature *Goebel à St. Petersbourg*

HITELIN, Eric   1789-1819   born in Borgå, (Swedish Finland), apprentice in Reval, from where he came in 1783 to St. Petersburg. Here he worked—before becoming master in 1789—in the workshop of Johan Sultov (267)

HUDENDORFF, Johann Andreas Heinrich   1800-18   came in 1787 from Hamburg to St. Petersburg, master 1800, in 1818 left the guild, his son Andreas Jacob Heinrich was apprenticed before 1825 to Keibel

HYPPEN (Hyppeen), Ephraim   1786-1816   born 1754 in Åbo (Swedish Finland), came to St. Petersburg in 1776, master 1786, died 1816 (266)

KARMARCK, Peter   1787-1803   born in Denmark (?Copenhagen), master of *galanterie* from 4 April 1787, still mentioned in 1795, died 1803 (315)

KAYSER, Johann Christian   1773-1801   from Gross-WieC near Leipzig, master from 1773, died 1801 (290)

KEIBEL, Otto Samuel   1797-1900   born at Pasewalk (Prussia), master from 12 October 1797, alderman 1807-8, died 1809. His son Johann Wilhelm managed the workshop after him. From 1836 onward it specialized in Orders and is still mentioned as a firm in 1910. In the early 19th century this was the best workshop for gold boxes. Imperial Warrant. A series of Keibel boxes bears only the signature and no assay marks (305)

KOLB (Kolbe)   1765-75, 1806-26   family of goldsmiths from central Germany, various members of which worked in St. Petersburg. Boxes with the signature *Kolbe à St. Petersbourg* date from the years 1765-75. These are often steel boxes with gold inlay. Friedrich Joseph Kolb, from Würzburg, came to St. Petersburg in 1793, master in 1806, Imperial Warrant between 1820 and 1825. Engraved signature *J. F. Kolb à St. Petersbourg* (307)

LANG, Alexander   1773-7   born in St. Petersburg, apprenticed to J. B. Gass, master from 6 August 1773

LILIEBERG, Johan   1827-55   born 1794 in Borgå, master 1827, died 1855, also sold foreign gold boxes in his shop (297)   .

LINCK, Benjamin Gottlieb   1791-1816   from Danzig, came to St. Petersburg in 1776, master from 17 October 1791, still a guild member 1808, died 1816

LOUBIER, Jean François   1776-1824   probably a Huguenot from Berlin, born 1744, master 25 April 1776, alderman 1792, left the guild 1816, died 1824. He was Court Jeweller and received the order to make a crown for Catherine II, which however was delivered only for the coronation of Paul I

METROT, Jacques François   1789-92   Frenchman, 1789 Master of *galanterie*. Had J. A. Hudendorff as a journeyman in 1792

NICOLAS, Antoine   1789-1831, 1789 master for gold and *galanterie*. Alderman of Foreigners' Guild 1824-5. Still mentioned with his journeymen in 1831

PANNASCH, Emmanuel Georg von   1809-37   in 1796 had a Saxon passport, master in 1809, specialized in enamel painting, and later (1821-33) almost exclusively produced Orders

PAUZIÉ, Jeremie   1740-64   born 1716 in Geneva, from 1729 in Russia, master workshop 1740, Court Jeweller, left in 1764 and died in 1779 in Geneva. His gold boxes are distinguished by their fine chasing and often lavish use of gemstones.

RUDOLPH, David   1779-96   from Copenhagen, master of *galanterie* from 9 December 1779, alderman 1793 (265, 320)

SAINTE-BEUVE, Nicholas Pierre   1787-93   born in Paris, master 30 May 1787, still a guild member in 1793

SCHARFF, Johann Gottlieb   1772-1808   born in Moscow, master of *galanterie* from 27 February 1772, alderman 1798, still mentioned in 1808, worked now and then for or with Master C. G. Goebel

SEGUIN, François   1779-95   born in Paris, master in St. Petersburg 9 December 1779, alderman of Foreigners' Guild 1790, called himself *Maître d'apprentissage* (276)

SPIEGEL, Andreas Ferdinand   *c.* 1830-62   born 1797, master from about 1830, died 1862, made gold boxes with chasing as well as with semi-precious stone mosaics (235)

TAPPER, Henrik *c.* 1815-27   master from about 1815, known until 1827 (324)

TASCHNER, Hieronymus Friedrich   1786-95 from Erfurt, master from 18 January 1786, in 1795 left St. Petersburg

THEREMIN, François Claude   1795-1801   master of *galanterie* from 15 January 1795, still working in 1801 (273)

THEREMIN, Pierre   1793-1802   born in 1764 at Gramsow/Gross-Ziethen in Prussia, son of a Huguenot pastor, apprenticed engraver and jeweller to his brother (François-Claude?) in Berlin, journeyed to Geneva and Paris and finally settled in 1793 in St. Petersburg. Here he was alderman of the Foreigners' Guild from 1800 to 1801. In St. Petersburg he married Marianne Duval. His son writes in a biographical note (Bibliothèque Publique et Universitaire de Genève, Ia 697): 'As *Bijoutier de la Cour* he quite quickly made a fortune which he found adequate and in 1802 came to establish himself with his wife in Geneva, where he recovered his health and ended his days.' In 1801 Theremin delivered four gold boxes to the Court Office and received for them 1,580 roubles. His boxes are predominantly in the Geneva enamel style (317)

Master's signatures not identified:

Master's initials C N, 1840s (Christian Naukkarinen?) (Translucent blue enamelled gold box in the form of a cartouche, 1842, Collection of H. M. Queen Elizabeth the Queen Mother) (261)

Master's initials I B, about 1800 (288)

Master's initials W G, about 1830 (328)

Moscow

LAJOIE, B.   *c.* 1765. Signed *Lajoie à Moscou* (247)

SCHWARTZ   *c.* 1790. Signed *Schwartz à Moscou*

TURKIN, Ivan Petrov   1771-9. Silversmith and goldsmith (116)

Russian Town Marks

	Arkhangelsk	84·t·
	Astrakhan	
	Chernigov	
	Dorpat	
	Galich	
	Irkutsk	1677-1678
	Kazan	1710-1711
	Kaluga	1726
	Kamenets-Podolsk	МОСК ВА 1737
	Kharkov	1741
		1742

Kherson		1777-1779
Kiev		1783
Kostroma		
Minsk		
Mitau	84	1880-1899	Moscow
Moscow		Narva
		Novgorod
	1787	Nizhniy Novgorod
		Novocherkassk
		Odessa
		Orel

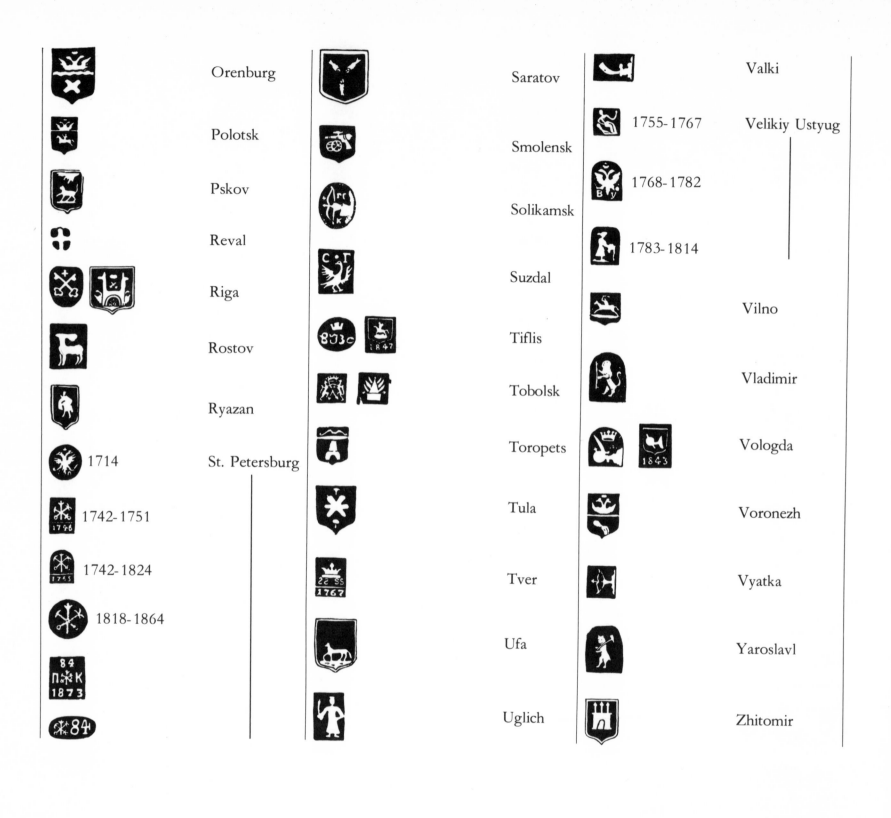

Orenburg

Polotsk

Pskov

Reval

Riga

Rostov

Ryazan

St. Petersburg

1714

1742-1751

1742-1824

1818-1864

Saratov

Smolensk

Solikamsk

Suzdal

Tiflis

Tobolsk

Toropets

Tula

Tver

Ufa

Uglich

Valki

Velikiy Ustyug

1755-1767

1768-1782

1783-1814

Vilno

Vladimir

Vologda

Voronezh

Vyatka

Yaroslavl

Zhitomir

Index of Marks and Signatures

Б

41	БОКъ	210
42	БРАГИНЪ	210
43	БР.ГРАЧЕВЫ	193, 207; Pl. 221
44	БРИЦЫНЪ	210; Pl. 140

В

45	ВА	192
46	В·А	Pl. 19
47	ВА	206
48	ВА	206, 215
49	ВЛО	230
50	В·М	210
51	ВМ	207
52	В·П	209; Pls. 35, 89
53	ВП	209
54	ВП	209
55	ВР	216
56	ВС	193
57	ВС	209, 216; Pls. 124, 128
58	В·С	209, 216; Pls. 124, 128
59	ВС	209, 216; Pls. 124, 128
60	В.С.	209, 216; Pls. 124, 128
61	ВШ	215

Г

62	ГЗ	210; Pl. 38
63	ГК	207; Pl. 57
64	ГЛ	192
65	ГП	215
66	ГР	215; Pl. 40
67	ГР	21
68	ГР	21
69	ГРАЧЕВЪ	193, 207
70	ГС	230
71	ГС	230
72	ГС	230
73	ГС	230
74	ГС	209
75	ГУ	217
76	ГУБКИНЪ	207, 215
77	ГУБКИНЪ	207, 215; Pl. 217
78	Г·Ч	210
79	Г.ЧЕРЯТОВ	210

Д

80	ДН	207; Pl. 127

Е

81	Е·Б	Pl. 87
82	Е·I	Pl. 18
83	ЕI	Pl. 18
84	Е·К	210
85	Е.Ч	210

И

86	И·А	214
86a	ИБ	210
87	ИЗ	216; Pl. 120
88	И.ЗУЕВЪ	216; Pl. 119

89	И·К	216; Pl. 107
90	И.К	207
91	И·Л	230
92	 84 (assay mark)	169
93	ИМ	216
94	И·М	214; Pl. 13
95	И.ОЗЕРИЦКІИ	208
96	И.П	193
97	ИС	205
98	ИС	208; Pl. 78
99	и.х	199, 217; Pl. 78
100	И·Ш	215
101	иθ	Pls. 30, 132

Й

102	ІБ	209
103	І·В 1815	230
104	ІГ	214
105	І·Г	214
106	ІГ	214

107	ІЯ	214
108	іжс	214
109	ІЗ	216
110	І·О	215
111	ІШ	215
112	іп	215
113	І·Р	135
114	І.Р.	193
115	НІС	Pls. 22, 41
116	І·Т	220
117	ІЧ	217
118	ІШ	Pls. 21, 25, 43

К

119	К.БОКЪ	210
120	К·ГАНЪ	194, 211; Pl.142
121	КК	230
122	КФ	192; Pl. 243
123	КФ	192
124	К.ФАБЕРЖЕ	192

| 125 | К.ФАБЕРЖЕ (with eagle) | 192, 206; Pl. 144 |
| 126 | К.ФАБЕРЖЕ (with eagle) | 192 |

Л

127	ЛА	209
128	1765 Л·В	Pl. 111
129	ЛОРІЕ	211
130	ЛЮБАВИНЪ	207

М

131	МАРШАКЪ	211, 212
132	МБ	230
133	М·Б	Pl. 126
134	М·ГРЕЧ	215
135	МД	215
136	МЖ	214
137	М К	216
138	МК	185, 214
139	М·К	Pl. 46
140	МК	Pl. 21

141	Мл	216
142		230
143	1767 МО	Pl. 112
144	МОРОЗОВЪ	199, 208, 211
145	М.П	193; Pl. 134
146	М·П	193; Pl. 135
147		Pl. 111
148	МС	Pl. 37
149	МС	217
150	МС	209; Pls. 52, 60, 61
151	М·Ц С	210
152	МЧ	217
153	МЧ	217
154	МЯ	217
155	МѲ П	215

Н

| 156 | Н.А | 206 |
| 157 | НА | 206 |

158	И·А 1825	Pls. 107, 213
159	НЕМИРОВЪ КОЛОДКИНЪ	208
160	НЗ	Pl. 60
161	Н·И 1832	Pl. 117
162	НМ	216
163	Н·М	168; Pl. 36
164	НСС	Pl. 25

О

165	ОК	207
166	О.КУРЛЮКОВЪ	207; Pls. 67, 150
167	О.С ЕИ	208

П

168	ЛВК	214
169	П·Г	230
170	ПЖ	214
171	ПИВ	213; Pls. 95-6
172	ПМ	207
173	ПМИЛЮКОВЪ	207

174	ПОВЧИННИКОВЪ	201, 208, 216; Pls. 51, 55, 58, 68, 71, 72
175	ПС	215
176	ПС	Pl. 38
177	ПС	Pl. 38
178	ПС	Pls. 14, 43
179	84 П.Т	168

С

180	1769 С·А	Pl. 40
181	САЗИКОВЪ	205, 209, 216; Pl. 225
182	САЗИКОВЪ	205, 209, 216
183	СВ	194, 211
184	С.В.	209
185	С·К	230
186	СПК	214
187	СС	216
188	С.СКРИПИЦЫНЪ	216
189	СУМИНЪ	211

T

190	Tİ	214
191	TI	214
192	TC	210; Pl. 18
193	T·C	210; Pl. 18

У

194	УВФ АСП	185; Pl. 112
195	У В Ф АСП	185; Pl. 112

Ф

196	ФА	192
197	ФАБЕРЖЕ	192
198	ФА.ЛОРІЕ	211
199	ФБ	214
200	ФБ	214
201	Ф.В	211
202	ФВ	211
203	ФВЕРХОВЦЕВЪ	209, 211
204	ФЛ	211
205	Ф.ЛОРІЕ	211

206	Ф·П	230
207	Ф·Р·	193, 208; Pls. 54, 69, 149

X

208	ХЛѢБНИКОВЪ	199, 207, 217
209	ХЛѢБНИКОВЪ	199, 207, 217

Э

210	ЭДУАРДЪ	39

Я

211	ЯА	192
212	ЯГ	214
213	ЯГ	214
214	ЯГ	214
215	56 ЯЛ	169
216	Я·М	209; Pl. 38
217	Я·М	209; Pl. 38
218	ЯМ	214
219	А·М	214
220	ЯЛ	Pl. 50

221	ЯР	211
222	Я.Ф МИШУКОВЪ	207

Ѳ

223	Ѳ·К	Pl. 36
224	ѲИ	230
225	Ѳ·М	230
226	Ѳ·П	230
227	ДП	230

A

228	ADLER	206
229	AH	192, 212; Pl. 243
230	A·H	192
231	AH	212
232	AM	192
233	A.N	192
234	AR	193
235	A·S	212, 220; Pl. 208
236	AT	193, 212; Pl. 243

237	AT	194, 211, 212; Pl. 142
238	AT	194, 211, 212
239	A.W	193

B

240	Barbe	217
241	B.C.Schlepper	Pl. 44
242	BEREL	136
243	Bergqwist	230
244	BOIANOWSKI	211
245	BOIANOWSKI	211
246	BOLIN	191, 210
247	B★L	220
248	BUNTZELL	230
249	BUCH	218

C

250	·C·A·S·	Pl. 228
251	·C.A.S·	Pl. 228
252	CE	218
253	C.E.BOLIN	191

254	CF	192
255	CFW	210; Pl. 87
256	GG	Pl. 41
257	C.Heyne	230
258	CIE	230
259	C.J.K	230
260	·CMS·	230
261	CXN	220
262	C.T	Pl. 216
263	CT	Pl. 216
264	CT	Pl. 216

D

265	DR	219; Pl. 181

E

266	EH	218
267	EH	218
268	Eiler	218
269	EK	192
270	ER	Pl. 22
271	ES	193

F

272	FABERGE	192
273	F.C.T.	220; Pl. 187
274	FK	Pl. 214
275	F★K	211; Pl. 212
276	F.S.	219; Pl. 190
277	FX B	217; Pls. 180, 192

G

278	GK	207; Pls. 53, 74
279	GN	193
280	G·G	215
281	G·S	210
282	G·S	230

H

283	HS	168
284	H·S	Pl. 37
285	H.W.	193; Pl. 133

I

286		189, 217; Pl. 183
287		189, 217; Pl. 132
288		220; Pl. 197
289	ICA	193
290	I·CK	218
291		21
292	IGK	210
293	I·H	230
294	IH	Pl. 131
295		200
296		200
297	I.L	168, 219
298	I·N	Pl. 36
299	IN	Pl. 141
300	J.Suew	216
301	JTB	Pl. 215
302	I.T.B	230

J

303	JY A B	136
304	J.W.	193

K

305	Keibel.	135, 194, 218; Pls. 151, 198, 202, 206
306	KLINGERT	207
307	Kolb	219; Pl. 214

M

308	MB	217
309	MC D	Pl. 30

N

310	N·P	200, 208
311	N&P	200, 208
312	N&P MAG·ANG	200, 208

O

313	OP	193

P

314	PK	200
315	PK	218
316	P·M	212
317	PT	220; Pls. 193-5, 200
318	PTen	212

R

319	RS	212
320	RUDOLPH	219

S

321	S·A	200, 210, 211; Pls. 218-19
322	Schlepper	Pl. 44
323	S·W	193, 215

T

324	TAPPER	220
325	TENNER	212
326	T.R	193

W

327	W.A.BOLIN	191, 210
328	W/G	220
329	W.R	193

ARTELS

330 **3ЯA**   206, 210

331 **6MA**   206

332 **IIA**   206

333 **20A**   206; Pls. 60, 78

Other Masters' Marks and
Signatures

No.

4   Moscow c. 1740
49   VLO   Moscow c. 1756
70-73   SEREBRYANIKOV, Grigoriy Ivanov Moscow 1745-68
91   I L   St. Petersburg c. 1870
103   VIKHLYAYEV, Ivan assay-master,
Moscow 1802-18
121   KONOV, Kuzma, Moscow early
20th century
132   BOBROVSHCHIKOV, Mikhail assay-master, Moscow 1755-68
142   Moscow c. 1720
169   GRIGORIEV, Petr   Moscow 1802-
24
185   KALASHNIKOV, Stepan Dmitriyev   Moscow 1762-95

206   PETROV, Fedor Moscow 1760-
89, simultaneously alderman
224, 225   MASLENNIKOV, Fedor Grigoriev   Moscow 1732-45
226, 227   PETROV, Fedor   cf. No. 206
243   BERGQUIST, Nils   St. Petersburg
1764-92
248   BUNTZELL, Jacob   St. Petersburg
1780-1823
257, 259   HEINE, Carl St. Petersburg
1823-38
258   ELERS, Clas Johann   St. Petersburg c. 1760
260   STAHLE, Carl Magnus   St. Petersburg 1830-63
282   SEPPÄIN, Georg   St. Petersburg
1822-35
293   HILDEBRANDT, Johann Gottfried   St. Petersburg c. 1760
302   BUNTZELL, Johann Theodor   St.
Petersburg c. 1810

Select Bibliography

Monographs and Articles

Bäcksbacka, L., *Narvas och Nyens Guldsmeder*, Helsingfors, 1946
— *St. Petersburgs Juvelerare, Guld- och Silversmeder 1714-1870*, Helsingfors, 1951
Bainbridge, H.C., *Peter Carl Fabergé*, London, 1949; rev. ed. 1966, 1974
Bernyakovich, Z.A., *Russkoye khudozhestvennoye serebro, XVII – nachalo XX veka* (Russian silverware from the 17th to the beginning of the 20th century), Leningrad, 1977
Berry-Hill, H. and S., *Antique Gold Boxes*, London – New York, 1960
Corbeiller, C. le, *European and American Snuff-boxes*, London, 1966
Fersman, A.E., *Les Joyaux du Trésor de Russie (Commissariat National des Finances)*, Moscow, 1924-26
Filimonov, T.D., *Opis' Moskovskoy Oruzheynoy palaty* (Description of the Armoury in Moscow), Moscow, 1884
Foelkersam, A.E., *Opisi serebra dvora Ego Imperatorskogo Velichestva* (Description of the silver works at H. I. M. Court), 2 vols., St. Petersburg, 1907
— 'Nekotoryya svedeniya o S.-Petersburgskikh zolotykh i serebryanykh del masterov za 100 let (1714-1814)' (Some information about the gold- and silversmiths of St. Petersburg over 100 years, 1714-1814), in: *Starye gody*, 1907, no. I, p. 7
— *Alfavitnyi ukazatel' S.-Petersburgskikh zolotykh i serebryanykh del masterov, yuvelirov, graverov i pr. 1714-1814 g.* (Alphabetic list of St. Petersburg gold- and silversmiths, jewellers, engravers, etc. 1714-1814), in: *Starye gody*, 1907
— 'Yuvelirnye izdeliya vremen Aleksandra I' (Jewellery of the Period of Alexander I), in: *Starye gody*, 1908, nos VII-IX, p. 529
— 'Novyi zal dragotsennostey Imperatorskogo Ermitazha' (A new exhibition-room of jewellery in the Imperial Hermitage), in: *Starye gody*, 1911, no. I, p. 26
— 'Inostrannye mastera zolotogo i serebryanogo dela' (Foreign masters of gold and silverwork), in: *Starye gody*, 1911, nos VII-IX, p. 95
Goldberg, T.G., *Ocherki po istorii serebryanogo dela v Rossii v pervoy polovine XVIII v.* (Sketches of the history of silverwork in Russia in the first half of the 18th century), Moscow, 1947

— *Chernevoe serebro Velikogo Ustyuga* (Nielloed silver from Velikiy Ustyug), Moscow, 1952
— 'Yuvelirnoe iskusstvo vtoroy poloviny XVIII v.' (Jewellery art of the second half of the 18th century), in: *Istoriya russkogo iskusstva*, vol. VII, Moscow, 1960, pp. 399-414
— 'Izdeliya iz dragotsennykh metallov (XVIII v.) (Objects made of precious metals, 18th century), in: *Russkoye dekorativnoye iskusstvo*, vol. II, Moscow, 1963, pp. 436-55
Goldberg T.G. and M.M. Postnikova-Loseva, *Kleymenie serebryanykh izdeliy v XVII—nach. XVIII v.* (Marks on silver in the 17th and early 18th century), Moscow, 1941
Goldberg, T.G., Mishukov, F., Platonova, N. and M.M. Postnikova-Loseva, *Russkoye zolotoye i serebryanoye delo XV-XX vekov* (Russian gold and silverwork, 15th-20th century), Moscow, 1967
Grandjean, S., Piacenti, K.A., Truman, C. and A. Blunt, *Gold Boxes and Miniatures of the Eighteenth Century*, The James A. de Rothschild Collection at Waddesdon Manor, Fribourg, 1975
Grinberg, L., 'Zametki o zhalovannykh gramotakh i geral'dicheskom khudozhestve' (Notes on nobility patents and heraldic art); in: *Vremennik obshchestva druzey russkoy knigi*, vol. IV, Paris, 1938, pp. 129-44
Habsburg-Lothringen, G. von and A. von Solodkoff, *Fabergé, Court Jeweller to the Tsars*, Fribourg-London-New York, 1979
Hinks, P., *19th Century Jewellery*, London, 1975
Ivanov, D.D., 'Starye russkiye kleyma serebra' (Old Russian marks on silver), in: *Sbornik Oruzheynoy palaty*, Moscow, 1925, pp. 108-109
Korsh, E., 'Russkoye serebryanoye delo XVII veka i ego ornamentatsiya' (Russian 17th-century silver and its ornamentation) in: *Starye gody*, 1909, nos VII-IX, p. 404
List of Russian gold and silver marks, ed. by Slavisches Institut München, Munich, 1971
Lobaneva, T.A., *Izdeliya nakladnogo serebra: Moskva, XIX vek* (Works of plated silver: Moscow, 19th century). *Trudy Gosudarstvennogo istoricheskogo muzeya*, Moscow, 1956
Martynova, M.V., *Precious Stones in Russian Jewelry Art in the 17th to 18th Centuries*, Moscow, 1973
Otchet Vserossiiyskoy khudozhestvenno-promyshlennoy vystavki 1882 g., St. Petersburg, 1883

(Pauzié, Jérémie), 'Zapiski pridvornogo brilyantshchika Pozie o prebyvanii ego v Rossii' (Memoirs of the Court Jeweller Pauzié, recalling the years he spent in Russia), in: *Russkaya starina* I, 1870, pp. 16-27, 77-103, 197-244

Pazhitnov, K.L. *Problema remeslennykh tsekhov i zakonodatel'stva russkogo absolyutizma* (The problem of the guild organization and legislation under Russian absolutism), Moscow, 1952

Petrenko, M.Z., *Ukrainskoye zolotarstvo XVI-XVIII st.* (Goldsmith's work in the Ukraine, 16th-18th century), Kiev, 1970

Pisarskaya, L., Platonova N. and B. Ulyanova, *Russkiye emali XI-XIX vv.* (Russian enamels, XIth-XIXth century), Moscow, 1974

Platonova, H.G., 'Usol'skaya emal'' (Enamel from Usolsk), in: *Pamyatniki kul'tury*, XXVIII, Moscow, 1959

Pomerantsev, N.N., 'Finift usol'skogo dela' (Enamel from Usolsk), in: *Sbornik Oruzheynoy palaty*, Moscow, 1925, pp. 96-107

Postnikova-Loseva, M.M. 'Kostromskoe serebryanoe delo' (Silver works of Kostroma), *Trudy Gos. istoricheskogo muzeya*, XVIII, Moscow, 1947

— *Russkie serebryanye i zolotye kovshi* (Russian silver and gold kovshi), Moscow, 1953

— 'Zolotye i serebryanye izdeliya masterov Oruzheynoy palaty' (Gold- and silverwork by masters of the Oruzheynaya palata), in: *Gosudarstvennaya Oruzheinaya palata Moskovskogo Kremlya*, Moscow, 1954, pp. 139-215

— 'Russkaya serebryanaya skan' (Russian silver filigree), in: *Russkoye khudozhestvennoye serebro XV-XIX vv., Pamyatniki kul'tury*, XXVIII, Moscow, 1959

— 'Prikladnoye iskusstvo XVI-XVII vv.' (Applied arts, 16th-17th century) in: *Istoriya russkogo iskusstva*, vol. IV, Moscow, 1959

— *Russkoye yuvelirnoye iskusstvo: ego tsentry i mastera XVI-XIX vv.* (Russian jewellery art, its centres and masters, 16th-20th century), Moscow, 1974

Postnikova-Loseva, M.M. and N.G. Platonova, *Russkoye khudozhestvennoye serebro* (Russian artistic silver), Moscow, 1959

Pushkarev, V. (ed.), *Russian Applied Art*, Leningrad, 1976

Razina, T.M., *Russkaya emal' i skan'* (Russian enamel and filigree work), Moscow, 1961

Rosenberg, M., *Der Goldschmiede Merkzeichen*, 3rd ed., Berlin, 1928

Ross, M.C., *The Art of Carl Fabergé and his Contemporaries*, Oklahoma, 1965

Rybakov, B.A. (ed.), *Sokrovishcha Almaznogo Fonda SSSR* (Treasures from the diamond fond of the USSR), Moscow 1967, 2nd ed., 1975

Shchukin, P.I. and E.V. Fedorova, *Opis' starinnykh veshchey sobraniya P.I. Shchukina* (List of antiquities in the P.I. Shchukin Collection), Moscow, 1895

Shchukina, E.S., *Medalernoe iskusstvo v Rossii XVIII veka* (Russian medal art in the 18th century), Leningrad, 1962

Shelkovnikov, B.A., 'Prikladnoye iskusstvo pervoy poloviny XVIII v.' (Applied art during the first half of the 18th century), in: *Istoriya russkogo iskusstva*, vol. V, Moscow, 1960, pp. 499-507

Snowman, A.K., *The Art of Carl Fabergé*, London, 1953, 2nd ed. 1962

— *Eighteenth Century Gold Boxes*, London, 1966

— *Carl Fabergé, Goldsmith to the Imperial Court of Russia*, London, 1979

Spassky, I.E. *Russkaya monetnaya sistema* (Russian monetary system), Moscow, 1957

— *Inostranniye i russkiye ordena do 1917 goda* (Foreign and Russian orders to 1917), Leningrad, 1963

Suslov, I.M., *Rostovskaya emal'* (Enamel from Rostov), Yaroslavl, 1959

— 'Moskovskaya emal' XVII v.' (Enamel from Moscow in the 17th century), in: *Sovetskaya arkheologiya*, II, 1960, pp. 208-19

Svirin, A.N., *Yuvelirnoye iskusstvo drevney Rusi XI-XVII vekov* (Early Russian jewellery work), Moscow, 1972

Tenisheva, M.K. *Emal' i inkrustatsiya* (Enamel and incrustations), Prague, 1930

Troinitsky, S. 'Farforovyya tabakerki Imperatorskogo Ermitazha' (Porcelain snuff-boxes in the Hermitage), in: *Starye gody*, 1913, no. XII, p. 14

— 'Sobranie knyagini Shakhovskoy' (Collection of Princess Shakhovskaya), in: *Starye gody*, 1914, no. VI, p. 3

— 'Tabakerki v pamyat' semiletney voyny' (Snuff-boxes in commemoration of the Seven Years' War), in: *Starye gody*, 1915, nos I-II, p. 51

— 'Deviz Imperatritsy Ekateriny II' (The motto of Empress Catherine II), in: *Starye gody*, 1915, no. III, p. 35

— 'Tabakerka Imperatritsy Ekateriny II s portretom sultana' (A snuff-box of Catherine II with the portrait of the sultan), in: *Starye gody*, 1915, no. III, p. 43

— 'Medal'nyya tabakerki vremeni Imperatritsy Ekateriny II' (Snuff-boxes with medals of the period of Empress Catherine II), in: *Starye gody*, 1915, no. VI, p. 41

Troitsky, V.I. 'Kleyma na russkikh serebryanikh izdeliyakh XVII v.' (Marks on Russian silver works of the 17th century), in: *Sbornik Oruzheynoy palaty*, Moscow, 1925, pp. 100-12

— *Slovar' moskovskikh masterov zolotogo, serebryanogo i almaznogo dela XVII v.* (Dictionary of masters of gold, silver and jewellery works in Moscow during the 17th century), Moscow-Leningrad, 1930

— 'Organizatsiya zolotogo i serebryanogo dela v Moskve v XVII v.' (Organization of gold and silver works in Moscow in the 17th century), *Istoricheskiye zapiski*, vol. XII, Moscow, 1941

Trutovsky, V.K. 'Boyarin i oruzhnichiy Bogdan Matveyevich Khitrovo i moskovskaya Oruzheynaya palata' (The Boyar and Keeper of the Arms Bogdan Matveyevich Khitrovo and the Oruzheynaya palata), in: *Starye gody*, 1909, nos VII-IX, pp. 345-381

Vrangel, N., 'Ocherki po istorii miniatyury v Rossii' (Sketches of the history of miniatures in Russia), in: *Starye gody*, 1909, no. X, p. 509

Vysotsky, N.T., 'Pashkvil'nyya tabakerki' (Snuff-boxes shaped as letters), in: *Starye gody*, 1913, no. I, p. 42

Waterfield, H. and C. Forbes, *Fabergé, Imperial Easter Eggs and other Fantasies*, New York, 1978

Exhibition and Auction Catalogues

Great Exhibition of the Works of Industry of All Nations, catalogue, vol. III, London, 1851

Ukazatel' russkogo otdela Vsemirnoy vystavki 1862 g. (Guide to the Russian division of the World Exhibition of 1862), London 1862

Ukazatel' russkogo otdela Filadel'fiyskoy mezhdunarodnoy vystavki 1876 g. (Guide to the Russian division of the Philadelphia International Exhibition of 1876), St. Petersburg, 1876

Krantz, M.C., *Exposition Internationale de Chicago 1893, Bijouterie-Joaillerie*, Paris, 1894

Prakhov, A., *Albom istoricheskoy vystavki predmetov iskusstva v 1904 godu* (Album of the 1904 Retrospective Art Exhibition at St. Petersburg, 1904), St. Petersburg, 1907

Catalogue of an Important Assemblage of Magnificent Jewellery, mostly dating from the 18th century, which formed part of the Russian State Jewels, and which have been purchased by a Syndicate in this country (124 nos), Christie, Manson and Woods, London, 16 March 1927

Exhibition of Russian Art, exhibition catalogue, London, 1935

Fabergé 1846-1920, Goldsmith to the Imperial Court of Russia, exhibition catalogue. Victoria and Albert Museum, London, 1977

An Important Collection of Early Russian Silver, sale catalogue, Sotheby Parke Bernet, Zurich, 22 November 1978

Russian Works of Art and Works of Art by Carl Fabergé, sale catalogue, Christie's, Geneva, 1973-81

Index

Photo Credits

The author and publishers wish to thank all the museums, institutions and collectors who kindly provided photographic material. The individual Plates were supplied by:

Baltimore, Walters Art Gallery   132

Buenos Aires, Museo Nacional de Arte Decorativo   191

Copenhagen, De danske Kongers kronologiske Samling på Rosenborg   154

Edinsor, Bakewell (UK), The Trustees of the Chatsworth Settlement   187

Frankfurt am Main, Karl Friedrich, jeweller   245

Geneva, Christie's   13, 18-23, 25, 32, 34-38, 40, 44, 51-62, 64-70, 72, 73, 75-78, 80, 83, 84, 86-88, 90, 99, 101-105, 108, 111, 112, 117, 119-130, 136-140, 143, 144, 146, 147, 149-151, 167, 168, 176, 181, 182, 198, 203, 211-213, 215, 216, 218, 219, 220, 227, 229-231, 236, 239, 241-244; 11, 39, 89, 91, 106, 107, 145, 197, 222 (Photos Claude Mercier, Geneva)

— Musée d'Art et d'Histoire   178, 238

Leningrad, Hermitage   30

London, Christie, Manson & Woods   6, 42, 43, 46, 63, 71, 74, 141, 152, 153, 155-157, 199, 206, 210, 214, 225, 237

— S. J. Phillips   131, 179

— Spink & Son Ltd.   217

— Victoria and Albert Museum   207

— Wartski's   195

London and New York, Sotheby Parke Bernet   1-3, 12, 31, 85, 109, 110, 112, 114, 158-161, 189, 192, 204, 228; 50 (Agent: Editorial Photocolor Archives, New York)

Moscow, Oruzheynaya palata (Armoury)   133, 134

New York, A la Vieille Russie   169-174, 194; 175, 188 (Photos Helga Photo Studio); 205 (Photo Taylor & Dull)

— Christie's   33, 148, 196

Paris, Léon Grinberg   4, 5, 7-10, 24, 26-29, 79, 92-98, 100, 162-164, 166, 200, 201, 221, 223, 224, 232-234; 115, 116, 202 (Photos Taylor & Dull); 118 (Photo Fernbrock Studio)

— Musée Cognacq-Jay   180

— Musée national du Louvre   184, 185 (© Arch. Phot. Paris/SPADEM 1980)

Turin, Rampazzi Ferruccio   14-17

Vienna, Kunsthistorisches Museum   47 (Photo Claus Hansmann, Gauting)

Washington, National Collection of Fine Arts, Smithsonian Institution   177 (Gift of John Gellatly; stolen 1979)

Special thanks for photographic work are due to Sir Geoffrey Shakerley (Pl. 193), Messrs. A. C. Cooper, London, and M. Hubert Salmont, Paris.